ADRIAN RYAN

This book is dedicated to:

Reina James – who foretold that it was possible to do it
Bet Balcombe – who showed a way to do it
Theresa Carlson – who said just do it

ADRIAN RYAN
Rather a Rum Life

Julian Machin

Sansom & Company

First published in 2009 by Sansom & Company Ltd.,
81G Pembroke Road, Bristol BS8 3EA
www.sansomandcompany.co.uk
info@sansomandcompany.co.uk

ISBN 978-1-906593-23-0

British Library Cataloguing-in-Publication Data
A catalogue record for this book is available from the British Library

Designed and typeset by E&P Design, Bath.
Printed by MPG Books Ltd, Bodmin, Cornwall.

Contents

Acknowledgements

The author wishes to thank Frances Fyfield for her support and immense kindness in helping to bring this manuscript to being. Many thanks go to Sarah Milan for her unparalleled editorial advice, and for his extreme graciousness to Richard Cuerden. Gratitude is felt for the efforts of Luke Florio, also for the unfailing solicitude of Geraldine Florio, and to the Estate of Adrian Ryan.

Much is owed to the recollections and the warm encouragement of Peggy Ryan. Others gratefully acknowledged for their contribution to securing the facts of this story are: the unstinting Polly Walker, the late Guy Roddon, Barbara Pitt-Ryan, the late John Kilbracken, Professor John Norris-Wood, Stephen Gardiner, Heidee Becker, Norman Coates, the late Valentine Goodall, and the late Joan Gillchrest.

For miscellaneous advice, kindness or for the loan of pictures for illustration, the author is also grateful to: Polly Walker, Carina Maitland, Anna Terrington, the Tate, Richard Selby, Chris Kelly, Catharine Phelan, Sotheby's, WH Lane & Son, Penlee House Museum & Art Gallery, the Potteries Museum & Art Gallery, Gulbenkian Foundation, the authors of *Fifty Years of Fressingfield 1952–2002*, Redfern Gallery, Gary Cady, Matthew Hart, and others numerous and forebearing.

Foreword

Once, long ago, I saw two paintings by Adrian Ryan for sale on exhibition and I stood where I was transfixed with excitement. I bought them. They will always be a delight, like the man himself, whom I came to know. He was seriously funny, stimulating, thoughtful, self-deprecating, humble; stoic and joking in the face of pain, illness and disappointment. He was born to privilege and entitlement and yet had seemingly nothing of either, only a small ego, an immense curiosity and a tiny sense of self worth for an artist of such bloody-minded integrity and talent. What he did have was almighty honesty, colossal kindness, no malice, but plenty of mischief and a native goodness, which meant that he was forgiven by everyone but himself. He had little hatred except of ugliness which he refused to celebrate or exploit. (Dirty talk was excepted as long as it was articulate.) He once said 'What is lovely is beloved of angels'. And so was he, a life enhancer, who left a legacy of Joy on canvas.

Frances Fyfield

Well-kept secret of the art world, 1987

...all you should learn about art is to know a good picture when you see it, and a bad picture when you see it.
Oscar Wilde, lecture to art students of the RA, 30 June 1883

In an antique shop in the historic shopping precinct of the Pantiles in Tunbridge Wells, I have over a period found a small number of paintings which have been inspirational. The first was *The Rally,* an oil on canvas depicting a political gathering in south London, painted in pre-Euston Road style c. 1932, by the little known consort of one of its founders. Elsie Few, or Mrs Claude Rogers, is better known as one of Victor Pasmore's early portrait sitters. Her painting was described as a wedding gift to Quentin and Olivia Bell of Charleston Farmhouse. It was loosely painted and too cheap and I was unsure about it. To my surprise, when I rang up Quentin Bell he more than corroborated its provenance, for with relief in his voice he declared 'Oh that's where it's got to! Well do come and see us and we'll take it off you...' Eventually we sorted out what had happened. In having a clear-out, he had stored the painting in the garage and it had been muddled with a group of things he sold to a dealer, then forgotten about. Years later, with Quentin no longer alive, I met Olivia at the private view of a show I curated at Charleston, and she told me that that sort of thing – she meant his unfortunate acts of muddle and forgetfulness – went on quite a lot. She was good enough to add that she was glad that I had given the painting an appreciative home.

Next from the Pantiles came an unsigned oil on board by Doris Zinkeisen called *The Fountain*. I took the shop's word for it, as there was much about this sketchy oil on board that appealed to me. I should have known better even then. One look at a real Zinkeisen should have been enough to make me realise the golden rule: the evidence is always in the painting. Having written to the ageing Ms. Zinkeisen and enclosing a photograph, I received her reply. She stated she felt 'almost sure it was the sketch for a [stage] setting I did for [Charles B., 'the British Ziegfeld'] Cochran'. It wasn't until the picture was up on the wall for sale on the stand I shared at the annual summer Olympia antiques and fine art fair, that the first sign of something not being right came in the form of a comment from Hans Lasson. He was a gallery owner of the old school with a very good eye, latterly from St James's. He wasn't the sort of person one mistook easily. Wheezingly, the patriarchal old émigré examined the 'Zinkeisen' then sailed on with a young woman in tow to whom he scoffed: 'Can't possibly be by her – the woman can't paint!' And the remark hit home, such that when an elderly couple then appeared – who knew a lot more than many art dealers – and unhesitatingly pronounced the picture a study for Charles Sims' great 1912 painting in the Tate, all became clear. The label was changed as soon as they departed and to my lasting regret the painting sold soon after to an Argentine banker.

There were other, unrecalled, pictures coinciding with other gentle Tunbridge Wells afternoons. Two haunt me like lost jewels: a haystack by Harry Becker and a Soutine-like painting of a fish, on which, a necessary part of the learning process, I managed to pass.

The third and smallest purchase was to yield most. Thick with impasto, muted greens covering a fine old Rowney board measuring just 6" x 9", it showed a Goya-esque fisherman, face hidden beneath his cap, sitting upon rocks, rod bowing while apparently drawing some resistant object from the foam. Of some interest was the rod's central, tensed position over what was below the frothy current: the unemerged catch from this fierce-running, emblematic stream of life – composed within a finely balanced backdrop of cool colours. Either prize salmon, or old boot – neither fisherman nor viewer can tell. In pencil on the back was inscribed 'Cornwall 1943 A. Ryan, Padstow'. To defray the cost of the painting, the impressive frame, carved and gilded in Brussels circa 1830, later sold separately and well, stifling the fisherman for not too many months more until another one was made.[1]

In life we own nothing and nobody. Everything is only on lease to us. I have 'owned' *The Fisherman, Padstow* outright and in half shares since 1986, have sold it twice and it has again come back to me. It sits on a shelf across the room now. It's 65 years old. Occasionally I consider where it might be in 65 more years from now. Pictures have independent lives and the benefit we derive from them is of our choosing.

'A Ryan' according to the painting's invoice (for £195), was Adrian James, born 1920, who was listed in *Who's Who in Art* with impressive credentials. As though he were a well-kept secret, people seemed not to have heard of him. There was, however, a studio address in Camden Street, London NW1 given, and although I felt I could offer little – a dealer starting out – I addressed a letter there. I could not know that this remarkable man would see me present, a decade on, at his deathbed, nor the extent that he would teach me, nor be sustaining me for years after that.

'Well kept secret' is misleading. Among fellow artists and because of teaching for decades at Goldsmiths' and Cambridge College of Art, Adrian was well known. But in 1988, when we first met, he had receded far into a protective shell as far as the art-buying public was concerned. Although it turned out that he had a dealer still, in the Redfern Gallery, since his first one-man show in 1943, they were not active on his behalf. His name did not appear on their list of artists represented. Their stock contained only a handful of his watercolours. Commissions were no longer heard of, unlike the old days when Rex Nan Kivell presided over the gallery at 20 Cork Street, London. Adrian had fallen off the register. There was only David Becker, a picture dealer from Suffolk, whose previous encounter with Adrian indirectly allowed my purchase of *The Fisherman, Padstow*. David Becker had elevated taste and low profit margins. A picture bought from him during the 1980s and 1990s would hardly fail to yield the joy of ownership or a healthy investment margin. He did much to prevent Adrian's shell from disconnecting him entirely from the art market, following the mixed results of his 1985 retrospective at The Minories, Colchester.

Adrian, in his twenties, had the early confidence of many of the great names associated with twentieth-century British

1. It turned out, much later, that three versions of this painting existed. They were painted in response to Rex Nan Kivell, of the Redfern Gallery, having in the 1940s for sale a little Matisse oil of the coast at Collioure for £100, which ended up in the Berggruen Collection. Adrian having £100 – as many then did not – asked to buy it; Rex, experienced in not saying yes while not seeming to say no, stayed demure and the Matisse appeared in more than one mixed show before Adrian realised that the picture wasn't ever going to be his. So, in his own vernacular, he painted the fisherman and its two compatriots.

painting. He emerged not inconspicuously from the Oxford-relocated Slade – presided over by the avuncular Randolph Schwabe (1885–1948) – where because of his mode of personal transportation he was unambiguously known as 'the Bentley boy'. Affiliated with the men's life room crowd – a discipline he advocated unequivocally ever after – Adrian was one of a group who, according to Dodie Masterman, Peggy Ryan's fellow-student, 'seemed not to move freely between women and male students.' As Peggy Rose, she was regarded as the best student since Augustus John and Stanley Spencer. She left the Slade in 1938 before the start of his first term, with their affair – resulting in a mostly amicable marriage – not beginning till the year after. Among his direct contemporaries were Bryan Wynter, theatre designer James Bailey, celebrated antiquaire Geoffrey Bennison and Patrick Heron. It has been said that Heron's favourable review in the *New Statesman* of Adrian's 1948 Redfern show, was first to earn public respect for his work, but in fact Adrian had for seven years already experienced this from fellow painters and distinguished art buyers. That apprenticeship had begun when Edward Le Bas, gifted painter and avid collector, bought a fine painting of a crayfish from the Redfern in 1941, now supposed to be in the RA collection. In the intimate infancy of the art world of the times, Adrian and Peggy were both well-regarded professionally by many who encountered them in Muriel Belcher's Colony Room or in the Chelsea pubs.

There is an early self-portrait on canvas 14" x 10", one of a series done over about ten years. It was bought by the novelist Rosamond Lehmann from the pre-eminent, long-defunct dealers, Arthur Tooth & Sons. It was later lent by her to their 1956 exhibition of his work 'Paintings 1942–55', was illustrated in the catalogue and dated there 1947. Adrian's dating of his own work could be unself-consciously approximate. Sometimes this was to achieve numeric harmony, sometimes not. Looking out on the world from the wrap of a splendid Cornish fisherman's jersey, the portrait has an earlier feel to it. It seems to rely on composition and painterly qualities more than psychological, which was the basis of the others painted in the same decade, virtually all of which he destroyed. A self-portrait with beard from July 1941 survives. His never having had a beard, it is partly interesting for the dismissive critique it later elicited from him: 'That's another bit of lying nonsense… I just couldn't get the jaw right.' In fact the Lehmann portrait is dated 1945 by him on the reverse and ownership of the unmistakably spotted off-black and white jersey dates from 1944 when he wore it plentifully. It is most likely that this is when the self-portrait was painted, during the summer when he, Peggy and baby Geraldine went to a house in Constantine Bay specifically to avoid the Blitz.

The very earliest self-portrait of all is painted on the grainy pine of his old Architectural Association drawing board. It is also one of his earliest surviving works of any kind. Sad, wary eyes half turn to the world; wild almost inflamed hair with orange; the right arm is missing; the depths of the shadowy right side, tucked away but not invisible, are what make it totally different to the later, 1944, example. It's a sketch in oils, but a vital one and a good likeness. The teenage face it depicts looks out onto a world newly immersed in war.

If the two paintings are looked at together, fusion occurs. Not in style – he has truly become an artist in the intervening period – but in terms of personal drama revealed in both. If dated 1944, the portrait means that the deaths of his mother and godfather have not occurred yet. The only close relative to die by this time was cousin Michael, a 20-year-old fighter pilot shot down over the North Sea in 1940, a fact which did concern Adrian lastingly. More of his unease is revealed by the knowledge of his depiction of self as a man whose discharge from the army exposed him to the charge of cowardice – made certainly by his mother – when really he was a pacifist. In the absence of commitment to either cause, he is left in isolation while containing the situation in his head. Isolated in Cornwall, cocooned within a fisherman's jersey, his eyes stare gravely out at universal unrest and express his personal dilemma over his role. A true record of a 24-year-old's place in a terrified world, very different from the apparent security of his origins.

'Sans Travail Rien': the Ryan family

For Adrian, on the surface, life growing up seemed easy. He said that until he was a teenager, he thought that the whole world – apart from the gatekeeper, whom he'd visited at home – lived as his grandparents did, where he partly grew up. Hintlesham Hall, near Ipswich, Suffolk, is a Tudor manor, almost too pleasant to be stately, though it was *e*stately in 1909 when Adrian's grandfather Sir Gerald Hemmington Ryan Bt.[1] bought it as a lifestyle adjunct to his status as actuary-supremo to Prime Minister Lloyd George. The baronetcy came as a result of working out the government risk on insuring aircraft during the First World War. Plenty suggests that Sir Gerald was razor-sharp and hardworking. His motto was *Sans Travail Rien*. Also he was rich enough in his lifetime (he died on 27 May 1937 leaving £203,753 14s.6d – then an immense sum) to smooth any undulations along the path to ennoblement. Since his death the Hall has been more of a flourishing concern than a private residence. It is today a private hotel with a well-subscribed golfing facility. Not that golf was not played there in the old days. Adrian's father Vivian, gullible and good for practical jokes, was told by his son before the Aga Khan came to visit and play a round or two, that this man was a sort of eastern god and under no circumstances should he take his eyes off him or a curse would impose itself. There ensued a very odd spectacle around the course: of Vivian driving and putting erratically in his fevered efforts *not* to keep his eye on the ball.

1. Cr. 1919; Kt. Order of the Thistle cr. 1911

Sir Gerald's tenure of the Hall was the longest by an individual in the twentieth century. He earned significant praise for his management of the estate and for his gentlemanliness from the late Valentine Goodall, son of the gamekeeper. As opposed to Lady Ellen Ryan, whom Mr Goodall described as 'Very Victorian. Shooting-stick and rod of iron – an unlikely couple.' In his 1995 memoir *Some Recollections of Hintlesham*, Adrian corroborates a sympathetic view of his grandfather, whose nickname he affectionately gives as 'BG' short for 'Bravo Grandpa!' in recognition of his outrageous puns, forever promising his six grandchildren sixpence each for every 'Bravo!' whenever he made a joke – although not necessarily delivering. Whereas Lady Ellen, perennially sporting her auburn wig, was the person he 'dreaded' a visit from at Eton: 'Granny in the back of the Daimler, all done up in furs, rattling necklaces and bracelets...' The auburn wig but once failed to crown her forbidding demeanour, when Adrian aged 15 found her in her bedroom, bald, crying – soon to be dying, although he didn't realise it. Not then above a bit of bribery, she gave him some gold cufflinks in exchange for his silence. He later pawned them to raise funds for his under-age marriage to Peggy. Most of the family had reason to feel warm towards Sir Gerald, a short, twinkly-looking man, from whose liberal views and deep pocket they derived continuous benefit. Peggy Ryan says that when she first got to know Adrian, he 'talked about BG a lot and used to walk with one shoulder *up*', as his late grandfather had. As elderly men, they shared a physical resemblance and an old-fashioned courteousness, which Adrian displayed unfailingly when offering a Christmas box to the Camden Town trades people.

There are no Ryan paintings of Hintlesham Hall. After Sir Gerald died and his eldest son Gerald Ellis Ryan had the house and estate auctioned off in parts, the almost magical place Adrian remembered from childhood was transposed into 'a sad and lonely shell'. He declined to return to it, despite for years living nearby at Holbrook. That he came near is evidenced in two tiny paintings of Chattisham Hall. Dated 1942 and inscribed verso 'To Pammy with love', these were gifts to his cousin Pamela, the first wife of Sir Peter Green, a popular and faintly tarnished former Chairman of Lloyds. Chattisham, whose fine-sounding name promises more than the squat, 1820s house architecturally delivers, was the home of Pam's father Gerald Ellis (2nd baronet) whose seemingly un-obvious influence upon the Ryan dynasty is deceptively significant. Pam's energy, from early childhood, resonated with Adrian though not with all of his direct family. BG's household with the two sons Gerald and Vivian, their wives Hilda and Kit and the six grandchildren, despite Lady Ellen's formality, ran along relaxed lines relative to the times. BG offered love, as with money, generously, but without seeming to nurture the development of his children's qualities.

BG's gifts could be splendiferous. To Vivian and Kit on their marriage came 3 Hampstead Hill Gardens, Adrian's birthplace, or 'Charlcote' as it was named by the man for whom in 1893 it was built. He was Charles Green R.I. (1840–1898), illustrator of many books, whose major success was Dickens' *The Old Curiosity Shop*. Charlcote is described in *Giles Artists' Houses in London* as 'a cross between a Queen Anne rout-house and a Renaissance casino'. It remains a most impressive, unconventional dwelling place and was no less so in Vivian and Kit Ryan's day, who together hardly fitted much of a mould themselves. The religious, long-suffering Kit rather fitted the pronouncement of the American suffragette Elizabeth Stanton: 'The Bible teaches that woman... precipitated the fall of the race... [and] marriage for her was to be a condition of bondage, maternity a period of suffering and anguish, and in silence and subjection, she was to play the role of a dependant on man's bounty for all her material wants.' Were money not to have overflowed from Sir Gerald's heaping sackfuls, it would have hit her hard. Vivian, generous to the heart, didn't value money in the same way at all, and had less difficulty in spending his unwisely.

Vivian's childhood had not been easy. At three years old, one long night such as parents dread, their wretchedly ill second son was diagnosed with meningitis. It was the source of all his being a person 'with disabilities'. 'Deaf and dumb', Adrian said of his 'lovely dad, who was just like something out of Scott Fitzgerald,' although he could in fact hear and talk restrictively. Adrian's elder brother Desmond has written an unpublished account of the Ryan history – some of it too vivid for Adrian, who issued a staunch rebuttal of certain details. Its virtue is that it is seldom dull, but it is romanticised prose. Meandering through it, however, the reader catches some sparkle of truth-telling. Desmond clearly loved his mother and enjoyed her confidence, disconcerting though that can be. Where Adrian was wary of saying much, from Desmond plenty can be learnt about their upbringing.

In part he is upbeat. Both brothers 'felt that to have a deaf father was something special and one up on other boys' and that 'as they grew their love for him began to have a protective side...' He refers to rivalry between his father and uncle to beget the first grandchild. There is a moot remark about the baronetcy and to Vivian having the first boy. Desmond also notes the hopelessness of Kit's situation, having everything decided for her, nurse, nanny, all by Lady Ryan with BG's backing. According to Desmond, Vivian felt that he and his wife were not listened to or respected, and it was small wonder that he veered in the direction of having 'to have fun' above all. It was a mixed blessing so often to be thanking BG for things, never depending on themselves.

The feeling grew in Vivian that he was entitled to a life of enjoyment. One early painting by him was a well-executed, unintentional pastiche of a court jester. Merry and bright, it might as well have been a self-portrait, for he was always joking. His distinguished painter friend and near neighbour Frank O. Salisbury might not have thought much of it. Ditto Seymour Lucas his private teacher, but as such more obligated toward circumspect praise. In a letter from the RA dated 20 April 1916 Lucas wrote: 'My dear Vivian, your picture is beautifully hung on The Line in the Green Room and looks quite worthy of its place.' Adrian, observing a similarly adequate daub of Vivian's of a terrier sitting on his haunches beside a dog bowl on which was inscribed the legend 'Doggie', wistfully chuckled: 'That was my dad alright; he didn't care about *Art.* If it said Doggie, that's what he put in.' Conversely, when he was aged fourteen, Adrian poignantly reported taking home a book about Van Gogh and showing it to his father who, remarkably, had never seen Van Gogh before. 'Oohhhh!' mumbled Vivian equally wistful, '*I* should have liked to have painted like that...'

Desmond's book informs us: 'Vivian managed with his antics and mimicry to become the hero of the three young ones'[2] who found in him 'a kindred spirit'. His childlikeness is seen as endearing by others, but increasingly not by Kit who was incorrigibly 'army'. Peggy Ryan remembers Vivian laughing, staying seated and light-heartedly banging the table with a spoon in time to *God Save The King* during the annual radio broadcast[3] mainly to defuse Kit's overriding seriousness at the opposite end of the long table. Also his frequent and less harmless flirting with every woman he met. Furthermore Peggy recalls that Kit thought she was doing Vivian a good turn by being married to him at all. Valentine Goodall simply said that 'Vivian was a lovely man'. Yet according to Desmond,

2. Including sister Jeannette, 1929–2005
3. He could hear loud music via the vibration of furniture

it was Kit who 'sensed the sadness that lay hidden behind his optimistic exterior.' Kit had reason to be sad herself. It was the role of the nanny to bring up her children, while she watched from a first-floor window as they were taken out each day at four o'clock – longing to be with them, observed Desmond, but hardly ever doing so. What she did do is unclear. Despite her view to the contrary, she had married way above herself. Respectable red brick, Berisal, her home in Normanton Road, south Croydon, was not remotely a patch on Charlcote nor even on Sir Gerald's apartment in St James's Square, let alone Hintlesham. Her once diligent water-colouring in when-did-you-last-see-your-father revival style has not resulted in any extant work and probably petered out. She missed contact with her family early on. Then each one of her relations systematically died, leaving only her severely military brother Reggie. She felt lonely in the wake of all the sequent deaths, angry, depressed and inert. What cannot have been any comfort to her, again according to Desmond, was Vivian's feeling, since life owed him, that he was entitled to enjoy himself. A party is alluded to at which Vivian gathered together some of his 'livelier young friends' while seeming to exclude her, unless she did so herself. Of supporters she seemed to have but one: John Englebach, a family friend of some years standing, so often a presence in their photographs, on holidays, feeding off the crumbs of their better provided-for table. They also came to feed off each other physically, a moral lapse she became unable to deny. Whether her well documented 'illness' was the result of an abortion remains unknown. Desmond writes candid details about sex between John and his mother, intruding equally on Kit and Vivian's wedding night. In doing so, he paints a picture as vivid in detail as his mention of the 1918 German attack on the Somme. In neither instance was he present, whereas in the detailing of his own wedding night, he shows a remarkable reticence.

1927 was a bad year for Kit. Even Vivian took account of it. A 'talk' between her and Sir Gerald is reported with ominous precision to have taken place on 5 January 1928, before the latter's annual winter cruise to South America. In order to assist the marriage – things must have been bad for Vivian to act responsibly – a plan for them to live abroad for much of the year and buy a house in the south of France was enacted in March 1928. Santa Lucia, the villa in Cagnes-sur-Mer, was finished and moved into by the spring of 1929. Kit, by Desmond's account, was 'intoxicated with new freedom.' Pregnant and then with a new baby to care for (Jeanette was born 2 August 1929), this seems unlikely. Vivian was again painting and exhibiting work, such as *Nicolai of Cagnes – Epicier* (in hindsight, there seems to have been a slight mistake in the title of this painting: 'epicurien' or epicure in English, seems more suited to this palpably self-indulged grocer friend of the artist).

Howsoever the Scott Fitzgerald idyll concluded, it enjoyed little duration. Perhaps Vivian's infidelities started anew in response to her denying him sex (in Cagnes he was known as 'The Lord Mayor', according to Adrian 'because he poked everybody') or in response to the renewal of extended visits from John Englebach, well represented in Kit's photograph album through the autumn of that year. Spousal communication, always compromised, became selective and finally foundered. When Vivian failed to notice Kit and the children leaving the train at Cagnes and the eight-year-old Adrian pointed out that Papa remained on board, she showed neither surprise nor concern. Vivian carried on to Nice where, a well-dressed Englishman in spats and having borrowed money off the hotel porter at the Negresco, they caught up with him a couple of days later. Vivian turned to the cocktail combination of local women and alcohol. Desmond, often ready to clock rivalry with Adrian, makes unequal comparisons between Vivian's lifestyle and Uncle Gerald's, making his father seem envious of the lack of 'Title [presumed] money, career'. It does not sound much like Vivian, for these are not things he valued consciously. Desmond continues: 'Is it any wonder that trapped in deafness, unable to fully express himself, he should drown out the unjust world in drink?' Kit turned one more time to his parents: specifically, woman to woman, to Lady Ellen. She knew about the money set aside for his grandchildren by Sir Gerald. She was, writes Desmond, 'scared to admit to… her lapse of morals' and about the effect it could have on their inheritance. She knew, via her upbringing, what it was like to have insufficiency of money and would probably have feared a return to that (John Englebach having none, was no real rival to Vivian). She feared for herself and for her infant daughter. Lady Ellen seems to have responded. In her will, made 28 December 1931, she leaves Kit £2,000, exactly the sum she provides for each of her six grandchildren. Jewellery, furniture and personal chattels go to BG. The residue is divided scrupulously between her sons. Kit used this money to buy a property for herself, which she later sold to acquire Longstaff's – an extended cottage at Iden – where she lived apart from Vivian. Lady Ellen's will is very simple. There was only one other bequest – of £200 – to a spinster who may have been a servant. In some ways, Kit may have regarded herself, and been regarded, as some kind of glorified servant. For taking Vivian on, begetting the first grandson and later a spare, to inherit the land and title, only to be superseded by the birth of Gerald Ellis' son Michael. It made for a terribly unhappy, depressed woman and mother for much of the time. But not all of it. A kind of scrapbook kept from Adrian's birth – at 6.35am, on Sunday 3 October 1920, weighing 7¾ pounds – gives the details of his early existence, of his illnesses, which are regular and often severe, and for which she evinces little, if any, sympathy: 'Very ill in February (1932) – Apendicitis[sic] peritonitis & pneumonia – in Nursing Home – Broadstairs.' There is no suggestion that she bothered to visit him in these extreme circumstances. She does not say he was kept in isolation either. Then there are passing references to his progress – 'Getting on alright at St Peters', which is not Adrian's own view, and jubilant ones to his success in achieving rugger and soccer colours, boxing and swimming – all documented in her legible handwriting with occasional flourishes. It is notable that she fails to refer to Adrian by name throughout the book, but always in the third person. Information lessens with the passing years. Entries result from pride – her own – not tenderness. For the year 1934, she writes 'Went to Eton... very happy' together with a healthy list of consequent achievements, including being 'top of division and 1st in Tests & 3rd in Harmsworth drawing prize'. Thereafter, and by sinful omission one of the most revealing things about her, there is no entry and it is assumed no pride at all, no 'sexed-up dossier' to follow.

For Kit, sex of any kind must have been a difficult subject. Vivian, if we are to believe his son Desmond, 'wanted his sex nightly'. The gentle idealism of the newly-engaged Kit's May 1915 photograph album contrasts sharply with this catastrophic obligation (presumably exposed along with everything else on their honeymoon in St Ives): the unsullied west and south-east facades of Hintlesham; Vivian dashingly posed on a horse or dashing in a smart suit; boating on the gentle lakes in the Home Wood. Serene calm radiates from photos of the well-kept gardens, the interior of the ancient church, chauffeured cars and respectful, smiling servants. The reality must have presented her with a shocking contrast. But a later, often told, story is of young Desmond and Adrian creeping out of bed to witness scantily clad revellers at a party held by their parents at Migvie Lodge, 2 Porchester Gardens[4] and the consequent

4. Their next house after Charlcote, near Vivian's brother's home in Bayswater

fury of Kit following their discovery. Humans attack whenever they are afraid. Kit caned the two of them, Vivian having refused to oblige her. Even after Adrian and Peggy were married, Kit used to pull apart the single beds when they stayed with her at Iden. Peggy said they laughed at it, but not to her, and pushed them together. Later they would find them pulled apart again. Not a word was said. Yet her proprietorial remark, when Geraldine was born in May 1943, was 'You couldn't have given me a better present', which sounds a perfectly grandmotherly cliché. Until, according to Peggy's recollection, you consider that in the short period of Geraldine's life before Kit died of cancer, in November 1945, she met her first grandchild only once and was not the doting grandmother on that occasion.

Moreover, Peggy feels Kit's apparent gratitude was for other reasons. Geraldine, being a girl, countered the troublesome possibility of another highly sexed Ryan male. And although of course she knew that Peggy was pregnant (having offered her a sole piece of unsolicited advice – 'It's not *done* to shout out when you're giving birth...'), the advent of baby Geraldine was tangible proof for Kit against the charge of Adrian's homosexuality – so deeply shaming for her – the cause of his 'expulsion' from Eton and of misunderstanding ever since. Desmond writes breezily about homosexuality; his own, Adrian's and also Pamela's. (Paradoxically, a memorandum in Adrian's diary, 16 July 1938, records 'Had my first woman! Feelings on subject mixed. Very hard to compare with boys. Amusing experience.') What Desmond has to say about Kit's response to being summoned by telephone to see housemaster Mr Rowlatt is far from breezy. 'For Kit the train journey to and from Eton... over a matter she found sickeningly indelicate, marked her life, so that she found it nigh impossible to forgive her son. Unknowingly he had subjected her to one of the most humiliating moments in her life!'

This subjective statement raises questions about the hierarchy of Kit's league of humiliations; whether Adrian's 'expulsion' – which is nothing short of a misrepresentation – was as humiliating to her as say, Vivian's seduction of his niece Pamela aged 16 (assuming that she, like everyone else, knew of it). Or Desmond's subsequent partial seduction *by* Pamela, his cousin. Or Adrian's seduction – in Flat B1 Albany – by Sir William Brass, a rich and powerful man she may rather have died for than dared to cross in any way. Or Kit's receipt of the court warrant for Vivian from the woman (who became his second wife and the mother of his 'bastard baby' according to Kit) while she refused to countersign cheques for child support. Or the self-humiliation she might have felt for doing nothing except take money from the Ryans all her life and putting curiously large sums aside for unequal distribution to Jeannette over the two boys after her death, while never admitting to anyone – excepting Lady Ellen, out of dire need – the extent of her affair with John Englebach. Added to this could be Adrian's getting himself out of the army and instead becoming a fire-watcher (despite receiving at least one commendation for bravery), for which she held him in the utmost contempt. 'You yellow-bellied little toad', she called him, and in his absence sold his Bentley for £5 for the war effort out of vengeance. Her love for him for so long had been conditional. Not as a mother's should be. Kit's life may not have been easy – though to some it could appear as a doddle – but there is no evidence that she chose to make it easier by seeking to resolve its difficulties instead of acting them out and projecting them onto her children. Adrian received at best a very chilly mothering, and the often uncomfortable power women could hold for him sullied much of his conduct around them. He was more at ease with men, the acquiring of three wives and three daughters notwithstanding. For him, with such parents as teachers, life was not easy as once it had seemed.

Adrian drew Kit on her deathbed. He hurried up from Mousehole, where he had been for over a month since leaving London, following the memorial for Willy Brass on 10 October, having last seen her a week before that on his birthday. What sort of a likeness he achieved is hard to tell, but he certainly captures that stillness and peace which comes to human remains when the spirit has newly departed. It is clearly hurriedly worked and must have taken a few minutes only. The paper is not taken from a sketchbook and it seems unlikely that he went with the intention of making a drawing, but did so spontaneously, using a small sheet of paper given him by someone from the nursing home. It is worked from the left-hand side, the right side consigned to blank emptiness, a powerful metaphor in itself, except for six desolate words he has written at the bottom: 'My Mother on her death bed'. (The stark entry in his diary in small handwriting says 'Mother Died'.) He has had trouble with the first 'm' of 'my'; he gives her a capital 'm'; he makes two words out of 'deathbed', adding stress while in the rarified presence of death. There is a flat matter-of-factness about the statement; also a rhythm not unlike the virtually contemporary (1942) opening sentence of the novel

L'Etranger by Albert Camus, existentialist chronicler of the human condition and expert in the matter of despair: 'Aujourd'hui Maman est morte...' and deploying the same seven syllables. There is one other departure from his normal drawing style. He faces this unique subject matter head-on and close-to; not customarily rising above it, but directly confronting a painful scene of utter irrevocability and final rejection. Face to face for the last time, possibly also for the first time in long years of her registering disapproval of him; finally without her registering anything at all – except an end to all hope of receiving mothering from her. His drawing is unsigned.

Kit died, relieved no doubt to have seen the end of the great world conflict, and Vivian buried her in the new ground opposite Hampstead Church. A prime plot was selected, brick-enclosed, of modern design, except for a traditional stone cross, set beneath an ancient beech. The tablet reads: 'TO MY DEAR WIFE / KATHLEEN F. RYAN / A PRECIOUS MOTHER / WHO FELL ASLEEP NOVEMBER 15 1945 / AGED 53 YEARS'.

When it was Vivian's time to die, he too was buried in that graveyard, 40 graves apart in the same row as his first wife. The inscription is faded on his tombstone. What can easily be read is: 'IN / LOVING MEMORY OF / VIVIAN DESMOND / RYAN BORN [unclear] / PASSED / AWAY / DEARLY BELOVED'. The double-banded decoration and the headstone's lettering bespeak the cultured genius of Guido Morris, the once famed St Ives printer – Adrian's doing. The grave, like Guido, has suffered badly with time, unlike Kit's, which is in good condition. There is something Hardy-esque about the relationship of these two in death. About Vivian's public display of marital correctitude – sorrow after the event of their marriage but not seemingly during it – or was it just simple-minded sorrow, well-intentioned? Apt are the lines from a Hardy poem: 'No shade of pinnacle or tree or tower, while earth endures shall fall on my mound and within the hour, steal onto yours...' Nothing on either grave would reveal to a stranger the fact that the two of them were related. Despite Kit's inscription appearing to be tender, if sentimental – a thing widowers, especially guilty ones, fall prone to being – the word 'precious' with its alternating connotation cannot fail to play on the minds of those knowing the brittleness of her nature. Vivian's tomb indicating neither marriage nor progeny is neatly unsentimental – Adrian again – and ingeniously ironic.

After twenty-two years of marriage with Adrian, his third wife Sue Ryan was surprised to learn that these graves lay within two miles of their Camden Town home. Of his grandparents' grave at Hintlesham Church, she said he had spoken. Indeed they had visited with Pamela and her husband that tall, tapering, elegant cross and the brass plaque inside St Nicholas' there commemorating the presentation of the church clock in Lady Ellen's name. Geraldine, Adrian's eldest daughter, knew of her paternal grandparents' Hampstead burial only through Desmond visiting from Canada. Yet Adrian was far from averse to grave-spotting. He would visit Braque's grave in Normandy, recommending others to do the same, Wilde's in Paris, and when told that his granddaughter Martha was going to Kensal Green, he remarked what a lovely time she'd have looking at the stones. And in the same graveyard as his un-parentlike parents lies Slade Professor Schwabe, and just opposite Constable, one of Adrian's greatest heroes and whose travelling easel, formerly Vivian's, he owned. This detachment from both parents' resting place is an example of his, at times, private and impersonal-seeming nature. It is unlikely that he would visit there silently. It is more a reflection of his uncertain feelings for them – justifiable in view of their being unsafe territory. He would not see the point in revisiting his mother's blend of rejection and pitch-black envy for his independence. His father's more agreeable feelings he could access without graveyard visits.

Before Vivian's death, in 1950, he too was ill for some time before the cancer wrenched the last bit of life out of him. Admitting him to hospital in Hampstead, they told him to stop smoking. Discharging him, they told him he could smoke again. There was nothing more to be done for him. Adrian with Polly Walker[5] the consort he would never marry, was at home in London at the time, at 48 Tite Street. They were visiting Vivian in his Finchley Road Mansions flat often, and towards the end, according to Polly, every day. Adrian's diary records 'see daddy' on Sunday 5 February; on Friday 17 'Daddy very weak'; visiting again on the 18th; on 22nd, which was Ash Wednesday, through to the 25th when he simply writes: 'Daddy died', thickly underlined. It then indicates his staying with Nan Ryan until the day after Vivian's funeral, Thursday 2 March, presumably choosing to be alone with Nan and, possibly, John his half-brother, before returning to Tite Street.

Nan, Vivian's second wife and widow, took great care of him and was curiously strong and matter-of-fact, coping without

5. Daughter of Alec and Kaye Walker, founder of Crysède Silks where Tom Heron, father of Patrick, became manager c. 1925

apparent emotion with the certainty that awaited them. Polly felt that there was very good feeling between Vivian and her. Underneath Nan was not just sad, however, but devastated when he died. She simply didn't give in to it. Nan also cleared up the place so very quickly, Polly said, and had burned her husband's bedding by the time they arrived that morning to find that he was dead. Through disabilities similar to Vivian's – which is how they met – Nan was unable to use a telephone, so there was no choice but to attend his last days by rote. The last time she saw Vivian alive, Polly said that he held out his hand to her, so she came near and then he gently kissed her cheek. She kissed him on the cheek also. It was not their normal practice. It seemed a soft gesture of affection from a person not historically given to shyness when approaching the opposite sex. Polly does not recall Adrian's manner of greeting his father, or how they parted that day, because she said he always sat in with Vivian on his own, she having gone in and come out before him. She said that his grief was dignified and unconcealed, openly weeping and deeply saddened. An orphan aged twenty-nine years. Polly did not go to Vivian's funeral, but cannot now recall why. The reason can only have been that Adrian for some reason prevented her, which she would have minded. His diary indicates that he stayed with Nan and his half-brother for the next six nights until after the funeral. He then returned to Tite Street. A habit of blocking out unpleasant events is something Polly will admit to. As much a past figure of controversy as one devoid of affectation, something particular struck her about arriving at Hampstead to find that Vivian had died. It was the strong feeling – a conviction which has remained with her – that Nan had smothered her husband with a pillow to end his suffering. Out of love and with great courage, if so. It is an insupportable feeling; but from everything that has been said of her, Vivian seems to have experienced from Nan a level of unselfish love and brave self-sacrifice he had not previously enjoyed in his life.

The only Ryan painting of Hintlesham is by Vivian. Like the majority of his works, and by most standards, it is of small importance and may be listed as 'whereabouts unknown' without great sense of loss. A photograph is all that is left of it, and yet this reveals something about the author of the work. Vivian's enclosed world, concealed behind the jovial mask, is difficult to fathom. It is safe to say that one thing he was not was any kind of a snob. His perspective on Hintlesham confirms this and is refreshing. He takes as his subject not any of the famous garden fronts; not the Thorn Walk, not the ornate Orangery; no gleam of Bentley or Lagonda on the gravelled drive. His view is of the drive alright, but looking away from the house, disregarding of almost everything that would indicate status of any kind – with the possible exception of a semi-circle of grass in the foreground – and it depicts what truly was closest to his heart: the land. Vivian was a fine shot, he was a horseman, he enjoyed golf, he rowed, he fished, he was athletic, he cared about the servants, he was the son of a man who was passionate about his estate and without doubt who wanted it maintained after his death. But Vivian was not only a damaged and frustrated man, he was the second disinherited son. As in so many aristocratic English families, merit and aptitude is often on a collision course with the shortcomings of actual birthright. Gerald Ellis Ryan, Bt., succeeding their father in 1937, had no interest in the estate. He didn't have in him what Vivian did, whereas Vivian didn't have it in him to protest any wished-for claim upon the land. Whether he saw his potential abilities is questionable. He was probably too used to doing what he was told. Between the brothers, after all, they had an inheritance that would last each their whole life. Hintlesham was auctioned, piece by piece, its eighteen indoor servants and countless outdoor staff were dismissed, the farm workers' lives put into uncertainty; as well as the working lives of the two brothers who would draw from its proceeds.

Vivian's picture also polarises the extremes of his character: the bright sunny demeanour and the dark shadows creeping beneath the surface. The way forward is fenced and gated (in photographs, the gate is more often open). The drive out appears to terminate (it actually turns both left and right, but his painting does not show this) and even the vertical trunks of the trees in the park echo the ironwork in the foreground to suggest bars as the main subject of the painting. Its use of false perspective, a rising above the subject, a self-aggrandising, is untypical of Vivian's style; but it becomes quintessential of his son's. This sad depiction of the absent presence is a poignant summing up of the life of a man who was trapped inside the cage of having to paint 'Doggie' photographically. Not only that, there was the issue of others – brother, sons, nephew, servants – all going in uniform to two wars from which he was debarred, penned inside a house where the cocktail hour came as regularly as the sun going down across the park. His frustration and, underneath, his anger cannot fail to have overspilled before it merged with, and finally drowned in, drink. He wasn't useful. It cannot have gone unsensed by any one of his children. Indeed it formed a considerable part of their uneasy inheritance.

The distribution of assets of one person's estate, in any family, is a potential minefield. How familiarly heard is the cry of 'That was always said to have been left to me!' in the absence of any scrap of supporting piece of paper? How is the same human cry stifled, held back by propriety and unwillingness to show avarice? Vivian is unlikely to have asked for anything at all. The extent to which he withheld crying for help, pain, attention or for equality is unknown. His tendency to hold back, because of his physical inability of expression or because of a natural generosity of spirit, is more guessable. In the circumstances, instead of equal[6] divisions, it might be expected that Vivian would receive more than being shunted through art school and left shares in a fortune he was not schooled in controlling. If Kit or anyone else thought they were being short-changed, they may only have rumbled in corners amongst themselves, not saying anything openly. Nothing about Vivian managing the estate is known to have been suggested. His brother Sir Gerald Ellis Ryan's dispersal of Hintlesham brought to a close its happiest period in the last century. His natural heir was Pamela, and his eldest son Michael was shot down over the North Sea in 1940. His inheritance from his parents was big on privilege, low on responsibility to those less fortunate around him. Sir Derek Ryan Bart, his son, was 'a pale shadow' compared to his vibrant sister.

Vivian's real inheritance is more unpleasant than his brother's to contemplate. On the surface, rich and married off, satisfactorily providing the first male heir, then to find, with Michael dead in the war and Derek reportedly shaken into sickness by it, that there was a chance of the title being diverted. Though initially applying himself to his unheart-felt way of painting, it was not his forté. In reality, he was wrapped up like an awkward-shaped parcel, unconsulted, without responsibility offered him, a prisoner in civvies, expected – even encouraged – to play the clown, hindered and unhelped and, with few exceptions, unloved and misunderstood for his true self.

The solution for Gerald and Vivian should have been obvious. If only they had found work that suited them (in some ways, they tried). The clue underpinned what had made the Ryan family what it was, *Sans Travail Rien*... In the matter of work

6. It was not equal in that Vivian was never remunerated, unlike his brother, with being made a Lloyds' Name

at least, Vivian's example taught Adrian how not to be. It is not an easy thing to be a painter, but work and creativity bring their own lasting rewards.

Family epilogue

Aileen Pamela, Lady Green, died on 24 August 1985 and her ashes were scattered into the estuary at Stutton. A good friend, Carina Maitland, said of her that she laughed more with Pam than with anybody. Also that she was outrageous and could be embarrassingly so, combining a powerful mix of danger and fun. Mrs Maitland highlights the story of Pamela, as godmother to her daughter, attending her school confirmation. After forty minutes of the school chaplain droning on, in the silent space of a longish pause so that everyone would hear, Pam said in a loud voice: '*How* much longer is this fucking old fart going on for!' The whole school liquefied into suppressed giggles and the disconcerted chaplain – realising his audience was lost to him – wound things up. Mrs Maitland said that Pam was too much without affectation to be a snob in the normal sense of behaving differently towards different classes of person. She was as likely to be good friends with the gillie as she was with the laird, as long as neither was stupid or boring. At Pam's flat in Burton Court, Chelsea, it was her habit while entertaining to keep the talk unbroken by not leaving the drawing room to relieve herself. Instead she was known to move behind the sofa where a pot was kept, into which she peed standing up like a horse. Chamber pots were apt to be put to use by Adrian too, as when new oil works struck him as being too bright, too fresh, so he strategically placed them under the bed 'just to age them a little'.

Cousins Pamela and Adrian were very connected in their lives and in their being. Whereas she was astringently outspoken, he was more introverted. His intention was not to hurt people, but his humour could be mis-read and others became upset when he was just trying to be funny. He too had a speech impediment of a form: he was a malapropist.[7] This affinity between cousins who are also friends – the antithesis to the phrase *cousinage, dangereuse voisinage* – lasted the two of them all their lives. Adrian missed her and the family connection after Pam died. For twenty years he had lived less than three miles from her at Lower Holbrook, rent free in a cottage Pam and her husband Peter had provided for him and Sue. They

7. He once introduced Eunice Palmer, the wife of his painter friend Frederick Palmer, both of whom he held in affection, with the rather annihilating commendation: 'And this...' – pointing at her but confusing her name – 'is Useless...'

loved and respected one another for their innate similarities as well as their differences. Adrian may have felt as ambivalent a love for Pamela, as he undoubtedly did for Vivian, wanting to display a hero-figure view of his dad, while being very conscious (while trying to be seen as reasonable and brave) of his father's over-spilling frustrations and unhappiness. Adrian would have anxiety about exciting any envy in this unhappy, damaged and disinherited second son.

Although he may not have been able to access the darkness of his father and his father's secret and self-deprecating world, he would always have been aware of it. And also of the restraint it brought him: namely, how much can Adrian James Ryan allow himself to get to be Van Gogh? A painting of late summer flowers, painted in Mousehole (from diary records) seemingly begun six months after his father died – the stretcher is faintly dated in pencil, 11 September 1950, four days after what would have been Vivian's 57th birthday – contains an answer. The composition is based on a pyramidal diamond. What appears to be a vase is a glass, aggrandised like the flowers it contains. The glass looks like a rummer of his father's, passed down from BG. It's an object that Adrian often incorporated into his still lifes. The painting reads as a celebration of summer's passing, but it also heralds the inevitability of the winter to come. The foreground, in reality a tablecloth, has the look of stone tiles, while the background is quite abstract and unclear. White (representing the outer self; more silvery, is associated with the human spirit) is in places thickly painted and in abundance. The style is very free. Overall there is a feeling of joy tinged with sadness. It is reminiscent of the practice of placing flowers in remembrance on graves. If subconsciously this is a painting for Vivian, for Adrian's recently found freedom from his father, and in liberation to work towards his full potential, then it only required him to try. Overall the painting is under worked, unsigned and, it must be assumed, unfinished.

In regard to being Van Gogh, the only way it seemed safe for Adrian to try, was ironically to follow the dictum of BG and to lose himself in work. Early on, it drove him passionately. Later, for very clear reasons, there was less passion, and more volume of work, much of it still the body of the legacy in his studio. He worked to save himself from his nebulous inheritance. He worked because without it he feared he might, like his father, amount to something that could look like nothing. *Sans travail rien.*

The Godfather: 'Uncle Willie'

An immense archetypal influence on the teenage Adrian was his godfather, Cambridge athletics blue, Sir William Brass, long-time MP for Clitheroe,[1] and governor of the British Film Institute. His nickname 'Sounding Brass' suitably catered to the differing on-screen/off-screen complexities of his character. Although he knew everybody who was anybody, the likeliest way of his entering into the periphery of the Ryan family was via his directorship of the Guardian Assurance Company. They were not otherwise obviously of his sphere, which was a thing of shifting boundaries, ranging from the relatively open to that which was closeted in darkness. He was born on 11 February 1886, and having inherited from his father a blind manufacturing company and the proceeds of a product equivalent to the morning-after pill, he had a comfortable fortune. He was a born communicator and for Adrian, he was the wind of change: unpredictable in an exciting way, rebellious and inventive. For Uncle Willie, from the supply of Ryan youth in the vicinity of his comfortable former rectory at Chattisham, Suffolk, his pronounced focus on Adrian would have been a thing of intrigue and excitement on a mental level well before the suggestion of anything else arose. Airy and detached, Sir William Brass was not a man to be pinned down to an arrangement, political, business or amicable. Lord Denham[2] whose father, the first baron, was friends with Billie [sic] Brass tells of him fitting the mould of politicians 'who are very

1. First Conservative member, elected 1918, for 40 years
2. Government Chief Whip in the House of Lords 1979–91, and Extra Lord in Waiting to the Queen since 1998

influential but never want to be near the front bench; who would much rather work and stay brilliant behind the scenes, and not be tied down.' He further described Billie as 'likeable because he was an amusing and amiable uncle figure, unfailing in the provision of chocolates from Fortnum's and toys from Hamleys.' Being amusing extended to the recollection of his singing to piano accompaniment the song of the Lord High Executioner from *The Mikado*, operating in a high tenor.

'There was never,' said Lord Denham, 'any suggestion of him being a notorious homosexual; but it was always clear that he wanted to be well thought of' – including by the first Lord Denham, who would not have approved of a homosexual aspect to his friend. This will have been why there were 'girlfriends' regularly brought or alluded to for cover. One of the most universal things to be said about Willie Brass is his cars and manner of driving them. 'Rather like Toad,' said Lord Denham, 'always in a snazzy Rolls with a blind rising at the back which said 'Thank You' to motorists who gave way.' 'He drove a Bentley,' said Valentine Goodall, the man who tended it, recalling its registration YR4070 and that of his other vehicle, a Hillman, 'and was very proud of the fact that he was antagonising the police by driving very fast.' He also mentioned a pull-screen fitted to the back of the car which thanked all those that he rather recklessly overtook. Mr Goodall portrayed Sir William with a mix of deference tempered with the critical observation of a former employee, and regarded him not as 'Lord Chattisham' (thought up for him by Adrian) because he evidently didn't have time to get used to the new title, announced on 14 June 1945, before his lordship's sudden death that August. 'Obstinate old bugger,' said Mr Goodall, 'He died of peritonitis because he wouldn't rest like he was told to', although Peggy Ryan positively recalls his death being due to an aneurism. He said he was likeable 'at times' but 'had a funny temper', noting that he 'wasn't overgenerous with the estate accounts,' but was 'close to the last pound.' Sir William, like many,[3] used to carry a flask of whisky, 'and his shooting perhaps suffered…', unlike Vivian, whom Mr Goodall said was a fine shot. Adrian, a middling shot, once totally impressed Eardley Knollys by shooting two woodcock with one shot at Long Crichel House, Dorset. Valentine Goodall volunteered information about Sir William having 'a feminine sort of voice' and voiced a long-term feeling that he might have been 'a misogynist'. Evidently, then, Uncle Willie was discreet in front of the servants, although his unshakeably faithful butler, Taylor Shiers, 21 stone of him,

3. Lord Dunsany being his example of 'a boozing shooter'

who served him at Albany as well as at the Old Rectory, and whose wife worked as cook, may have been privy to far more. Shiers more than once told Valentine Goodall that 'he'd be looked after' by Sir William after his death. Accordingly a bequest of £500 perhaps went some way to reward the lack of the butler's clacking and potentially damaging tongue.

It also put him on an equal financial footing with the money left to Adrian – the Brass esteem on the one hand for the value of discretion and his price on disappointment at Adrian's early marriage to Peggy on the other. A photograph of Uncle Willie, Adrian and Doris Colman,[4] one of two mustard heiress sisters, taken at Longstaffs, Iden, in July 1939, shows Adrian at his most awkward and unsmiling. He is standing in an embarrassed pose against the Bentley, his legs not fully supporting him, wedged for the purpose of the photo against the much older Doris and yet at the same time pulling away from her; linked behind the scenes as it were with Uncle Willie, who has much of the smiling puppeteer about him – a man well-used to assuming innocence without, while pulling the strings. If the person memorialising the occasion of these visitors in their stately car were Kit, and since it is usual for the photographer to place the subjects, the interposition of Doris between Adrian and the wholly misogynistic Uncle Willie (who contrives to pull as much apart from her as he can, while retaining possession of Adrian unseen) seems almost like Kit pulling apart the beds of her son and daughter-in-law. There is nothing casual about the photograph, and certainly not in the careful composition of her principal subjects: house, people, car. Adrian would have realised her motives and felt uneasy at her hypocrisy, or his own, especially in regard to Uncle Willie. Overall he stands crucified.

Eight days after being removed from Eton (see next chapter), Adrian's diary entry for Friday 8 April 1938 (inked in and ahead of infilled information in pencil) states: 'Off with Brass.' A neat reference to an alternative tour taking in unambiguous licentiousness, a much talked about boys' brothel in Algiers being only one of the educative stop-overs along the way. Perhaps this trip was the first time that the two of them conjoined – with the mutual satisfaction Adrian confided years later to the writer Frances Fyfield. There is nothing new or exceptional in the diary amongst its many observations about faggoty flotsam and jetsam. It is neatly ironic to be punished for homo-sex by removal from school, then catapulted into Sodom by a high-standing Parliamentarian,

4. After Sir Gerald Ellis Ryan's wife died, Doris moved in with him as his mistress

one for whom the lyrics of W.S. Gilbert held great appeal: *'My object all sublime/ I shall achieve in time/ To let the punishment, let the punishment/ Punishment fit the crime...'* After a 58-year interval, once more at Eton for his exhibition 'Dwelling Places' in the well-adapted gallery space, the Brewhouse, Adrian was confronted by four fifth-formers keenly serving wine at the private view. It seemed churlish not to invite the boys to help themselves to the odd glass. Except that later on, they clearly had had too much. Asked why they had volunteered to help out, the now tipsy quartet confessed to its being in lieu of punishment. They met the inevitable follow-up question – What were you to have been punished *for*? – with unguarded candour. 'For drinking!' they gurgled happily.

The Brass trip lasted twenty days. Returning via France he records buying *Salome* and 'The Portrait de D.G. [sic] (O. Wilde)' specified as gifts. They returned to Albany at 11.30am on 27 April, when apart from recording that it was dull, cloudy and wet and that he went to bed at 11, he simply states: 'Should have gone back to school, but – .'

The fact is that energy bordering on confidence was strong, on the surface, in Adrian in 1938: 'The arrogance of youth' he often mentioned much later on, when referring to the bickering among upcoming St Ives artists who couldn't bear the old-school figurative painters. A good part of his well-being was provided by Uncle Willie. Whether at that time a 52-year-old unmarried MP keeping company with a 17-year-old boy would arouse a degree of suspicion, if the media had been developed enough to observe and bring it to public attention, is debatable. The two of them spent enough time together for people to notice. There are 35 references in the 1938 diary to – mainly solo – encounters with Uncle Willie, setting aside their north African tour. The first is given dated 16 January, the last on 15 December. The obliqueness of the entries makes it impossible to gauge the extent of what went on: 'October 13 to play with Willie – quite good... Met Bell[5] and Boys at Queens [Theatre] – Night with Willie.' This may well be innocent, as seemingly, was 14 July: 'Work in the morning – haircut, then out with Willie and 2 girls from RADA.[6] 'Dined Ivy then to Albany.' From 3 June he refers almost exclusively to 'Willie' as opposed to 'W.B.' 'Uncle Willie' or simply as 'Brass'. The first mention of staying the night is on 7 May (but after the African tour) '...out with Brass to dinner and play – Excellent show... Slept at Albany.' As opposed to (9 July) 'Out with Willie

5. The entry continues: 'Bell v. charming – wants me to share flat studio with him. Saw Picasso's Guernica... we want to stay at flat together and use it as a studio – He says he's a masochist'

6. Where Desmond was studying at the time

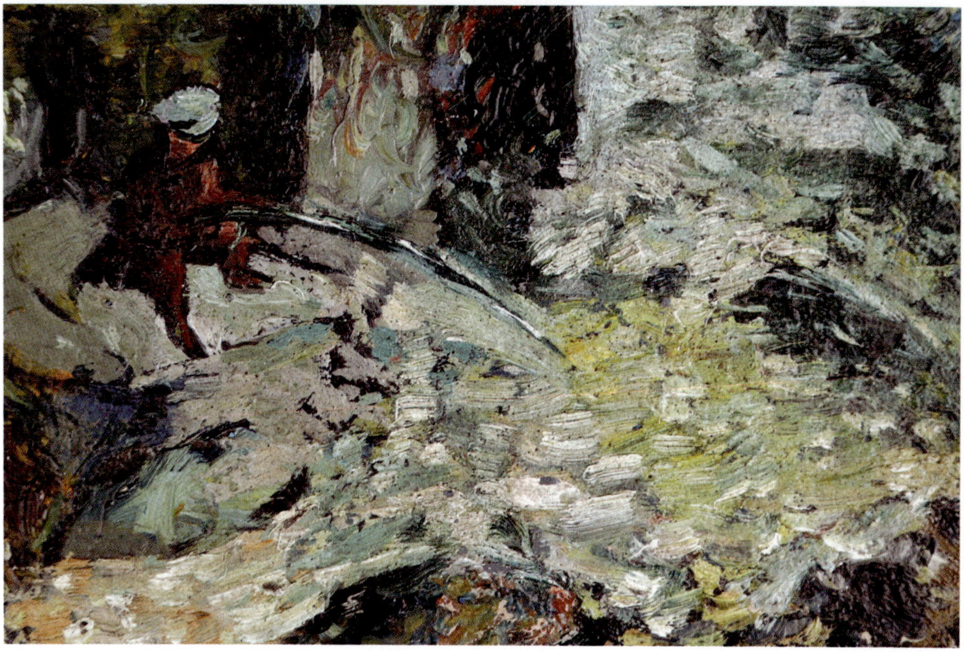

Fisherman, Padstow
oil on board, 1943

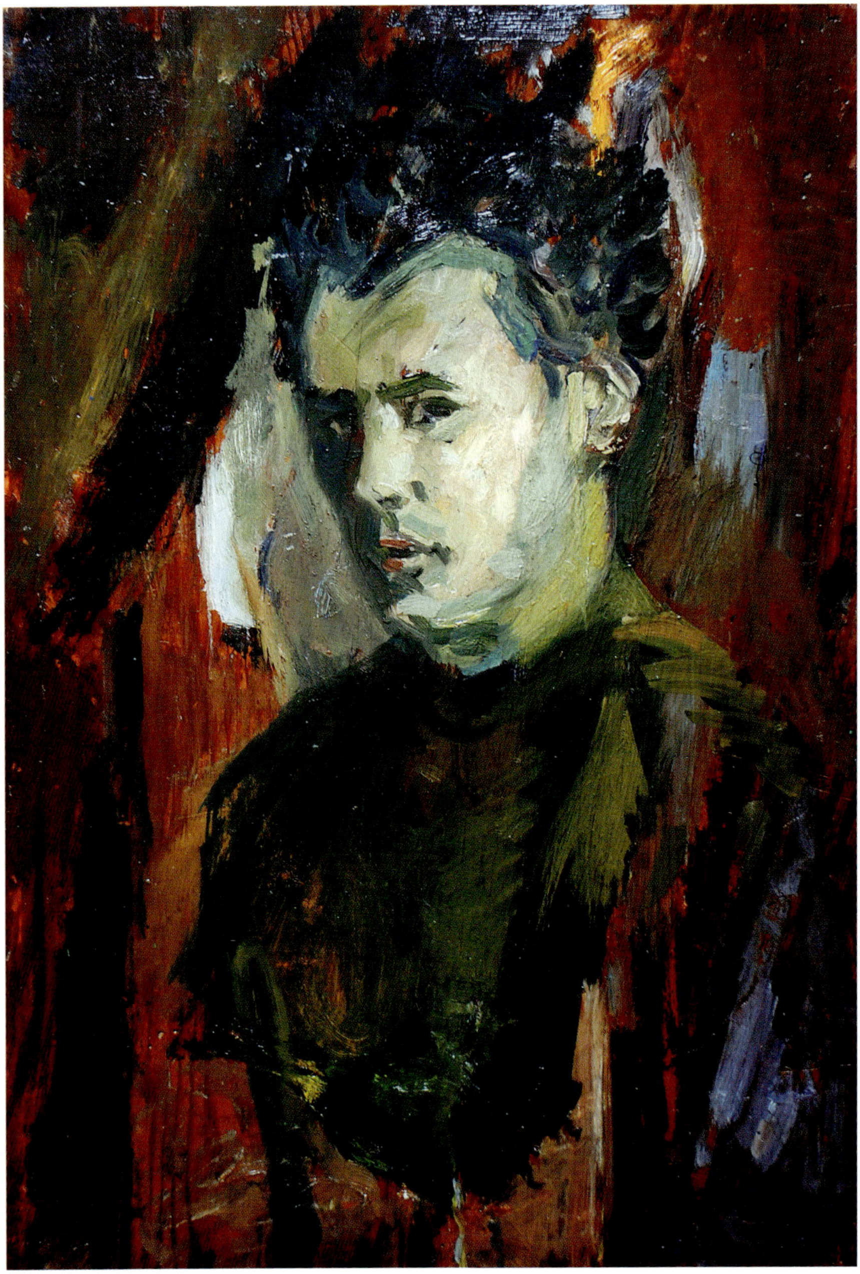

Self portrait
on Architectural Association board, 1938

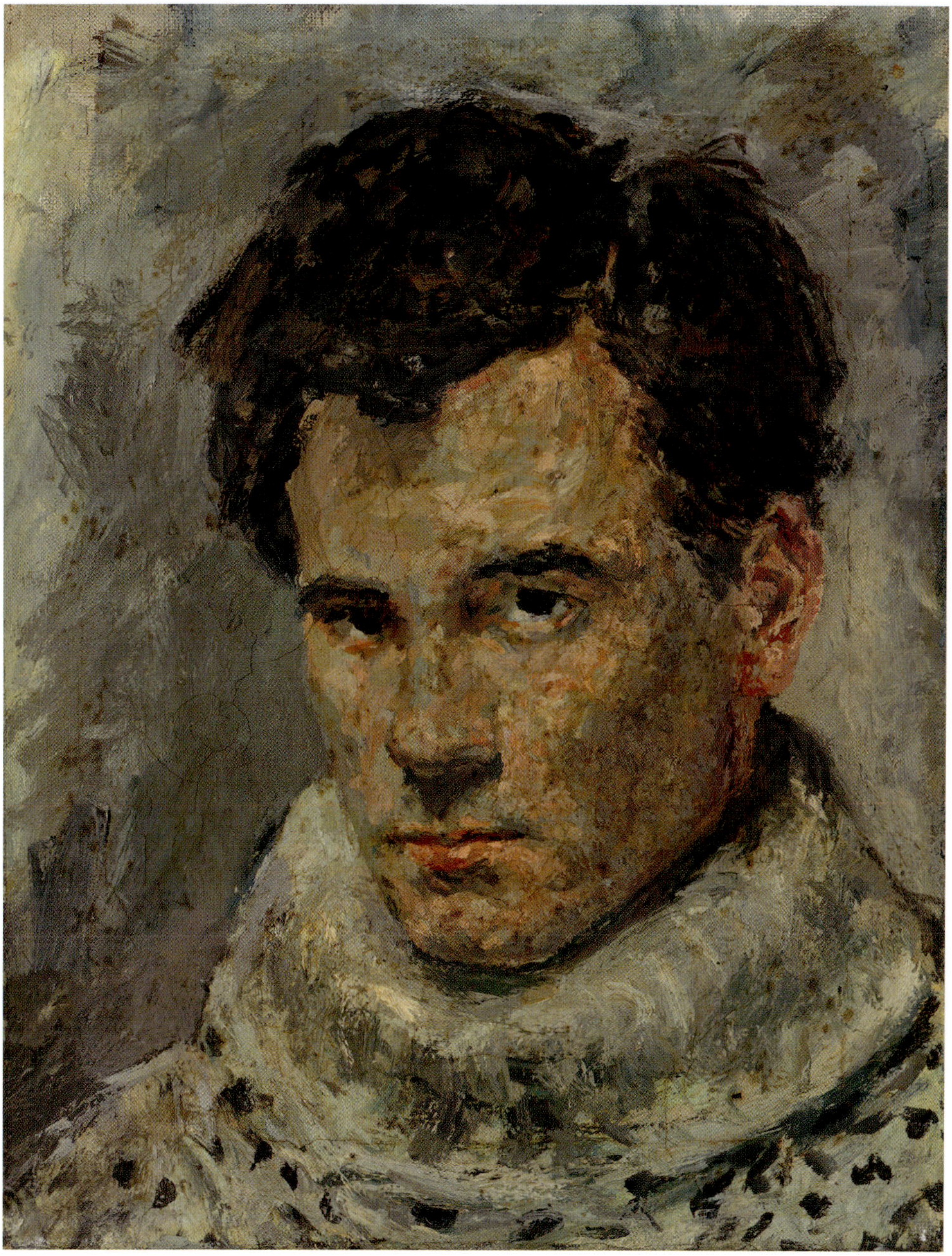

Self portrait
oil on canvas, 1944

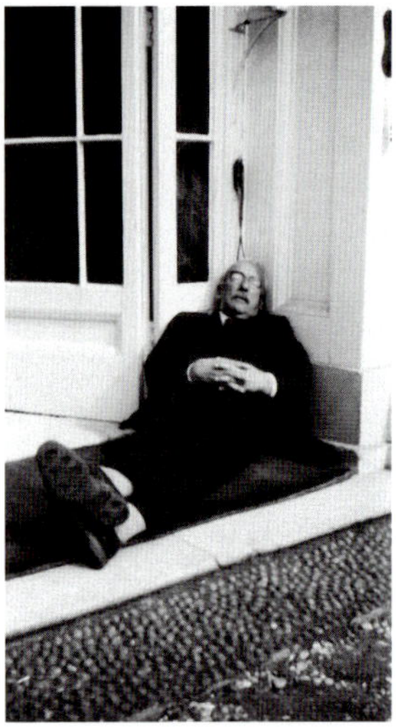

Sir Gerald Ryan Bt., c. 1930

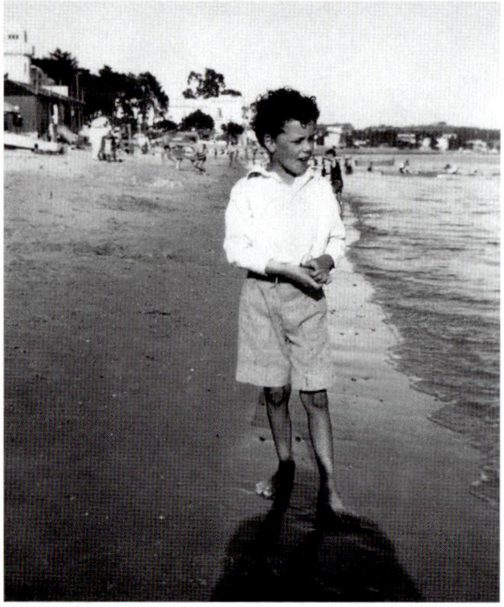

Adrian, Cagnes-sur-Mer, c. 1928

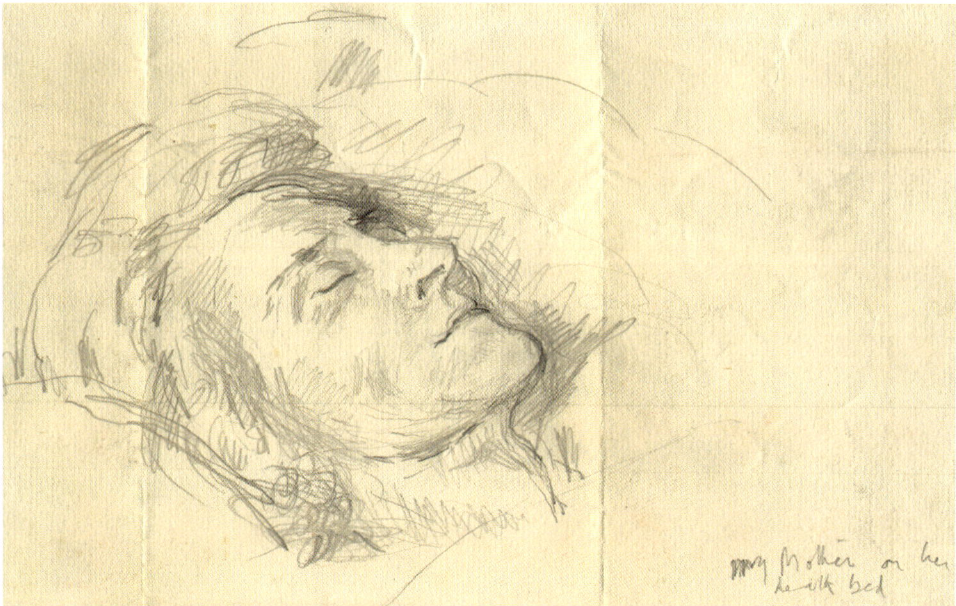

My mother on her deathbed
pencil on paper, 1945

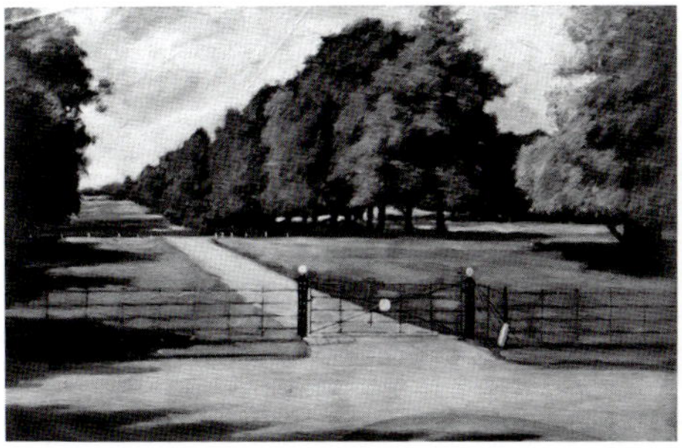

VYVIAN D. RYAN
The drive from Hintlesham
c. 1910

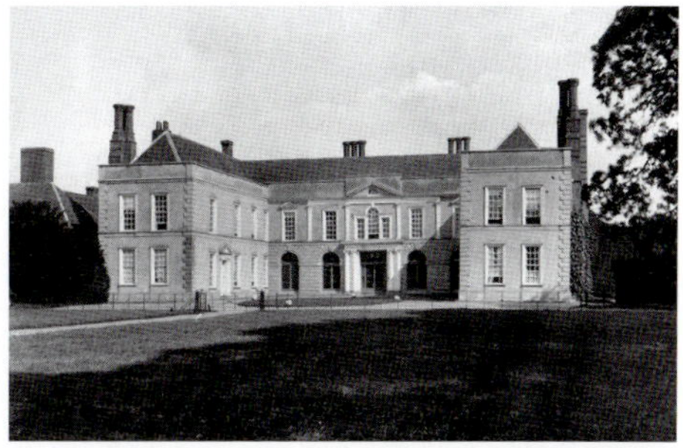

Hintlesham Hall, c. 1915

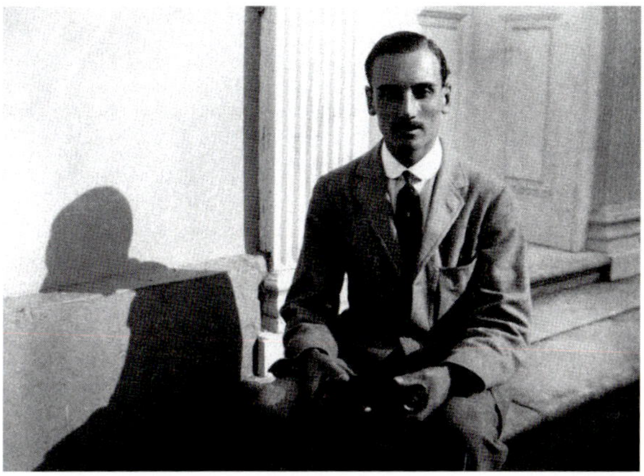

Vyvian D. Ryan, c. 1915

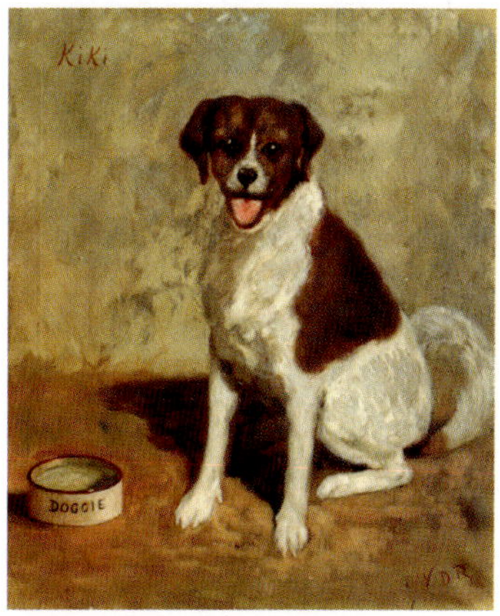

VYVIAN D. RYAN
Dog painting
oil on canvas, 1934

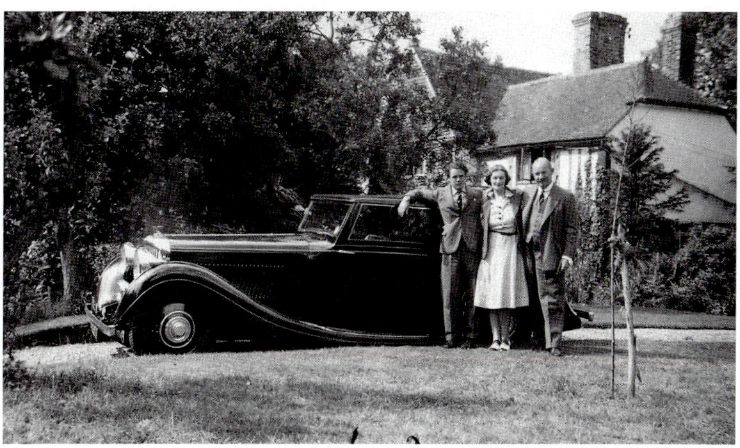

Adrian, Doris Colman and Sir William Brass, Longstaffs, Iden, 1938

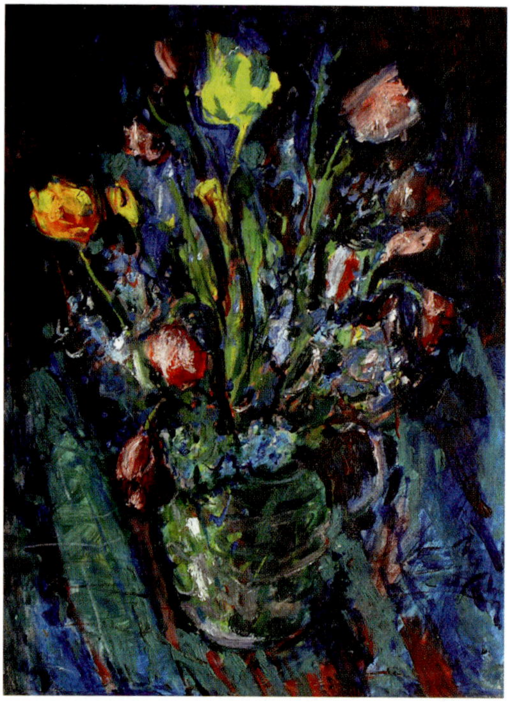

Mixed flowers, night time
oil on canvas, 1949

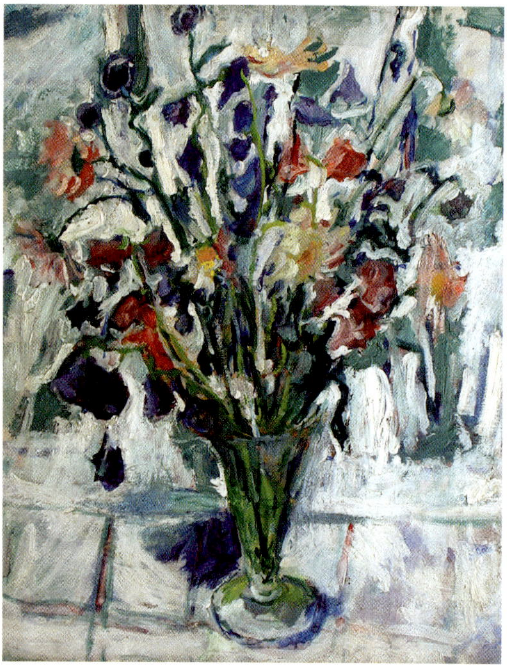

Late summer flowers
oil on canvas, 1950

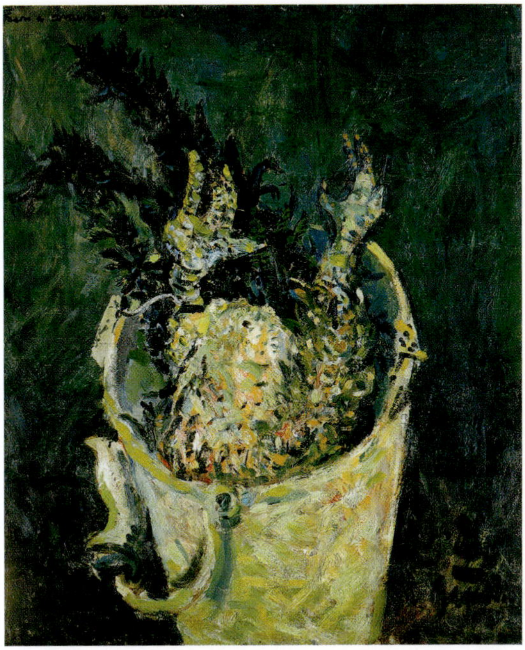

Chicken in a bucket
oil on board, 1944
courtsey of Redfern Gallery

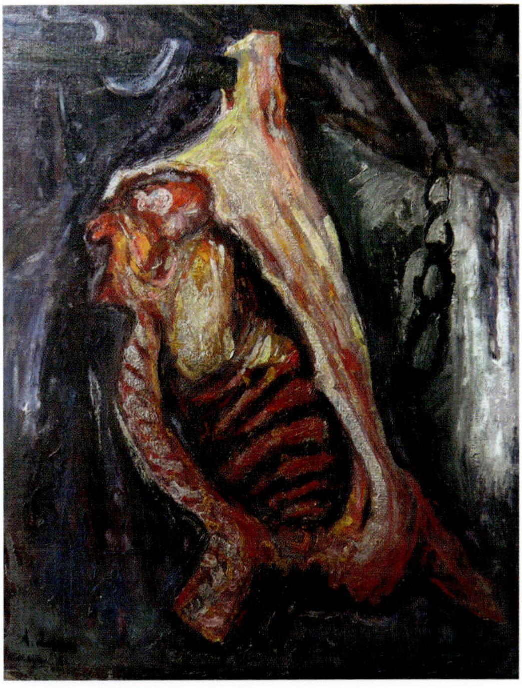

Side of beef
oil on canvas, 1951

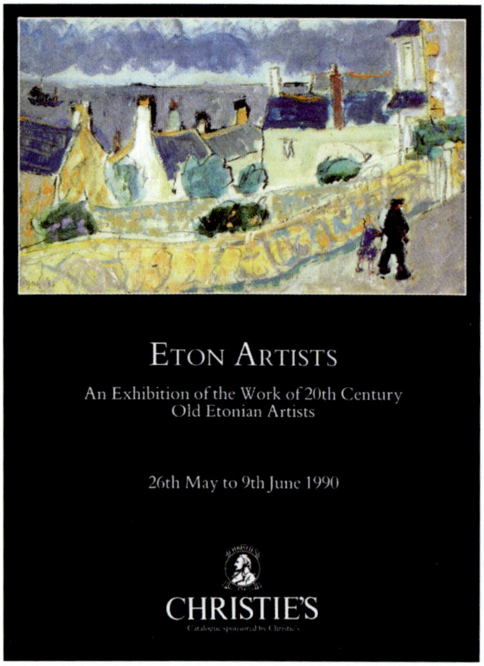

'Eton Artists' catalogue cover, 1990

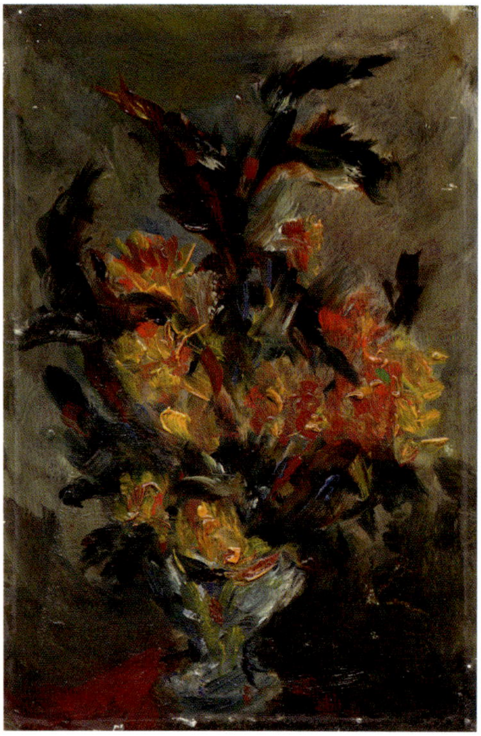

Still life of monbretias
oil on board, 1938

and party, to show. Stayed night with W.B.' Once more in July, and again in September, October and December, he spends an ambiguous night either 'with' Willie or 'at' Albany, plus other occasions when they dine together but it is unclear where he beds down. Feelings are barely alluded to except (13 August memo): 'Letter from Willie – looking forward to seeing him again.' And somewhat excited (29 November) having on the 27th driven à la Brideshead[7] to Oxford in a Lagonda reaching '102 mph!': 'believe Willie is getting me into the Reform.'

William Brass did get Adrian membership of the Reform Club, but he didn't much remember him in his will, though Adrian said he had always told him 'Your Dad will see you all right Jim'.[8] As the will was made on 28 March 1939,[9] it more or less coincides with Adrian taking a room in Earls Court, where his love affair with Peggy began. He did give Adrian an MG and a painting by Soutine, the Utrillo and maybe a Modigliani, and all in the period up until 1941 and his marriage. There are no extant diaries for those years. However, on 4 May 1944, Adrian writes in his diary: 'Ask U. Willie about Rembrandt', which most likely indicates an etching at Zwemmers whose expense he sought to diffuse in lieu of a birthday yet to come. Less a 'falling out', more that, upon marriage, Adrian 'wasn't quite what he'd thought he was' is how Peggy describes the response of Willie Brass to her becoming Mrs Adrian Ryan. She personally always got along well with him. What more could have been W.B's commitment to 'Jim' out of his considerable fortune is inestimable. The chief beneficiary – he was given the Old Rectory and everything in it and in B1 Albany, plus a substantial sum of money – was a distant cousin named Geoffrey Bassett Palau. Valentine Goodall said that the butler's daughter-in-law had but briefly mentioned Palau, who converted all goods and chattels into cash and was otherwise unseen in the neighbourhood before or after. Two other cousins-removed, John Schlottel and John Bassett, each received the same amount of money. The last codicil removed land previously gifted to Palau, transferring it willy-nilly to Schlottel. The first gives to the Old Etonian Trust one thousand pounds 'in grateful memory of the happy and useful years I spent at Eton', a curious linking of felicity and utility. Closer Brass relatives – sister, first cousins, three nephews and the mother of Geoffrey Palau and father of John Schlottel – each receive smaller gifts of money. With a grand total of 41 individual bequests (excluding servants' wages paid for one year from his death) of chattels or money, Willie Brass shows

7. Published 1945
8. 'Jim' was how Adrian was known to family and friends since boyhood
9. Codicils added 6 March 1940 and 20 November 1940

himself emotionally very partial to help and happiness going his way during his lifetime. Listed second of seven godchildren, all receiving £500, Adrian could probably, but for that underage marriage, have done better – and he ever alluded to that possibility. He had at least the consolation of greater bounty and a real connection with this free-spirited dynamo having come his way while they were both able to enjoy it.

As far as the Security Services records go, there is no file on Willie Brass in the National Archives. Whether they would have considered him as 'vulnerable' and worthy of being watched, then or now, is not open to debate by their Press Office. Declassification of files can occur after 75 or 100 years. The archives cast a little light upon his activities, foremost his engagement on deception work for the Political Warfare Executive – specifically Churchill's propaganda intended to inform the German people that an Allied victory would be for their benefit. Valentine Goodall believed him to have been in charge of the Balloon barrage around London during the war. Elsewhere he is listed as PPS to the Minister of Transport and Minister for Aircraft Production, 1941. Certainly his lofty and freewheeling position both before and during the war gave him priority of access, without obstacles, in the taking of a handsome young Eton-ejectee in tow. Adrian's diary (30 September 1938):

> *Willie rang up. To lunch Quaglino with Lord C + Lady – then to Heston to meet N.C. All Eton Ambassadors there etc. Dined – saw flick Willie.*

Neville Chamberlain's famous *Peace in our time* return from Berlin – 'waving that bit of paper' as Adrian put it – indeed took place on that day. Why Brass went in the official chauffeur-driven car to meet him and taking his protégé, is a mystery. His role as PPS was long past. *Dod's Parliamentary Companion* dates it from December 1922 to January 1924 and then from December 1924 to 1927. Adrian did not forget and would mimic the repeated cry of minor officials as they were escorted towards the 'plane: 'Make way! Make way for Sir William Brass!' A photograph in the collection of the Imperial War Museum showing Mr Chamberlain waving the Pact shows also his former PPS and protégé smiling at the peace that it apparently connoted.

Whatever they had, it seems for the most part to have involved a natural empathy and fun times. Certainly so in 1938. Set against the backdrop of a war in whose proceedings he was involved at a stimulating level, W.B. must have defused much in Adrian's home life that he could have wished otherwise. What sort of role model he provided is more questionable. A feeling endures of there being too much of the mercurial about his godfather, that would not, ultimately, benefit Adrian's difficulty with commitment, nor do much to nurture his inherent kindness.

There is no lasting memorial to the Right Honourable Baron Chattisham of Clitheroe. His un-entailed two month-old title died with him, unexpectedly in a London nursing home on 24 August 1945. He was 59. Lord Denham recalled the difficulty of the times, the shortage of money in wartime and after it.[10] His death was subsumed into the intensity of world affairs, his name lost to posterity. Announced in *The Times* on the 27th, personal tributes were printed on 28 and 29 August. They gave no details of his work. His friend Major Arthur Talbot-Ponsonby (fellow executor and equal beneficiary with the first Lord Denham) alluded, quite without irony, to:

> *his magnificent hospitality at his home in Chattisham to hundreds of young men from the Dominions serving in the forces...*

being 'but an index of life spent in unselfish endeavour.' Mr I.S. Amery[11] corroborated:

> *his country house [was] a home from home for men from all the overseas services... the number of those who spent their leave on week ends with him ran into many hundreds...*

This practice of giving temporary accommodation to troops may on some level appear more self-serving in hindsight. Also, according to Valentine Goodall, there were three sailors from nearby Holbrook naval school living permanently in the Old Rectory's attic – having been billeted out while the school was taken over – an arrangement confirmed by Audrey Lorford, a local historian. In addition, W.B. had at some time become close to a young man called Derek Booth, the brother of Mr Goodall's wife Violet, and sought 'to adopt him', but was somehow prevented from doing so. The demands on his time can have known few bounds.

Adrian wrote in his diary for 24 August, less than three months before he was so flatly to record the death of his mother, and

10. £1,000 bequeathed to his father by W.B. – like Adrian he received £500 – would not have come through until after the will was proved in January 1946

11. Rt. Hon. M.P. and former Secretary of State for Dominion Affairs

with some contrast: 'Uncle Willie Died in London' occupying the maximum space, thickly written, like a banner headline, heavily boxed in and underlined. He received the news in Mousehole, where he had been since the second week of July, less than a week after Kit went into a nursing home. Two days before his departure, on 13 July, he records 'lunch with Willie' for the last time. He had made an extended visit to Chattisham from Friday 15 June, the day after the Barony was announced, till Sunday 24 June, although on five of those days (until 7pm on Thursday 21) his lordship was out of the house, being congratulated elsewhere. Over the five-month period from January to May 1945, Adrian met Willie on at least six occasions, twice staying the weekend at the Old Rectory, once for five days. Whatever the differences between them – not least their strongly Conservative versus Liberal political views – and which may have less concerned Peggy than did Adrian's war record, the mutual fondness was lasting. The two were by choice inextricably in each others lives, and the sudden demise of the one was both shock and loss to the other. Despite the quotation 'It is always a silly thing to give advice, but to give good advice is absolutely fatal' having appeared in a diary memorandum of Adrian's following a visit to Chattisham seven years before, it said nothing against the *receiving* of the same. It is unlikely that wily Willie Brass would have declined to give Adrian the ameliorating benefit of his experience, if called upon, as no other of his acquaintance. The 25-year-old had much to learn, and his next role model (and far less suitable one, Augustus John) was not yet a presence, so with his godfather now out of the picture, some learning came the hard way.

Eton

Before Eton Adrian was sent to St Peter's Court Preparatory School, Broadstairs (first attending the Doreck Kindergarten, beginning in September 1925), about which he had not a single good thing to say. He learnt there, aged eight, that it was supposedly normal and acceptable to be isolated from one's parents and unacceptable to object. He also learned how to box. One further thing he culled from the austerity of this unhappy time concerned the rationing of chocolate. Where other boys would seize upon the weekly chocolate bar issued to them and devour it, Adrian would cut his into small pieces, take one in his mouth, slowly suck it, put the rest carefully away and thus make the whole thing last until the advent of the next tuck rations. In old age, after lunching at the studio and if there were chocolate – and there often was – he would sweetly deploy the same tactic.

It was of great pride to Kit and the source of much envy to Desmond languishing at Bryanston – yet of seemingly little or no consequence to Adrian – that he began at Eton in September 1934. Much has been written about Eton between the wars concerning the vanishing upper classes, upon which the school was reliant to attract new wealth and ensure demand for its particular brand of education. 'The count of boys from the peerage was not much less in 1930 than it was in 1900, with 64 boys either peers or sons of peers in a school some 75 boys larger'[1] and excluding ten baronets. In Adrian's final year there

1. *Eton Renewed* by Tim Card, John Murray 1994

were no fewer than 97 peers or sons of peers comprising four dukes, five marquises, 19 earls and five viscounts. There was one royal prince and as healthy a percentage increase of baronets as ever a headmaster could wish to top and tail the bill.

Fees were paid not to the school but to the housemaster, who sublet his premises trusting to make a decent profit from the 45 boys in his care, ensuring not to 'lose' one without an adequate reason. This could only be by breaking school rules, which officially included vice – homosexual relations – but since most of the policing and punishing was not initiated by masters, and a fair margin of sin was neither frowned upon nor discouraged, a prevailing tolerance made homosexual encounters quite normal. Lytton Strachey circulated his recollection of the one obliging adventurer who locked himself in the lavatory as the school train left the station so as to receive visits from every single boy before they all got out at Eton. John Kilbracken 1920–2006 (formerly Hon J.R. Godley), a long-term friend of Adrian's in the next-door house Hedlams, said of their time there: 'To have a romantic feeling about a pretty boy one or two years younger was commonplace and acceptable among the boys.' He was for two years forbidden from seeing a boy of whom he was very fond, although in truth his fondness was on an idealistic, unsexual basis. He thought that there was no likelihood of feeling guilt for acts of homo-sex, though; getting caught would be alright and dealt with by a senior boy or member of pop.[2] What very nearly *did* cause his own expulsion was becoming the school bookmaker. But that was another matter.

Ludovic Kennedy (entr. 1933–38) – one of five boys who snuck off to Le Touquet in a private aeroplane belonging to one of them and got back again before anyone had realised they were missing – once contributed to a book of celebrities' so-called 'First Loves'. Where others provided lyrical descriptions of the scent of this or that on such and such a day, month or season under whichever oceanic breeze etc., Sir Ludovic commended a simpler truth from the past, and straight-forwardly named the boy in question.

In later life, having attended a party with Sue, Adrian later reported the circumstances of a sudden realisation: 'Some awful red-faced colonel-type,' he said, 'droning and trumpeting about having been at Eton…' Disbelief turned to doubt, until he could get discreet confirmation of the name:

2. Eton prefect

a faint memory; Adrian bowed his head in shame at such a questionable lapse in good taste: 'How *could* I?' he mourned.

Some answers are contained in that 1938 diary, underlined 'Strictly Private' at the opening page. The first memorandum contains quotations from Oscar Wilde, beginning: 'To reveal art and conceal the artist is art's aim' and throughout the year, the thoughts of the Anglo-Irish writer pepper the pages at intervals. 'Young men want to be faithful and are not, Old men want to be faithless and cannot' punctuates the ending of January's first week. By the first weekend in March it is signalled that 'The only way to get rid of a [sic] temptation is to yield to it.' Less than four weeks later, temptation had taken its toll (31 March): 'Mother tells me that Rowlatt has asked me to leave Eton...'

Here the myth of his expulsion can be exposed. The painter Guy Roddon (1919–2006), who also taught at Goldsmiths', once said on this subject that 'He used to joke about it, and to refer to it [his expulsion] in such a way as I wondered if it were true.' But knowing Adrian well, he added: 'I always felt that Adrian must have gone over the top and seduced a new boy' with the possibility of its being a rather important one.

No evidence points to an august event. There is only a diary memorandum dated 26 March which may be read as evidence of some encounter: 'Recieved [sic] a charming note from Mike S.' (Thought to be J.M. Spooner, also at Eton 1934–38) 'Began "tonight I feel as if I had been shot to the Heart" Continues – "I hope the sexual monster has not lost his victim?" Charming boy.' The memo asterisks an earlier note: 'Heard Mike got 10 up! i.e. 17 up in 3 days. Flogging should be abolished.' It was the last day of school before Easter break and it wasn't Spooner who didn't return.

Long before Captain Charles James Rowlatt MA, MBE, son of a judge in the High Court, was housemaster at Eton in September 1930, he had been a pupil there. His listed credits include membership of Eton VIII, Field XI, and College Wall. Thereafter he was a Scholar to University College, Oxford. He served as Temporary Captain and Staff in France 1914–19, and as assistant master at Eton immediately after. He gave up his house in 1945, retired as master in 1952 and promptly died. There is a certain type of whom, with minor interruptions, it can be said that Eton was his life. Mr Rowlatt was such a man.

The Earl of Harewood (Viscount Lascelles, Rowlatts House 1936–42) has written:

> *I think it was in general an agreeable and happy house, ruled with a certain asperity by the House Master, who had been badly wounded in the first war and, as was customary in those ancient days, was inclined to allow his personal prejudices to colour the life of a house. He had no languages and rather despised those who did, and he disliked noise penetrating from our side of the house to his. But he was very fair and I think we all rather liked him, in a distant kind of way. He had been a 'wet bob', preferring rowing to cricket (unlike me), but we were quite a good cricketing house although I think we were beaten in the finals of the house competition. I don't know if Adrian Ryan was much of a cricketer or indeed anything about his sporting activities, which... bulked reasonably large in one's Eton activities.*

Lord Harewood's personal recollection of Adrian carries a disclaimer. 'I have a good memory of him in the sense that I don't have a hostile one, though as he was three years older than I we were not in any sense of the word friends.' Neither he nor John Kilbracken could remember anything about Adrian having been in any way disgraced, expelled or even taken out of school. School records would show expulsion, but no more than that. They do not. Why Adrian had come to believe in the idea of his expulsion seems only the result of Kit's intensely vituperative dislike of the circumstances behind her having been asked for his brief removal, and the blend of his feeling of rejection and of being unfairly singled out – a poisonous cocktail to his egalitarian sensibilities. On 24 March 1938, Adrian writes in his diary: 'Rowlatt came... and talked 1 & ¾ hours about sex. I told him plenty! Left room 11.15.' Three days later, a Sunday, he records: 'Rowlatt did not come round!' suggesting change in habit. Two days after that he dined with the housemaster, together with Allen (M. Allen – 'Mike'), Lewis (R.W.A.P. Lewis – 'Robin') and Bobby (unknown) on which occasion Rowlatt 'appeared all right.'

Next day they all left school, and the day after that, Kit received the housemaster's phone call. In consequence, on 9 May, Adrian apparently wrote to Rowlatt and less than two weeks later, went back to Eton to see the Headmaster and collected the famous leaving book of Gray's poems. His diary entry for 21 May concludes: 'Lunched with Rowlatt. Met all my friends.

Had photo taken. Humphrey F (F.H.M. Fitzroy) in good form ventured that 'Homosexuality is the Rich man's priviledge[sic]'. From here on, unsurprisingly, Rowlatt is not mentioned. It is noteworthy that much later Adrian visited the town of Eton and nearby Marlow with Tite Street doctor Karly Prekop and Polly on the afternoon of Sunday 12 June 1949, but according to Polly they didn't go inside the school. Rowlatt is only obliquely referred to in the staunch rebuttal of facts issued to his brother over half a century later: 'Then there is the nonsense of Eton, Homosexuality and the Headmaster whom Mother never saw. It was the homosexual house master that for some reason (jealousy?) decided to ask for my removal (why not the rest of the boys?) and who yet invited me down to lunch... and to meet the Headmaster and receive my leaving book. No doubt to relieve Mother's worries you told her about yr love life at Bryanston?' The significance of this is hard to miss. The sense of the sins of the many had been visited upon the few, and the passing of many years silent of complaint but rather of jokes directed to Guy Roddon – for humour is a kind witness – has not latterly dulled the injustice felt. What a terrible example of a role model the envious Rowlatt was, and how damaging. Not just to Adrian, but also to those who went unpunished for participating in the selfsame 'crime'? It was an event of incalculable consequence. An outright betrayal and the fixing of a theme of being envied for his independence which his mother always felt, hence the pulling of beds apart, that haunted him. Adrian's eldest daughter Geraldine grew up with the sense that her father hated Eton, hated fagging, and that it was a gothic and genuinely negative experience for him. If this is so, he didn't broadcast it widely. Neither, however, did he precisely broadcast disenchantment over Kit's mothering. In each case an archetype had let him down, fitting his stoic and largely suppressed method of dealing with extreme pain.

In 1990, the 550th anniversary of the founding of Eton College was marked by many special events celebrating all aspects of school life, including an exhibition at the Drawing Schools of the work of twentieth-century OE artists, sponsored by Christie's auctioneers. Some of the artists were noteworthy: Sir Gerald Kelly, Lord Methuen, Sir Robert (Robin) Darwin, Sir Roger de Grey, Sir Howard Hodgkin, Sir Edmund Fairfax-Lucy and Francis Farmar (who also catalogued the exhibition). Others were less well known, but the very varied range gave great interest, since all that the individual artists had in common was so extraordinarily limited. Adrian's painting *Mousehole Cottages* dated 1986, appeared on the front cover of the catalogue, with Howard Hodgkin's *Lotus*, 1978, on the back cover. As perhaps no other painting in that exhibition, the scene it depicts so perfectly conveys an impression valid for the span of the century. Not the little boat, neither the cottages, nor the appearance of the fisherman and child can be pinned to a particular era. The composition, with many vertical and diagonal lines to the viewer strolling with, not straying from, the two figures, is complex. The curious colour harmonies and traces of thin oil and mixed media give the effect of a deceptively light touch.

It accomplished one seemingly impossible thing in addition. It softened Adrian towards his old school. He didn't go to the exhibition, but he did want to hear how it was (and how was the art of the students of the day). Also, according to his wife, Sue, he was pleased that the Queen not only toured it, but that she could hardly have missed his painting stuck on the front cover. He had taken extra care over the frames surrounding the two pictures (the other was of Etretat, Normandy) he consigned. Rejects of his pupil Haidee Becker, for him they were uncharacteristically ornate, but just the thing, he felt, for that setting. Thus having been singled out again but in a good way, it helped when the time came, six years further on, in seeking a venue for a long overdue selling show – his first in 11 years – that via an initiative of the then Vice-Provost Tim Card, the College offered its own gallery space for an external exhibition for the first time in its history. Though it didn't seem so then, in retrospect he must have swallowed bravely to submit to that rehabilitation. At the earliest discussion stage of the show, however, an immediate invitation by the Vice-Provost – to whom Adrian did not much warm – to a reunion dinner which threatened to involve some of his peers caused consternation. He declined it as promptly as it had been issued.

Eton during the last century cannot be said to have much supported the arts compared to other parts of the curriculum. That is not to say that there were not inspired art teachers, only that there was not opportunity in the timetable allocated by the authorities to allow them fully to do their work.
If Vivian – and to an extent Kit – had not been a painter, if Adrian had not grown up with 'the smell of paint, and pictures everywhere', would he aged 14 have taken home the book about Van Gogh? Would he at 17, and no doubt before, have casually recorded in his diary (15 January 1938): 'Painted afternoon' and on the next day: 'Rose 9.30. Painted.'? Would it otherwise have occurred to him, barred from returning to

school, to have enrolled in the art school local to 37 Platts Lane which at that time was the family home? Polly Walker retains a picture that is said to be the first one he ever painted as a result of attending this unknown school, of a still life of mixed flowers (not marigolds nor monbretias but not unlike them) in a glass she thinks to be a rummer, painted on an old Rowney's board of Vivian's. It is unmistakably a student work and the not fully recognisable nature of the flowers may be a failure to replicate them. Adrian, while later disparaging the picture, had given it his signature at the time. Polly, liking it when she first saw it, was told she could take it and did so on the basis that it might otherwise be thrown out.

Adrian cannot have stayed long at this school, for on 3 October 1938, his 18th birthday, he began at the Architectural Association. There are regular references to painting (and to painters) in the intervening pages of his diary, but more seemingly as exercises not to completed pictures; except once (7 August): 'Iden. Rained all day – stayed in – painted a picture. Hit or miss style – missed! Cleared towards evening.' This concurs with the still life given to Polly: the dark of a wet summer's day penetrating the small windows of an ancient cottage, country flowers resting on old-fashioned mahogany, and precocious talent dismissed as child's play.

Adrian's last day at the A.A. seems to have been 16 December 1938. There is no record of his returning for the following term. His time there seems far less distinguished than his social life, still busy with many school friends featuring in it, and nothing about the accruing of new ones, or of new skills either. He had a graphical mind[3] and a love of buildings. In some ways, he would have been suited to a career in architecture – which he incorporated as subject matter in his paintings, of which more later – although his natural impatience would have been an obstacle. At any rate, the apparent wish of his grandfather's for him to learn a trade did not lastingly pass muster with Adrian. He diverted to the Slade, one of a rather celebrated intake of students in the third term of the academic year 1938–39.

3. See his chapter on Composing in *Still Life Painting Techniques*, Batsford, 1978

The Slade and after

Adrian drove to the Slade – in London, before it relocated to the Ashmolean during the war – in his Bentley to have a look round. Suede shoes – as P.G. Wodehouse frequently reminds us – were less de rigueur than racy. Adrian wore such a pair. Peggy Rose was chosen to show him around the school, mildly thinking that he looked rather nice. She left, after five years, having won the John Nettleship Scholarship to travel, in the early summer of 1938, a prize-winner along with Dodie Masterman, part of whose joint reward for achievement was to go to Paris paid for by Goya Paints. With the £20 further prize money, Peggy went on to Brittany, where Adrian and Asgeir Scott were staying, more or less by chance. Joan Lawson, who later married Michael Young, was having an affair with Adrian. After the summer was over, Peggy went with Joan back up to Oxford to see all their friends. That is where the romance began.

To facilitate going up and down to Oxford, Adrian moved out of 37 Platts Lane and rented a room in Earls Court, where the relationship with Peggy developed. Those women who experienced it testify to Adrian's considerable powers of seduction. The process, for him, was inclined to be the Holy Grail in the majority of his youthful relationships, a fact of which he was semi rather than fully conscious. The less the likelihood of its going to happen, the more his craving increased. A Libran nature craves romance. He was no exception. It is after the first flush that things can get sticky. Adrian again was no exception. What changed circumstances was the no small matter of the war.

Meanwhile what the Slade did for Adrian perhaps can be summed up by an event that took place some years after he had studied there. 'Five Contemporary Painters' – an Arts Council of Great Britain Western Region exhibition – took place in 1950, aiming to introduce to a provincial gallery a group of painters who would normally show in commercial galleries in London. A second aim – intended to produce some unity in the work – was to invite five artists of roughly the same age whose careers had all started at the same art school (the Slade). The catalogue went on to explain:

> *It might have been expected... that there would be some visual common denominator in the work of the group, but... this has not happened at all. On leaving the Slade these five must have set off hurriedly like travellers in Grimm or Hans Andersen by different paths through the forest, and today, not so very many years since parting company, they meet almost as strangers, utterly unlike in their work and each to a greater or lesser degree with a marked personal flavour.*

The other four artists comprised Bryan Wynter, Patrick Heron, R.W. Treffgarne and Paul Feiler. All showed seven works except Patrick Heron who submitted six. The full extent that any of them can be said to have gleaned anything from the school is not for discussion here. Neither is it to refute that Adrian derived anything at all, but in Peggy's words: 'He owes nothing to the Slade – he never fitted that mould and in any case he wasn't there long enough.' In a letter he wrote to Polly Walker dated 31 August 1995, evidently responding to a question of hers, Adrian wrote: 'Yes, I knew Albert Rutherston – he was the principal at the Ruskin when the Slade moved in during the war. He actually taught me on the few occasions when I turned up in the life room! Kind little man, brother of Rothenstein the painter...'

What Adrian did garner from the Slade in his short association was more reckonable in people: primarily his marriage to Peggy. Artistic friendships also, initially very warm with Pat Heron, with Bryan Wynter and to an extent with Paul Feiler.

After Adrian and Peggy were married in 1941, they moved

briefly to Manchester Square, then via Maida Vale to the ground floor of 48 Tite Street. This place, effectively, for the milieu in which they found themselves – more enduringly for Adrian – was a form of education in itself.

Tite Street today, off the Chelsea Embankment and of unassailable respectability, is hard to reconcile with the louche – oft-times to the point of desperation – playground it once was. Blue plaques serve as gentle reminders: Delius's friend, the musician Peter Warlock, who gassed himself to death at number 30, Oscar Wilde at number 34.

Bastion of this bohemia was More House, the multi-roomed Hope-Nicholson mansion punctuated with a maze of corridors which was a lodging-house-from-home for the infamous or simply not yet famous. Mrs Hope-Nicholson, according to Slade Professor of Art History, John Richardson, her 'one eye looking at London, the other at France' was the matriarch, into whose foyer familial he had 'eloped' in 1941. Sir Clement Freud, tenured while working as a cook at the Dorchester, described her as being 'like a caped bat-witch and seeming most often to be standing at the top of the stairs.' Her son Felix and daughter Lauretta Hugo, who married Victor Hugo's painter great-grandson Jean, imported all sorts of interesting people. These included June Osborne, whose liaison in those petrol-rationed years with Charles, Duke of Rutland, offered a lifeline to many of the lodgers in the form of the car he would send in which they hitched a ride to the Soho pub of their preference, before it came to His Grace that she wasn't a virgin and she effected a marriage to Churchill's son instead. Adrian Liddell-Hart was also in residence. He was not only a contemporary of Adrian's at Eton, as was Felix Hope-Nicholson, but also one of the intimates being the cause of his having to leave it, which he made up for by being best man at his wedding to Peggy.

Even though he and Adrian each knew from the Slade both Geoffrey Bennison and another Tite Street neighbour James Bailey – forever getting beaten up by the soldiers and sailors he took home from the rougher pubs – John Richardson remains the only extant inmate of More House not to recollect Adrian fully. Conceding that he was sorry because 'he sounds fun', the New York-based scholar and biographer of his friend Picasso wrote that 'the name Adrian Ryan rings only the faintest of bells'. It is a pity that they didn't know one another. Adrian meeting Picasso could have gone either way and the closest he got was admittance with Bernard Hailstone to the studio in Antibes with the *maestro* not at home. That opportunity enabled him to 'nick a bit of chalk, hoping it might *do* something', he self-deprecated. And it seems unlikely, going by Clement Freud's flattering, quite un-self-interested, description of Adrian being 'one of the most fanciable of the beautiful people in Soho, with his fluffy hair and beautiful eyes' that Richardson would fail to remember if they had met. On the other hand, he did not recall taking Clement Freud to lunch in Vallauris to meet Picasso either, to the extent of questioning that it had happened. Sir Clement's account of the occasion is emphatic, made memorable by the question posed to him by Picasso in seemingly ungrammatical French – 'Comment va ici?' Its true meaning pivots on acronym superseding the adverb – Comment va *ICI*? – a simple enquiry after the performance of his doubtless considerable stock market interest, which Picasso imagined that Freud, coming from London, might know something about.

Adrian's appearance did not meet with universal approval. Clement Freud recalled that a prospective client Adrian tried to charge £1.15d to execute a mural, turned on him: 'For that money,' the man snorted, 'I can get a *proper* artist with long hair and sandals!' Elsewhere in evidence were the painters Colquhoun and MacBryde – 'they were drinking while I was painting' and were often the worse for it in or out of Muriel Belcher's Colony Room – and more substantively, Augustus John, nearer-to with his Tite Street studio at number 33 – for Adrian the next role model only waiting to be acknowledged. On another footing meanwhile, there was the presence of the young Lucian Freud.

'Of my contemporaries,' said Adrian in recorded conversation, 21 November 1990, 'the first person I thought was really good was Lucian – as a young man', singling out *Father and Daughter* dated 1949, a picture in which the face of a man is partly shaded by beads. He admired his vision and draughtsmanship, being very different from his own. The two of them had a number of oddities in common: less than two years in age difference, they were young, attractive and sexually unrepressed; they had ambition; they each had the reputation of a grandfather to precede them and a partly unexpressed sibling rivalry issue. Both had Peter Watson, publisher of *Horizon*, floating interestedly around them and both were photographed by John Deakin – although the images of Adrian taken for *Vogue* have long since disappeared. Only where Adrian had money,

Lucian was needful of it. Each of them was invalided out of the services very early on during the war. For neither was the painters' alternative of the camouflage corps optioned: disguising pill boxes seen from the air as caravans and haystacks, as ruins or a wayside café. Adrian fire-watched, and was commended for it, though it did not appease the embarrassed militarism of Kit one bit. Uneasy relations with their mothers was also a thing they shared. William Feaver writes that Freud only started painting his mother in 1972, in order to 'overcome a lifetime of avoiding her'. Around the same time Adrian took moons as recurrent subject matter, a universal symbol for the mother – 'Whenever a painting goes badly wrong,' he said, 'I just put in a moon'. By inclination, Adrian was all for the conscientious objectors; but a practical, less frictional course of fire watching and being at liberty to paint his own work provided the ultimate solution. Both he and Lucian had their first shows during the war: Adrian's at the Redfern in 1943, Lucian's at Lefèvre in 1944. They had met in the nightlife of the Chelsea pubs and, with John Minton, enjoyed a relaxed and easy intimacy which outlasted the duration of the war. 'Corroboratively vague' was John Richardson's verdict on talking to Lucian about his deeper relations with Adrian. According to Freud's biographer, Adrian is remembered by Lucian Freud for buying early works from him, for recommending a doctor for the clap, and for a willingness to lend money, rendered easier by having a rich 'uncle' as a benefactor. John Russell, in the catalogue essay for Freud's 1974 show at the Hayward Gallery, also pays tribute to the effect on Lucian of 'emotional immediacy' emanating from Adrian's two Soutines hanging on the wall at 48 Tite Street, where he regularly stayed over. In return, Lucian gave Adrian a picture, *Chicken in a Bucket*, painted in 1944, and now the property of a prominent Australian actress. Adrian appears to have been intrigued by the work, for he painted a larger and portrait-shaped version of it shortly afterwards. In paint at the top is written: 'From a drawing by Lucian Freud to whom this is dedicated, August 1944'. Adding words to paint, on the back or front of pictures, captioning them, was a habit of Adrian's, though by no means one that he overdid. He once explained that 'if you want to find out whether an artist is any good or not, try copying their work' and this finished repainting of Freud's picture – a poisoned chicken awaiting veterinarian autopsy – probably issued from admiration. There is something of early Modigliani about Adrian's rendition in view of the use of oil text. His signature, lower right, is defiantly bold. The prince of the damned generation of painters – peintres maudits – is being alluded to consciously or not; including in the way that he is also talent spotting. In *Modigliani, The Pure Bohemian*, by June Rose[1] the author writes: 'Modigliani showed exceptional appreciation of nascent ability. Years before others, he recognised the difficult genius of Chaim Soutine' and went out of his way to be of help. Adrian's picture both resolves his own mind and pays tribute to his less well-placed friend, as did Modigliani with his portrait, *Chaim Soutine*, 1915. Adrian's chicken is perhaps as close as he came – its portrait shape no accident – to depicting Lucian indirectly. He never was confident of his strongly psychological portraits, and even the best he regarded as failures, though it didn't always stop him from trying. Restructured as a pyramidal diamond, it presents its subject in the round. As paintings, the two accord in their title, subject, and not much else. Their connection was friendship, not art (Freud would have regarded ownership of a Modigliani as 'a lapse of taste' according to his biographer). As their lives coursed further apart – partly because of the increasing time that Adrian spent in Cornwall and also the suicide of their mutual friend, the painter Johnny Minton in 1957 – and as the Freud juggernaut grew, so did Adrian's own immolation. The last thing he'd have wanted was to claim connection by showing his picture after its first outing at the Redfern summer exhibition, July 1944. Lucian's gift Adrian regretfully under-sold, as ever sending someone to execute the task for him (Peggy took it to Sotheby's where in 1977 it fetched £750) during fluctuations in his finances. His own painting stayed stacked in the studio at the time of his death.

Sven Berlin was living in Cornwall at the outbreak of war. Largely untaught as an artist, and making abstract art 'without even knowing I was doing it', he was asked to join the local defence volunteers, which he was unwilling to do. An unofficial tribunal followed. The tough Cornish people proposed throwing him down the mine shafts. In recorded conversation (10 October 1990) Sven said: 'I was petrified but I was absolutely truthful; I told them I was a pacifist... they realised and let me go.' He was still living in his peculiar white tower in St Ives when he befriended Adrian towards the end of the war. Fifty-three years later, at Adrian's memorial service at St James's Piccadilly, which he was too infirm to attend, his memoir of their unbroken friendship was read out for him. Afterwards many in the congregation declared that it struck the right tone. In fact it had required heavy editing. Sven's production of purple prose has always been a nightmare for editors.[2] The underlying message was simpler and more effective. He held

1. Constable & Company, 1990
2. Affectionately confirmed by John Sansom, who published Sven's *Coat of Many Colours*

Adrian in high regard and had every reason to. Adrian had shown him enormous kindness, had been generous with money given – not required to be repaid – and sensitivity that included saying nothing when Sven's tendency toward cauterising truth-telling got him into trouble.[3] Sven admired what he saw as statements of truth in Adrian's painting, no doubt envying the lack of uncontroversial after-effects. Adrian also introduced Sven to Eardley Knollys – who for £100 bought from him when he was strapped yet again for cash, the Alfred Wallis table depicting a schooner sailing between two lighthouses. Sven raged in perpetuity against the memory of Eardley and Edward Le Bas sawing off the legs in order to transport it on the roof of their car. Sven gave Adrian a sketchbook by Wallis which had come to him via Adrian Stokes, as had the table. Adrian loved and approved of Wallis's unique way of throwing space around, 'provided,' he stipulated, 'that you treat him as something completely different.' Every page of the sketchbook was signed and much of the work was untypical: hunting scenes and strange-looking animals featured in it. As usual, he in time sold it at the bottom of the market when he was broke, flogging it 'to some crook' and regretting that he hadn't torn out a single page to keep. The one Wallis he retained, later the property of his middle daughter Scarlett, was acquired separately.

One evening in the bar room of the Ship Inn in Mousehole they called 'The House of Lords', Sven was introduced by Adrian to Augustus John. Sven called him 'larger than life, like Noah,' describing him both as 'a wild old sod' and – more rarified – as 'a completed personality'. Augustus was apparently not interested in Sven at all, but in the voluptuousness of his companion Jacqueline Moran. Putting a hand up a girl's skirt was the sort of thing Augustus did all the time, according to Peggy. Her experiences of his magnified persona include having stones thrown at her windows while he drunkenly implored to be let in; or his efforts to drive up the acute gradient of Sennen Hill, baffled by the car's unwillingness to move properly, whilst with the hand brake firmly on.

Adrian rated Augustus as the 'finest painter of *heads*', a compliment he turned into a joke in his 1954 portrait of the white-haired old patriarch's face wittily composed against all convention within a rectangle: everything from the neck down omitted – except the cheekily implied notion of some imperfectly executed pair of hands. More outright cheek was the fact of Adrian openly calling him 'Gussie' as few others

3. Publication of his book *The Dark Monarch* in September 1962 was withdrawn with a public apology to those 'libelled' five months later

did, but Guy Roddon said it amused the old man. Augustus's celebrity equalled his notoriety. In Chelsea, where he would take Adrian and Peg to the Pheasantry, or at Mousehole, where he spent one summer visiting his son Edwin and daughter-in-law Betty, Augustus's reputation preceded him. It legitimised Adrian's sketchily drawn boundaries regarding fidelity and sexual indulgence. Most of Adrian's conquests attest to his inclination toward polygamy. Adrian took Augustus as a role model quite consciously, in the opinion of Guy Roddon. Adrian's expressed view of him was 'a great man as well as a great artist and an intellectual.' The diaries contain few clear references to Augustus – drinks and dinner occasionally, visiting the Tate with him in June 1954 when his show was on; visiting him in Guy's Hospital in November the same year – considering the familiarity they are held to have enjoyed (although there are meetings with 'G' that may, or may not, relate to Augustus). Artistically, Augustus cannot be said to have directly influenced Adrian. Gwen John, whose work Adrian bought from Anthony d'Offay, did. He noted her dictum of 'the strange shape, like the little hat or whatever, which starts her off' [in a drawing] and from which a picture develops, a system he partly adopted for himself. Unlike others in the debate, including Augustus himself, he rated the sibling artists in their separate fields as equals: 'They were two different kinds of artists,' he said, and would not have considered the idea of putting them head to head. With the wider John family, he was also extremely friendly. First off he knew Edwin – who had introduced Adrian to his father – probably initially from Mousehole, where his wife Betty had a cottage, formerly the old fish store. That Adrian and Mary John, the wife of Caspar,[4] went to bed together was of small consequence other than a green-eyed and enraged Polly coming to blows with Mary on Mousehole quay, a spectacle appreciated by their paramour and other contented observers. Caspar's response was to buy Adrian's painting of a nude on the beach (Polly's head and Shirley Maiden's body), while Edwin merely reacted by buying Adrian's portrait of Polly on exhibition at Marlborough's. He and Adrian indulged in two sets of gambit-playing: chess and practical jokes, Edwin serving lunch at his Rue de Vaugirard studio upon a table laid not with knife and fork, but spanner and screwdriver. Guy Roddon quotes Henry Lamb calling him a 'farceur', adding that he was a surrealist one and original with it. A peculiar language manifests in the letters written to Adrian by Edwin: 'Are you yourself in fine fettle? Your letter seems, unlike mine, to exude the old verve of many yesterdays...'

4. First Sea Lord and Admiral of the Fleet, eldest son of Augustus

Beyond the influence of Matthew Smith's lively colours, the tone of a complex and possibly disappointed spirit are un-disguisedly found in the psychological portrait Adrian made of Edwin, circa 1955, evidently conceded something of a hit by the sitter, who bought it as well.

Sir Matthew Smith was the other person in this milieu whose work ranked high enough in Adrian's estimation for him to want to own it – in which endeavour he failed – and to yield to its influence – in which he succeeded. It seems odd that he never owned one. Eardley Knollys told of Matthew Smith being 'utterly unlike his pictures; quiet and remote...' and yet terribly easy about selling his work, and although very different, the two artists were at ease in each other's company and Adrian had ample opportunity to buy direct from his studio. They once spent the weekend in Hertfordshire, staying at Furneux Pelham with an election candidate whose walls were adorned with many beautiful early Smith paintings. An unusual artistic assault on the electorate ensued. Matthew Smith took the microphone, repetitiously calling 'Vote Liberal for Mister Hughes!' in his thin, piping voice, while Adrian took the wheel – rally-driving style, as was his wont – and thus they shot around the constituency at an alarming rate.

A still life of mixed spring flowers (tulips, irises, daffodil and lilac) at night, painted by Adrian in 1949, shows some of the senior painter's influence in the vibrant yellow and orange colours which enliven the energy of the flowers against the dark background of purple and blue. Adrian said he was envious of Matthew Smith's use of paint. 'Very difficult to copy,' he said, adding with a touch of sorrow, 'Not many people are fooled by my copies of Matthew Smith...' This still life is far from being a copy. It is an example of how his vernacular can openly incorporate what he carefully identifies as other people's language and ideas, and fuse with them. He once said: 'There's a *smell* about my paintings...' by which he was acknowledging devices culled from other painters before him, although his remark was as ever taking self-deprecation too far. The blue-black darkness of the painting may also reflect the fact of 1949 being in two unaccustomed ways difficult for him. The first thing was that, suffering a temperature of 101 on 2 January, he developed (for at least the third time in his life) pneumonia. He was hospitalised after a week and remained so for almost a month; at the mercy of a concerned stream of potentially conflicting parties whose thinly disguised antagonism would have enlivened the atmosphere no end, a situation he would have more relished than deplored. But Polly being unaccountably in Cornwall until the day he came out of hospital and was removed into her care, it was Peggy who presided daily at his bedside, and calm prevailed. Secondly he grew uneasy about money. Whether he was in fact harder up than he had been or whether it was just unease about his depleting bank balance and having to keep himself, Peggy, daughter Geraldine as well as Polly (who took part-time work to generate income shortly after he left hospital), he took the decision to sell one of his Soutines. *Le Lapin Ecorche*, 28" x 25" was sold by Sotheby's on 30 March 1949, lot 133. It fetched £400. This was the first time he parted with one of his joyfully bought artworks by acknowledged masters, but it wouldn't be the last.

Collecting and selling

Le Lapin Ecorche by Chaim Soutine (1893–1943) had been bought in March 1943 from Eardley Knollys, late of the Storran Gallery and had cost £225. The Storran Gallery, formerly situated in Albany Court Yard, plumb in the vicinity of Willie Brass's London flat, was part owned and part run by Eardley, and was managed by his lover Frank Coombs until his death in action closed down their operation before the end of the war. A friendly rivalry existed between most galleries at that time, but the proprietors of the Storran and the Redfern were on particularly good terms, despite very different personalities being involved. Eardley's relaxed, uncommercial, civilised and gentlemanly manner was all that the flamboyant and grand showmanship of New Zealander-turned-English-socialite Rex Nan Kivell was not. How Rex first landed the *Crayfish* painting is uncertain, possibly via the London Group, where in October 1941 Adrian exhibited two oils: *Ronsseng, poet prisoner of the 'Isle Joseph'* [sic in the ledger] and *Self portrait in a rugger cap*, which he later diminished (together with the 'lying nonsense' of the self-portrait with a beard): 'Putting that thing on my head when I was 21…' As good a place to start as any, Adrian's trawling of the dealers had begun with the esteemed dealership Agnews. They duly sent a young man to appraise his work, although after lengthy examination of it he was slow to offer an opinion. When Adrian pressed him for a response, it came with more candour than he was expecting: 'You see,' confessed the youth, 'I've just married the boss's daughter, and I don't know anything about art.' Everyone has to start somewhere, and this honest and accepting individual would become one of the great authorities on Turner, as well as chairman of that picture dealing firm. His name was Evelyn Joll.

The *Crayfish* was fairly imposing, measuring 36" x 24", and it cost Edward Le Bas 28 guineas. Either the gallery in those days wasn't taking fully half of the sale price of a picture, or the frame cost a guinea on top, because Adrian received 15 guineas for his work. It must have felt like a good start to his professional career, especially as the painting was later lent by Le Bas for the Redfern's 1942 summer exhibition, where it was praised in an article by Clive Bell (*New Statesman*, 22 August 1942). Adrian and Peggy's combined earned income for the year 1941 to 1942 amounted to just over ninety-eight pounds; her four works – three portrait commissions and a painting entitled 'Ballet Frock' as per his ledger – accounting for just under half of the total. Three works of Adrian's, it has to be said, were sold to family members, including two still-life paintings to Kit, one of which is then pointedly annotated as having not been paid for but given away. Adrian's twenty-first birthday, on 3 October 1941, enriched their bank balance by a further £4,225, excluding stocks and shares, and gave rise to their first forays into collecting. A coloured woodcut by Gauguin and a coloured lithograph by Vuillard were bought from the Leicester Galleries for 11 guineas. There was a gift from Peggy of six Japanese prints from Zwemmers bought for four pounds. His brother supplemented this with the present of a drawing by Gaudier Brzeska of Horace Brodsky, which Adrian asked to exchange to Zwemmer for one by Modigliani, priced at six pounds. The collecting instinct, a complex exploratory process balancing intuition with form, was ignited in him. Two vogue purchases followed in December 1941: tribal art wood carvings from the Yoruba tribe were bought by Peggy as presents for Adrian. He made a painting of one of these – *Still life of African Sculpture*, 20" x 24" – on the day after its purchase, although the purity of its form may have been easier to envisage than to capture, because by January he had painted over it.

Forty pounds that December added two more Modigliani drawings, one of Jean Cocteau, the other entitled *Portrait de Famille*, both from the Leger Galleries. An oil by Walter Sickert – in the ledger 'a present for Peggy'; in retrospect, a must-have purchase difficult to justify in other terms – added £168 to

December's expenditure. A chalk drawing – *L'Hotel de Quai Voltaire* by Sickert – seems to have been included in the price by Mr Willoughby of the Leicester Galleries, sensing the wisdom of setting sprats in order to land mackerel. Adrian, being partial to all fish, was reeled in again as early as the first week in February 1942. Susceptible as he was above all to Modigliani, an oil *Portrait d'une Femme au Collet Blanc* lowered his bank account by four hundred pounds and raised his collecting fever. More substantial acquisitions were inevitable.

It is not easy, even on an unrestricted budget, to form a collection of paintings that withstands dictates of fashion and endures by means of its own defences. Cohesion is everything. Painters, although there are exceptions, are not collectors in the general sense, no matter what they come to have in their possession. Collectors, generally, do lastingly well under the moderating influence of an experienced guide. Even Eardley Knollys, who consistently championed and sold Adrian's paintings and from whom he bought such as *Le Lapin Ecorche*, does not seem to have been called upon for advice in buying pictures.[1] Where Eardley's own collection has survived intact, Adrian's random-seeming Modiglianis and Soutines, his early Utrillo (dated circa 1912/13) of the Eiffel Tower bought with youthful optimism for £500, his Matisse woodcut from the Leicester Galleries in January 1943 and blue period Picasso drawing – quite faint, of a woman[2] – and numerous Picasso etchings, his sculpture by Merino and Bernard Leach pottery pieces, all adorned his flat for less than a decade after they were lovingly collected. They were casualties, when times grew difficult in the aftermath of war, of hasty buying and not taking a firm stance when selling. Adrian's sales standpoint was somewhat of a wholesale or discounted one, not wishing to be seen to be asking or expecting too much. The notion of disappointment was latent in the sale of things, regardless of what, although he never forgot the glowing pleasure gained from those paintings bought in the early years; of what it could mean 'to wake with a Modigliani smiling down at you; so different to spending 30 seconds standing in a gallery in front of one'. He also retained some flicker of acquisitive instinct almost until the last. A Sotheby's catalogue which he perused as late as October 1998, two months before death came to him, offered a harbour scene in oil by Christopher Wood at a tempting estimate: 'Now that would *really* piss Sue off,' he ventured, 'if I start buying pictures *now*...'

1. Except once, in the matter of a Bonnard for sale at Roland Browse and Delbanco's which was thought too expensive to contemplate
2. Sold on to Erica Brausen for £100

When he vacated Hill House in Lower Holbrook, Adrian burnt all of Eardley's letters, over which he nonetheless expressed much sorrow. Whereas over disposal of family heirlooms including a pair of Chippendale chairs from Hintlesham and John Constable's easel he was unsentimental, tears were shed over the destruction of these letters, which evoked the past much more personally. They are unlikely to have revealed much that was not already known. Eardley's romantic nature inclined him to idolise people, the more unattainable the better, and retain and treasure special friendships in return for which he asked very little. Twenty-two letters written by Adrian to Eardley are retained by the Knollys estate, however, and the tone and manner of them is deeply affectionate and wholly at ease (referencing wide-ranging subject matter from Lucian Freud going dancing at the Café de Paris with Princess Margaret and Graham Sutherland painting the Queen, to the Hanging Committee at the RA trying to get him to persuade Patrick Heron to send in). Much indebtedness is evidenced. Eardley was officially working for the National Trust's western region and living in style at Long Crichel House in Dorset with Eddy Sackville-West, Raymond Mortimer and Desmond Shawe-Taylor, but remained in the swim of the small and enclosed picture-dealing world. For years Eardley regularly sold Adrian's works without taking any commission, in addition to buying paintings for himself. Eventually, in March 1947 and at Adrian's suggestion, they came to an 'arrangement' that Eardley would take 20% of the value of future pictures sold, not in money but in pictures to keep for himself. The only oil known to have changed hands in this way is *The Canal at Moret*, 1948. The complementary and contrasting influences of Soutine and Utrillo are evidenced in it; also of Sisley, who had frequented the same spot. It is an original picture for all that, whose vibrant colour and use of paint imbues a quiet landscape with timeless drama.

Also in the spring of 1947, Adrian went with Eardley to the chic Hotel Welcome, Villefrance, near Nice,[3] patronised then as now by film stars, prime ministers and presidents, taking with them Graham Sutherland and his wife Kathy. The Sutherlands were ingénus who had only once before been abroad – to Paris, just after the war, also taken by Eardley when according to him 'everything was bursting in flower and absolutely at its best.' The second visit thrilled Graham as much, such that not too long after, he and his wife moved to nearby Menton. Adrian liked Graham, describing him as 'a really genuine, sweet person, very good with young people', but in common with

3. Eardley had spent the winter of 1928 there

others thought Kathy 'incredibly pushy; attending cocktail parties dressed entirely by Graham; serving tea [at their home in Trottiscliffe, Kent] in tea cups by Graham, in hat and scarf *by Graham*'. Eardley later agreed with him, finding that success got to them in the way that they 'were not interested in anybody unless they were concerned with his success.' It puzzled Adrian to recall Sutherland for the first time coming 'face to face with those cactuses which became what he did for almost the rest of his life.' He failed to understand this kind of art: 'His thorn motif adds up to nothing in my book,' he said, but in 1948 when Sutherland's sales took off and he wanted to relinquish his teaching at Goldsmiths', Adrian took over his one day from him and remained there for the next 35 years.

Eardley's views on art and Adrian's were similar, as were their backgrounds, and Adrian enjoyed dialogue with him and appreciated what Eardley wrote about art, including about himself in *Art News & Review*, 8 October 1949, to coincide with his Redfern exhibition. Adrian wrote to thank him for the article, letting him know that the editor, distinguished critic Bernard Denvir (1917–94) said it was 'the best one they've had' and shyly in a post script added: 'It was very nice to read what I try to do put so well into words. I can't tell you how much I like it!!' In another letter dated 5 February (without the year) Adrian writes: 'After reading it [your article on Matthew Smith] I looked through several books on Matisse and came to the conclusion he's not really a good colourist at all! And that MS was more serious! because any artist with taste could decorate a canvas – but the real problem of a colourist (a problem I couldn't find Matisse answering or even aware of) is "what colour is the shadow cast by (an apple) on the table- (cloth, coloured squares etc.)" Do you agree? Looking at Matisse it seems he always has to have a ready made object full of colours – those decorated vases, backcloths and striped dresses etc. – whereas a real colourist – such as Soutine – is *searching* for the colours in ordinary things, and especially in the folds, creases, and shadows those things create. Rembrandt's hands contain all the colours Matisse uses! There's a Rembrandt...in the N.G. in which the hands are ultra-Soutine! The pigment [is] madly scrambled and the colours amazing. How long did it take you to write the article? It must be very difficult to write exactly what one means! All I've been trying to say I see you've written in one sentence – "MS's... gift is that of creating three dimensional forms entirely out of colour" – which to my mind is the problem a colourist should face and Matisse doesn't. Oh dear! How long winded I am! But having got your 3 dim. form in colour the bloody thing casts a 3 dim. shadow!! ...lots of love if you've got this far – Adrian'.

It can be fairly stated that Eardley's attentiveness was without conditions; that overall his energy was of a giving and mothering variety and that Adrian felt the benefit of it and unfailingly showed his appreciation – the pure form of giving back. Only their 'agreement' of early 1947 does not overall seem to have been fully actioned. The small clutch of undated letters makes this clear. '48 Tite Street. April 25. My dear Erd. A thousand thanks for buying my picture of trout at the Redfern. It was very sweet of you to be so loyal. Only one other painting sold – & a few watercolours. Rather depressing...' Two letters in sorrowfully uneven handwriting emanate direct from his sickbed (entered 7 January 1949) leaving no doubt about where to visit: 'William King Ward – St George's Hospital – Hyde Park. My dear Eardley, I fell ill New Year's day, with pneumonia... I might be out about 24 Jan? I need to sell. This illness is wretchedly inconvenient. Lots of love yr miserable Ade.' Eardley visited him on Sunday 16th and sent a letter the next day with a cheque for £100 (visiting again on the 19th) in evident response to which he responded: 'St George's Hospital Jan 17th. Darling Eardley. What a sweetheart you are! Thank you very much indeed for the wonderful cheque – it certainly will 'help'! But I really can't accept it as a present – I'll consider it an advance on the pictures I hope you'll be able to sell for me...' And post-1947 (because of a reference to Eardley painting that it also contains): '48 Tite Street, Oct... I don't know quite how well I managed it with Bonham Carter [probably Lady Charlotte, a friend of Eardley's] but she is honour bound to buy a picture after the show... But she'll do it thro you (I do believe she thinks you make on it!!) – You are a fantastic man – you know you can have any picture you like (I owe you hundreds) and yet you talk of "paying some more"...'

When the tide of his relationship with Polly turned fatally and drowned him in drink – after the terrible binge had subsided – it was to Eardley that Adrian wrote bitterly and to Long Crichel that he repaired to be reminded of 'things other than bitters and bitches'; a place he had unusually – for female partners were not hugely welcomed there as the butler had made clear to her – once visited with Polly. There he enjoyed hospitality and kindness which his diary confirms to have lifted his mood. He writes on his birthday (3 October 1951) to thank Eardley, Desmond and Eddy, with some levity reinstated: 'I enclose a little present which I should like to give you all – tho' I'm afraid your church will have to work hard to look like its portrait.'

Adrian seeking, as did many, to paint Ram Gopal (1929–2003) – 'the Nijinsky of India' and an international dancing legend – Eardley paved the way and furnished him with the address and telephone number, and put Vanessa Bell and Duncan Grant onto Adrian when they sought partners in a lithography press. Amid all the kindness, and notwithstanding all the amusement that Adrian provided him, Eardley seems only to have asked one thing (the one time they went to bed together having been entirely mutual). In a letter written by Eardley dated 10 March 1947 and with marked timidity and lack of urgency he proposes: 'And one day I want to ask you if you ever felt like it to paint a picture of me.' It is a trait of those who seek to commission portraits of themselves that they feel insecure about the way they look and hope to be reassured. It is not thought that any sitting ever took place. Amity melded into more remote cordiality, initially influenced by the move from 48 Tite Street. Also as the years passed, the 18-year gap between them appeared to narrow. Five months before Eardley died in September 1991, he showed at Michael Parkin's gallery in Motcomb Street. Adrian attended the private view and there wasn't much physical difference between these two gentleman painters, bright-eyed still and friends to the end.

Rex de Charamboc Nan Kivell was a dealer who knew how to wield the occasional paintbrush. It was never the main thrust of his creativity, whose masterpiece – aside from the formation of the Redfern gallery – was his own transformation from New Zealand colonial to seigneur of English society. When some drawings with royal provenance turned up in the basement of the gallery, Rex, a friend of the then Sir Anthony Blunt, Keeper of the Queen's pictures, was informed that the Palace wanted them returned. Averse neither to the system of honours nor of barter, his unflustered response was: 'Mmmmn, I've always wanted a knighthood'. Although it took time coming and he had for a decade to make do with a CMG, he was eventually knighted in the Birthday Honours of 1976, officially by recommendation of the Australian Prime Minister 'for services to the arts'. He was able to luxuriate for a year in it. He died the following June, ahead of the vexatious public unmasking of Blunt. Rex vexed invoked a very different being. For reason of discretion, he kept an additional flat in a louche corner of Fitzrovia, where he periodically installed lovers, for as long as each lasted. The turnover is held to have been high. Following one unhappy ending, passers-by, including Mattei Radev, the picture framer and friend of Eardley Knollys, were entertained by the spectacle of some unfortunate youth's worldly possessions being vengefully jettisoned: records, clothes and books flew through the windows, cascading onto the pavement below, to the accompaniment of disembodied seigneurial swearing. Sir Rex normally combined self-possession with charm; valuable for giving him barely rivalled access to fine artworks. He was a pioneer of prints which, according to the sales-conscious Graham Sutherland, 'were nearer to his heart… not everybody can afford paintings' and notably presented Picasso's Vollard suite and Rouault's 'Miserere' series. Of particular pleasure to Adrian was the gallery's stock of paintings by Christopher Wood, who had died at Salisbury Station in 1930 by throwing himself under a train. Adrian regarded Wood as 'England's most poetic, lyrical painter', adding that 'for sheer joy I'd rather have a Christopher Wood than almost anything.' Rex could afford not to be precious about pictures. Adrian once walked into the gallery one day to find him doing a little dance and singing: 'I've got a ba-na-na in the Ta-ate! I've got a ban-na-na in the Ta-te!' In a quiet moment Rex had determined that a 1924 oil still life by Wood with an underpainted banana lacked vitality. Brightly he repainted it. A curator from the Tate Gallery then came in and promised to buy it for the collection. This was perhaps Adrian's favourite memory of Rex, the two of them as equally delighted by this minor deception and momentous accolade. His pleasure over the incident endured as the glowing banana did not. Either Rex (unlikely) or the Tate bottled out and the picture 'restored' to its underpainting remained as stock until several decades later.

As artist and dealer they did not mix socially, but it was a friendly business relationship. Rex cared feverishly for grand society – having eagerly contracted into it – whereas Adrian, partly through exposure at birth, was immune. As with other artists he – as Guy Roddon expressed it – 'was in the group but he wasn't', yet was at ease when called upon to fraternise. Rex's fraternity of rich, usually unmarried, often titled, gentlemen-collectors were keen to call on Adrian at Tite Street, in chauffeured cars that would return him after an outrageously extended lunch to the ever patient Peggy or, later, a piqued Polly. They came calculating that his place in the stratosphere of British art was more rising star than rocket waiting to be spent. The well-heeled artist friend of Gertrude Stein's, Sir Francis Rose, was of their number. That he ever bought a painting is in doubt. Sir Edward de Stein did, and also commissioned a portrait of himself. Dapper Sir Edward, ex-Eton and Oxford, was an attractive polymath; founder of what became the merchant bankers Lazards; President of Gallaher Ltd which merged with Columbia Gramophones and became EMI; philanthropic Chairman of the Finance Committee of the Red Cross; water colourist and author of books including *Poets in Picardy* and very keen on shooting and fishing. Numerous sittings occurred. Adrian happily recalled going to the neat house that Sir Edward shared with his sister at 25 Montpelier Square, where the butler shimmered discreetly away, and regretted that the only thing he 'never got to see' was the country estate. Sir Edward Marsh, classicist lover of Rupert Brooke and Churchill's private secretary, sunk Adrian's work somewhere into his vast collection, following a period of slightly over-enthusiastic calling. Adrian had his limits, and reached them early with predatory Peter Watson, backer of Cyril Connolly's *Horizon* and master of the expressive use of the deep pocket. Drinks and a concert at the Adelphi with Watson on two consecutive nights in March 1944 were the sum of association that Adrian could cope with.

Legendarily decent and shy, Lord Croft, a leading light of the Contemporary Art Society who was still buying Adrian's paintings 50 years later, came not via Rex but Eardley. The problem was that what Lord Croft liked above all wasn't rightfully Adrian's to sell, but Polly's. In a done deal by the time she came out of hiding in the bedroom, Lord Croft had departed, minus forty pounds, with the canvas *Lobster*, 1946, removed from its place above the dining table. Adrian insisted on giving her the money, but what she wanted was the picture back, in whose making she had had input on the crucial positioning of one of the feelers and which had been given to her in consequence. Had Edward Croft known the situation, the painting would have remained in situ. Instead, for 55 years it hung in Croft Castle, Herefordshire – the family seat since the Domesday book – apart from being lent to a show at Tooth's, until in 2002 Sotheby's auctioned it as part of the Croft Collection, when it found a buyer from its spiritual home in Cornwall. *Lobster*, 1946, shows a creature arrested in clear water among deep rocks. Water represents emotion. Adrian's narrow characteristic horizon line is absent; thus air representing freedom is lost, and all the lobster can do about it is look defiant and hope to save soft flesh beneath armour plating. Feeling trapped, got at and seeking a way out of darkness were familiar concerns. The war, the death of Kit, the people – wife, child, mistress etc. – who all desired a morsel of him are focussed in this embattled creature, and the lobster responds with poised claws, sensitive on all sides, gentle antennae wary, balancing the different aspects of his nature, victory with defeat. It contrasts with the tranquil nude asleep amongst the same Mousehole rocks, which is so symbolic of the extreme powers – security and by implication its opposite – that women awakened for him. This optimistic nude was begun in July 1946 at the Owl's Nest studio in Mousehole, at the start of his relationship with Polly Walker. Her serene face is cushioned (but by rocks) not unlike his rendering of Kit on her deathbed nine months earlier. Unusually, for anyone right-handed, he painted the face last, working from right to left. The model for the body was – as Polly does not fail to point out – an older woman called Shirley Maiden (whose claim to fame was having gone to bed with Dylan Thomas, which apparently raised her stock considerably and placed her in demand in Mousehole during the war; she later moved to Bognor Regis) who, shortly after posing and certainly maiden no more, demanded £150 from Adrian in payment for an abortion at a private nursing home in Blackheath. Polly was deputised to deliver a cheque for a doctor known as 'Pinky' by hand to London. It then got about that Shirley had contrived to receive a similar sum from a local dentist well known for his drilling abilities. Adrian was angered but did nothing. He maintained civilities whenever they encountered Shirley in the pub, which in turn annoyed Polly; the two women not just in paint remained at odds with one another. Whereas the painting's wistful, womb-like depiction of calm polarises Adrian's reality.

Meanwhile Rex put on Adrian's Redfern shows with customary flair. The *Evening News* reported his first private view, highlighting attendance by Sir Eddie Marsh and H.E. Bates, while Eddy Sackville-West, Oliver Gollancz and Lloyd George were among those who bought work from the show. Concurrent with which, occupying Room One from 11 March to 3 April 1943, Rex showed André Masson, Georges Rouault, and an impressive list of works by Matisse, Bonnard, Jongkind, Utrillo and Fantin Latour.

Some of the earliest exhibited of Adrian's pictures can only be imagined, their painterly qualities assumed to contrast with some fairly transparent titling: *Newspaper Boy* measuring

50" x 30" sold to James Agate and later appeared at auction, where it was bought by Peter Cochrane, director of the dealers Arthur Tooth & Sons; *Footballer* measuring marginally less; *Child with a Camera*; *Arab*; *Pierrot*; *Sailor Boy* (just 6" x 9", painted over in January 1944) and *Dogs Playing* all passed unphotographed, and to whereabouts unknown. Adrian's ledger lists many works from the early forties, against which the annotations 'destroyed' or 'painted over' considerably outnumber the fate of the rest. He was all for F. Scott Fitzgerald's dictum of never blaming failure, there being too many extenuating complexities in life – but of being merciless toward lack of effort; as sometimes he was toward effort too.

From 1943 to 1953 six exhibitions at the Redfern bore testimony to his effort in creativity. They are in retrospect easily lumped together, but they fared individually very differently. Not all were sell-outs, and the last two seem to have sold all too few. Thereafter he and Rex, undetectably, seem to have called a halt – and for some time. On the surface those shows collectively signified artistic achievement. In reality they were more correctly to do with endeavour. In a decade much had changed for Adrian and in the world around him. So much was expected of him as a result of that early success. Expectation leads to disappointment and Rex, always initially sympathetic to the woes of those around him, was too self-regarding to be anything but bored by their more long-term misfortunes. A crusading knight tires of long-drawn-out campaigning: Rex was diverted by wanting adventures with new young artists and new art forms. When Adrian most needed to show, Rex was not naturally offering assistance and Adrian would never have requested it. Similarly, in 1949, election to membership of the RA having been proposed – initiated by Robert Buhler – and which undoubtedly would have generated continuity, it required some push from Adrian to clinch it and foundered for the lack. In failing to bid for his own self-advancement, he showed no mercy either. Being taken up by Tooths for an exhibition in January 1956 must have looked like a welcome progression. It wasn't defection, but it must have given a temporary let-out to Rex whose ambitions were otherwise diverted. Not many people came at the start, which depressed him, and of the two paintings sold at the opening, one was to Edwin John, who of all people knew about having to battle against other's expectations and reputations; but he was later cheered by the 'quite good' write-up in *The Times*, which boosted sales, including one to

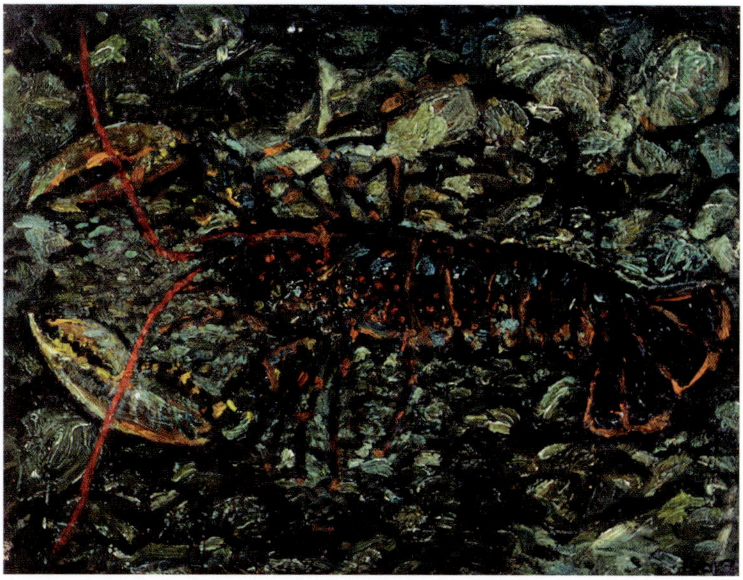

Lobster
oil on canvas, 1946

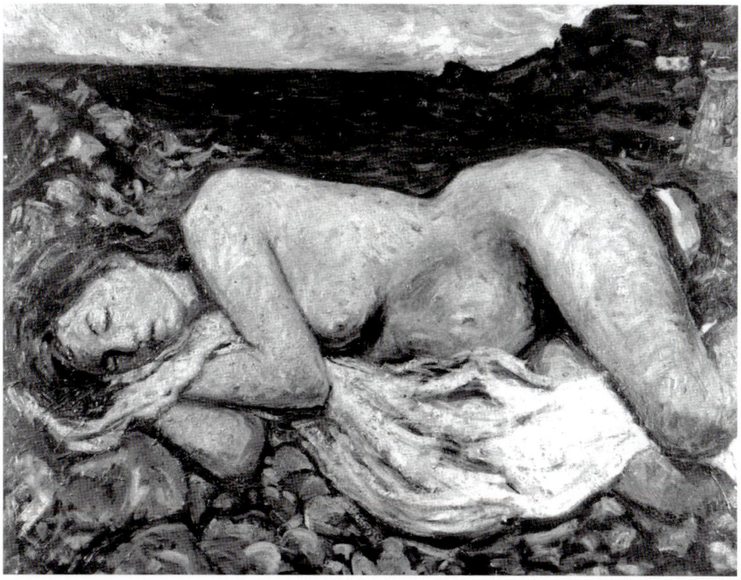

Nude among the rocks, Mousehole
oil on canvas, 1947

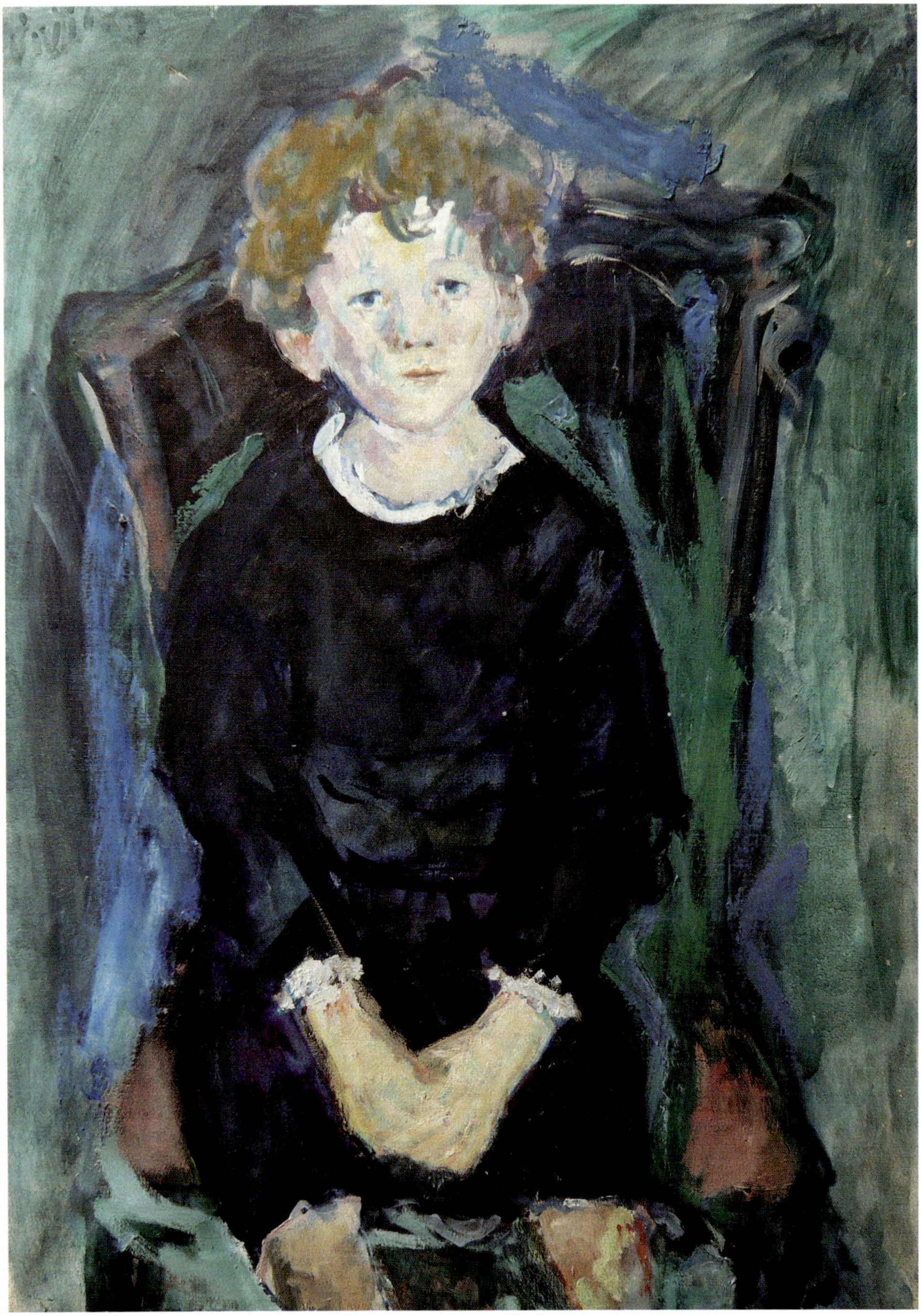

Portrait of Miss Vivien Ryan
oil on canvas, c. 1961

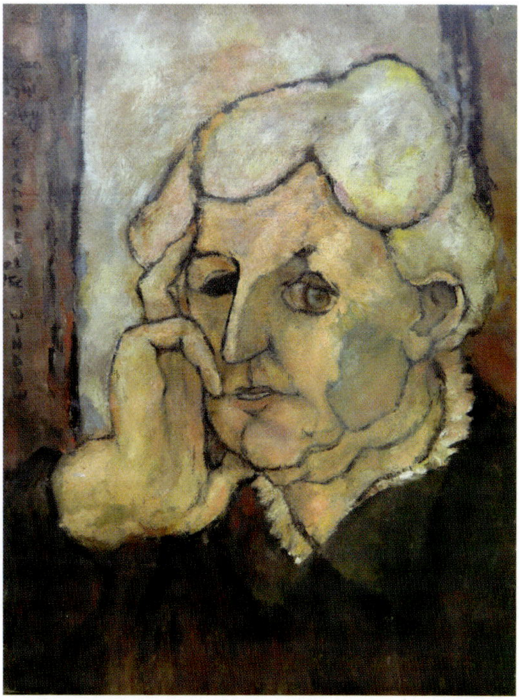

Little Grannie
oil on canvas, 1941

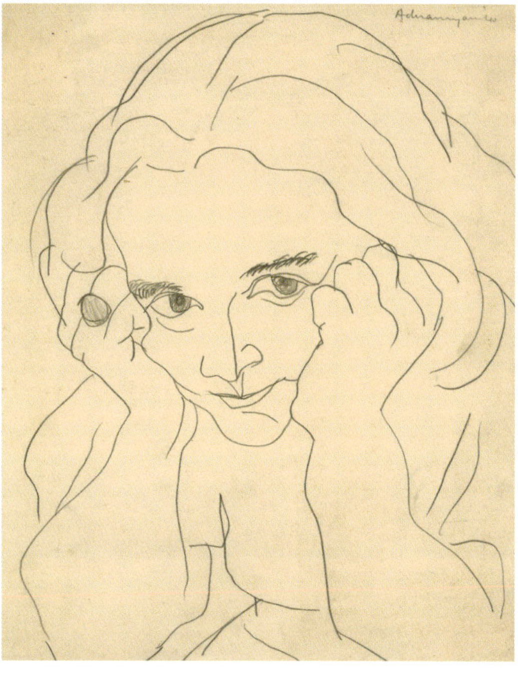

Peggy Ryan
pencil on paper, 1940

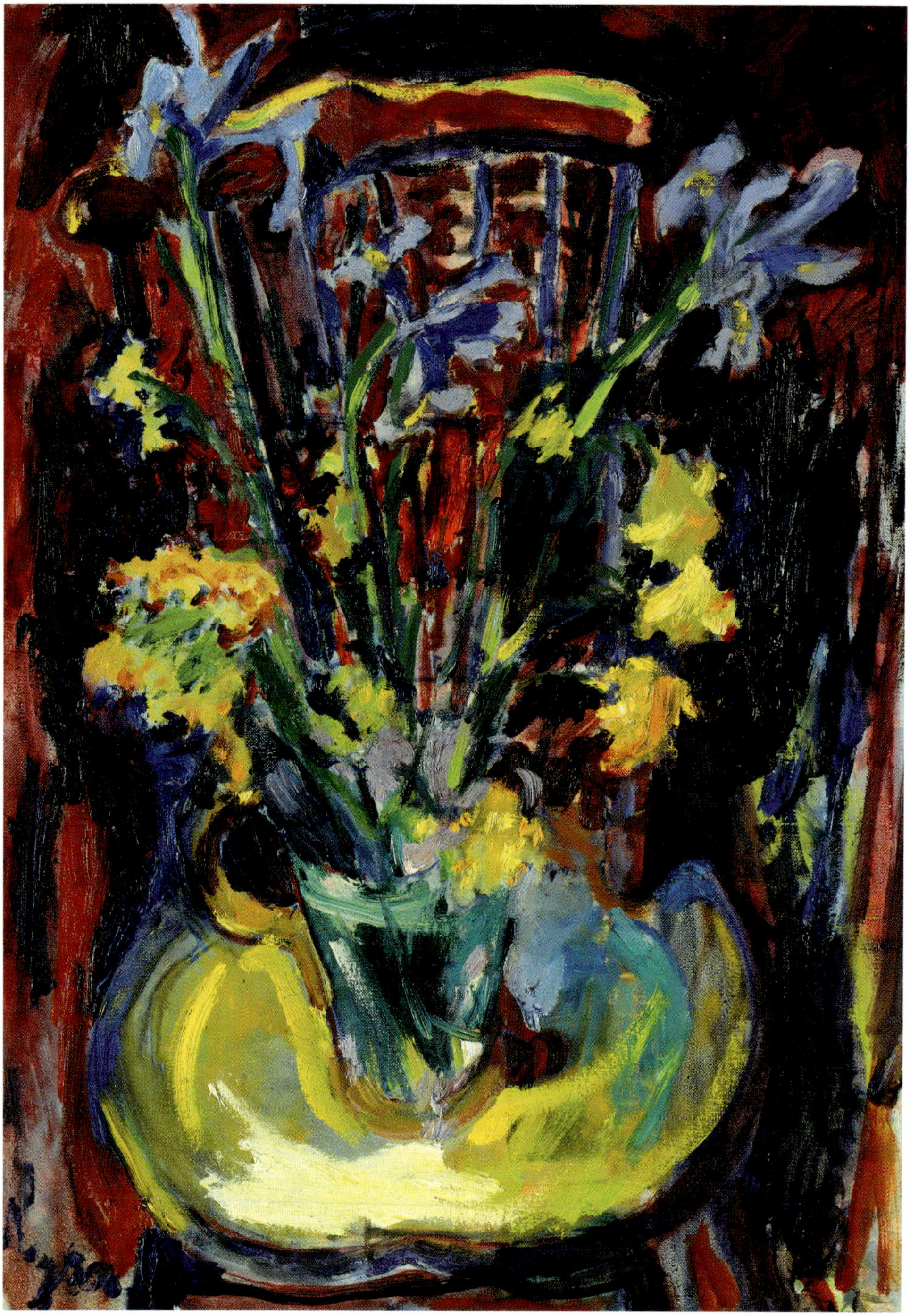

Flowers on a chair
oil on canvas, 1958

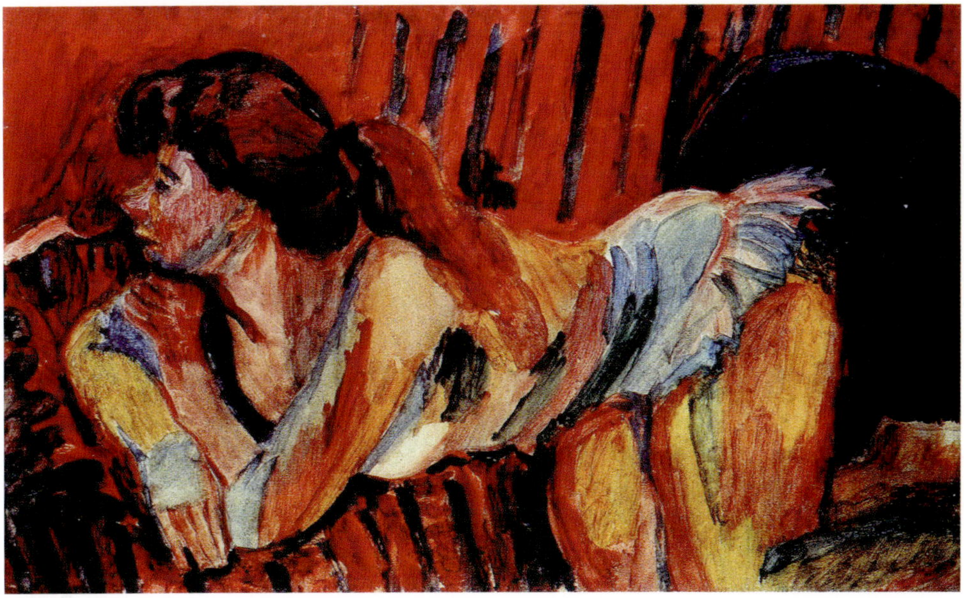

Joan Gillchrest kneeling
oil on canvas, c. 1959
courtsey of Redfern Gallery

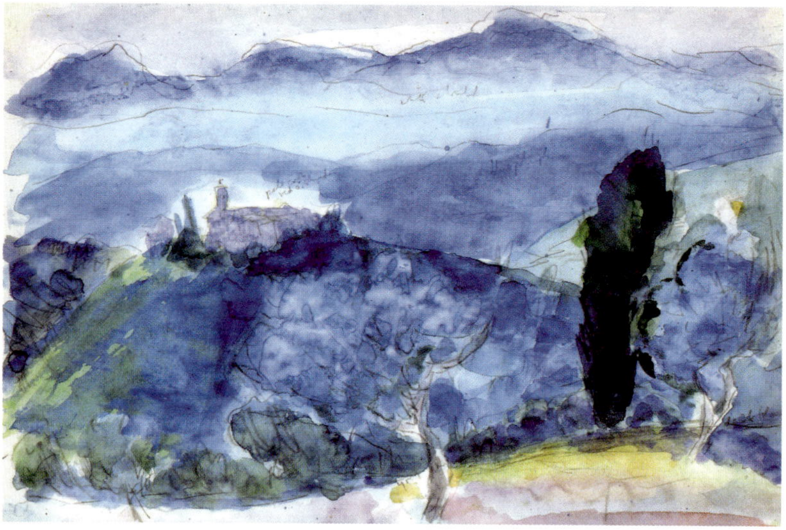

Callian
watercolour, 1968

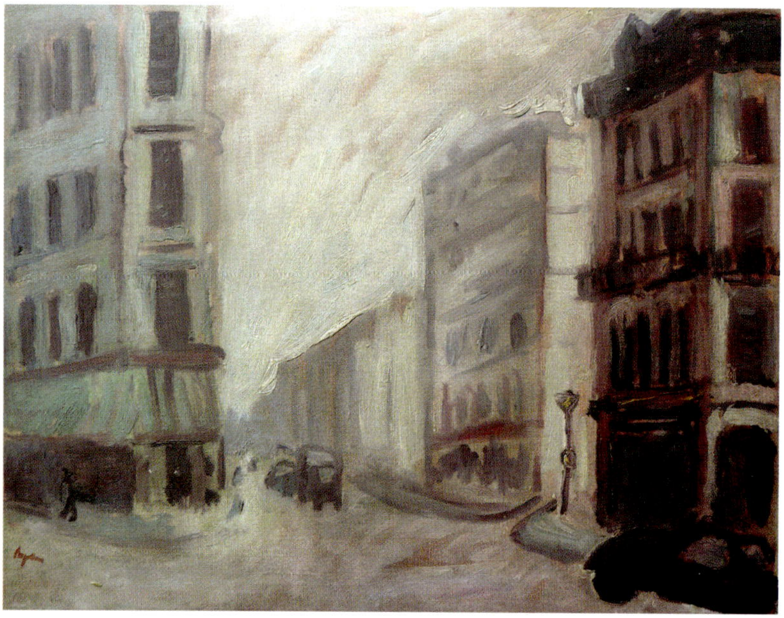

Rue de Vaugirard, Paris
oil on canvas, 1957

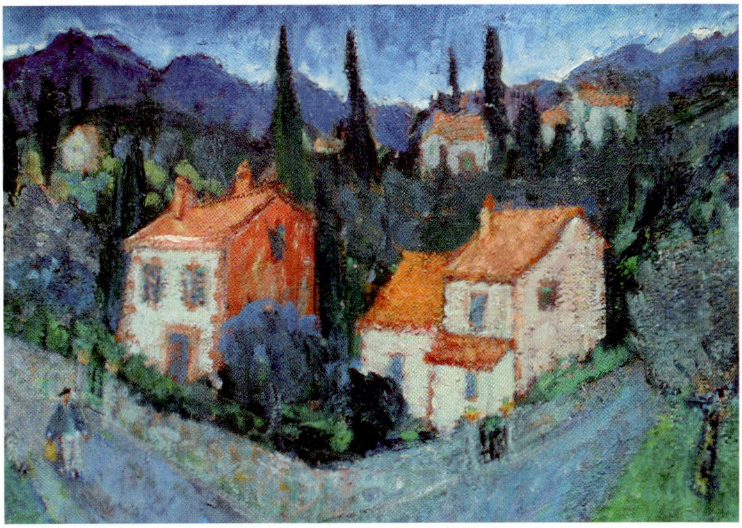

Joss walking, Montauroux
oil on canvas, c. 1970

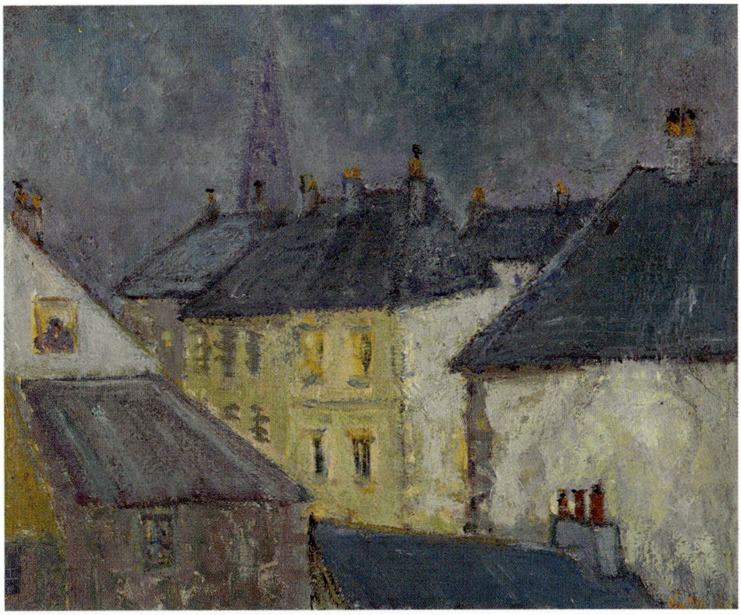

Brittany night scene
oil on canvas, c. 1980

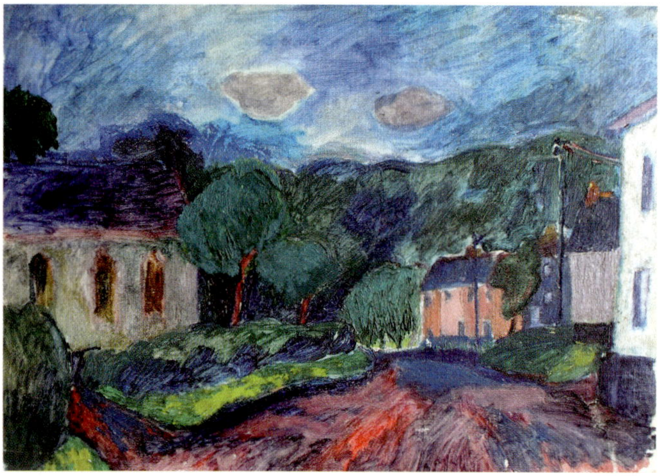

Suffolk street scene
oil on canvas, c. 1953

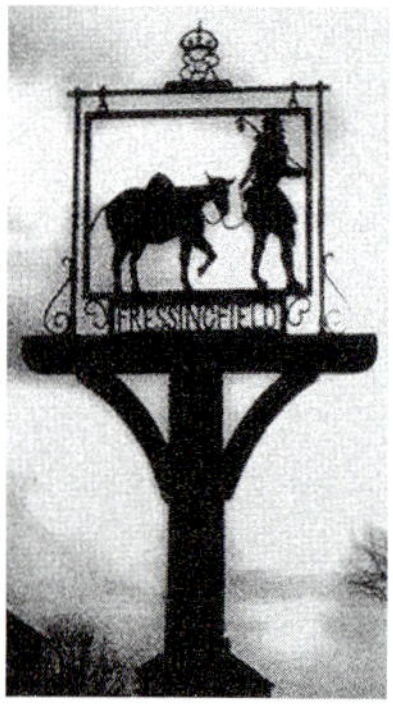

Adrian's sign for Fressingfield, 1952

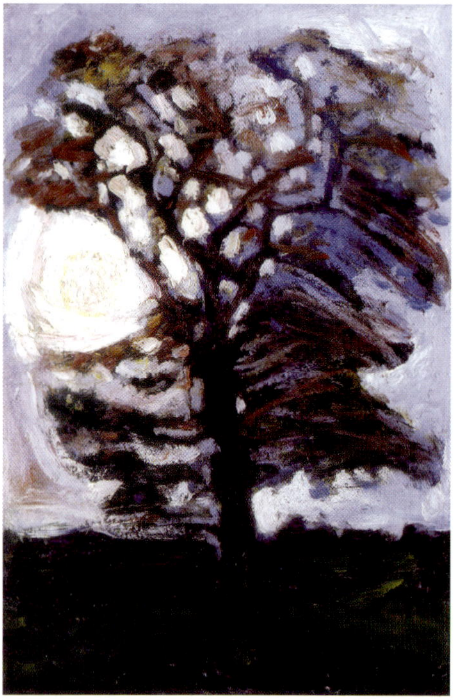

Tree and setting sun, Suffolk
oil on canvas, c. 1956

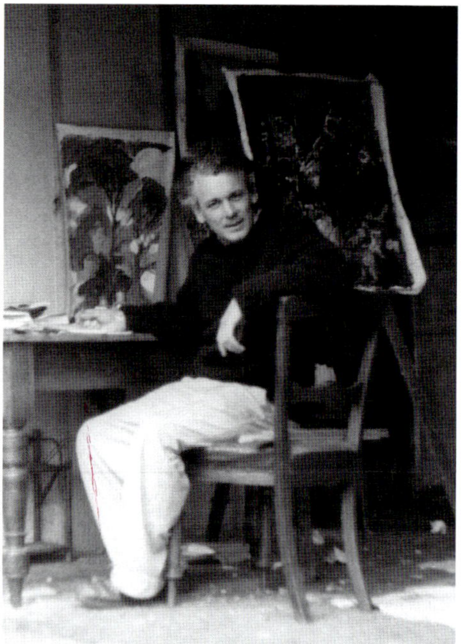

Adrian in his Camden studio c. 1961

the CAS, and one later still to the National Gallery of New Zealand, making nine in all. Tooths as a firm did not endure much longer. Financially, worse was to come.

Marriage and children

'You're married now so I'll have to marry Barbara – she wants me to,' said Adrian to Peggy, shortly after 29 January 1953, when – coincidentally on the same day as his sixth Redfern show opened – she married Richard Alexander at Chelsea Registry Office. In fact Adrian had married Goldsmiths' student Barbara Pitt nearly five months previously, on 4 September 1952, less than two months after settling a bitter legal wrangle over money with Polly, from whom he had broken almost exactly a year. What he really meant by this loaded statement is unclear. Peggy, however, lived long-term with its implications, not realising it as a disclamation, which at best suggests an ability to distance himself from marital estate. Nurtured by Vivian, his views on the marriage contract involved licensing the male party to unwritten, unspoken get-out clauses and extra-curricular activity as a matter of course. It was part of the child in him. He never intended to be destructive, but where women were concerned, Adrian was unconventional to say the least. Peggy has cited *Ariel or the Life of Shelley* by André Maurois as something Adrian loved and a good example of his utterly free-spirited, early beliefs in unchained love, and its references to the senselessness of 'Knight Errantry' and to marriage as 'a shameful and immoral action'. His three wives, also Polly Walker and Joan Gillchrest, agree that Adrian would have liked to have been a polygamist. Furthermore, if there was a woman to undertake a conventional domestic role while allowing him his unconventionality, his work flourished. Conversely, following a falling-out, work was temporarily impossible. But if they wanted to paint too, as Peg, Polly, Barbara and Joan all did, that for him was a problem: one that he acted out by turning their work to the wall when dealers or collectors came. This, as with his infidelity, has been misconstrued as unkindness, rather than pained inferiority – and for which he sought especially to make amends to Peggy, whose talent alone he forever rated highly. Sue Curnow, coming so much later on the scene, being no would-be painter and furthermore enabled to maintain salaried employment – the first bearer of stability in his life – was as consort and third wife unique in these advantages.

Meanwhile, wedding Barbara aged 19 years and 10 months, also at Chelsea, with as witness another Goldsmiths' lecturer and splendid painter – of boxing scenes especially – Sam Rabin, seems to have been impromptu. Adrian declared she had proposed to him (on holiday in Wales sometime during the summer of 1952) at which Barbara with dignity demurs. Ringed as Full Moon in his diary entry for the day, he first posits: 'to France?' and secondly reports: 'Get married to B. Fly to Paris after Mad Party…' the only premeditated part seeming to be France. 'Slept late. Eat, drink – St Germain. Met Moynihan Deux Magots',[1] was followed on day two by 'Orangerie, Jeu de Paume, to Delacroix Studio'. Thereafter they took the train to Cannes, were met by brother Desmond and after motoring to their hotel, finished up in the casino where, with manifest enthusiasm, he 'WON ON 27!!' Next day they included Cagnes-sur-Mer in a tour, presumably taking in Villa Santa Lucia, if it had not become a horseracing track by then, and next evening met up with Eardley at the casino, and also for lunch the following day. 'Eat too much – and F. too much!' is next day tempered by: 'Champagne in evening – walk along River with B.' Swimming and drinking and pleasant evenings in the square span nine days romancing in the south before returning to Paris for one day, where they saw John Minton. Long after emigrating without their two children to Cape Town, South Africa, Barbara recalled with pleasure a mutual love of music and poetry; of reading Dickens in the bath one to the other; of long English summer time and making a miniature bowls lawn together at Wood Farm, Fressingfield, and listening to Beethoven while the cuckoo in the garden echoed that in the *Pastorale Symphony*. Romance, however, as with family life, was far from being their bedrock; was rarely referred to by him, and of acrimony

1. Rodrigo Moynihan, painter, 1910–90

and resentment there was plenty, whatever love or understanding may have connected them initially, or reached them latterly. The interim years that continued, albeit remotely, to fashion their association were on account of their two children, Scarlett and Vivien, whose upbringing he undertook with the help of numerous females other than their absent mother. Ill-equipped by his own mother's inadequacies, the role came to him by default; by certain accounts he was delighted, finally, at gaining custody on the grounds that Barbara was unfit, rather than by his own suitability or desire for the task in hand. Guilt and feelings of inadequacy remained with him. In October 1993 he described an often recurring anxiety dream wherein Joan Gillchrest was again booting him out and in which his miserable task was hurriedly 'having to sew in the name-tapes of both girls on the eve of sending them back to school; and then of missing the train...' Geraldine being cared for by Peggy caused him much less stress. The existence of three different and sometimes conflicting daughters seems to have affected him in equally differing ways. That his work was challenged there can be no doubt. That he tried hard as a parent – which is not to say he was necessarily a good parent or an easy one – is undoubted, if hard to measure. Moreover he visited on all his daughters energy that returned high regard and unconditional love to their father – a valuable achievement – while they remained objective about much that they might have wished different about their upbringing.

Adrian's having been 'from the age of two... stuck up on a chair to be painted in a... vast studio with a balcony and suits of armour everywhere' recalled an act of enthralment which did not deter him from doing the same to his own daughters. The scale of these portraits seems to increase in proportion to their descending ages. Thus Vivien is most fully represented, Geraldine the least, who was mostly in the sole care of her mother and therefore less vulnerable, with Scarlett bringing up the middle ground. Drawings or paintings of his parents – except the death drawing already referred to – are there none, nor of cousins or other close relatives except of 'Little Grannie', his mother's stepmother, by all accounts a civilised and kindly early presence. Early, fluid drawings exist of Peg, some of them signed in handwriting 'Adrian Ryan', predating the simplified form of his recognised signature. Barbara, though often drawn, did not mature into more than a solitary oil (exh. at the Redfern, January 1953) and of Sue Ryan – so often incorporated into what he termed 'happy holiday snaps' with her sitting on beaches, or on steps, as a sketched figure in mid ground – nothing (aside of nudes) approaching a true portrait was executed. More of a muse than his three wives, ironically, was Polly, while bearing in mind that in this period there would most often not be the distracting element of children present. Of Joan Gillchrest, too, several portraits were made and have survived, as were certain others of other mistresses. Portraits, including of the self, often issue from the wish to explore the bonds of intimacy, but a glance at Adrian's *oeuvre* suggests that staying within the legal knot of marriage for subject matter seems to have held little interest for his sylph-like mind. While maintaining that he didn't 'like painting portraits' he nevertheless made them often enough, up to and including the very last picture he struggled with – 'just to say I've done some work today' – one week before he died. Re-inspection of his ledger, however, refers to a sequence of long-forgotten – including by her – oil paintings of Peggy, including two nudes (one with her pregnant), the largest 50" x 28"; also pictures of Peggy with Geraldine and of Geraldine as a baby in a pram and other depictions. Seventeen family oil paintings in all – including two exhibited at the Redfern in 1943 and 1944 – plus one of Kit – 'Mrs Vivian Ryan' 20" x 30" – neatly recorded, together with their fate. They are all listed either painted over or, in a few cases, destroyed; as though there were something that he disliked more in some than in others. An oil on wood of Patrick Heron dated 1944, which the artist long remembered and after Adrian's death asked the Tate Gallery St Ives to try to recover, is also given in the ledger as having been destroyed.

A portrait of daughter Vivien, circa 1961, her round little face topped with abundant curls of hair, is reminiscent of Adrian in photographs at a similar age, an effect enhanced by her wearing what could be taken for period boyish apparel. Her hands are clasped in a bid to stop her fidgeting, her body is slumped, her legs do not carry her and her knees – the body part representative of submission – seem most animated. But it is the dullness of her expression that registers differently from her father's shining, mischievous intelligence captured in photographs of him throughout childhood. The inspirational brightness is not in her but is in all the colours surrounding her; whereas she has been clothed in blue-black, in all languages associated with 'the blues', and there is blackness lying behind her – literally her *background* – visible through the chair's slats thereby reinforcing depression. If Adrian's mothering was uncertain territory, growing up, for little Vivien, was as well. This at times served to make guilty and depress Adrian further. The painting suggests a suppression of two necessary operations: his requiring to paint and she having to be child-minded away from Joan, who was unaccountably unfond of Adrian's youngest child. The chair on which Viv sits partially reinforces the earlier period feeling to the work. More significantly, since it barely registers in other portraits – though so many other upright chairs *do,* while his sitters derive no comfort from easy chairs, ever – it precisely confirms the atavistic act: for it is one of the two period chairs Adrian garnered from Hintlesham. The distinctive seat embroidered with the family coat of arms by Lady Ryan has its deep red background revised, however, almost beyond recognition, as comfortably rose-tinted as ever the past can be. Expunging the family seat, so to speak, but not the connection, is a distinction he could easily have chosen to avoid snobbery. (Another painting of 1948 showing the second of these two chairs further corroborates the reworking of the seat fabric.) He similarly deploys one of the chairs in portraying Geraldine in childhood.

Atavism may be hard to by-pass whilst being charming to recognise. A photograph taken near Tregonce Cliff, near Padstow, in 1944 recalls an earlier one at Cagnes-sur-Mer, almost twenty years previously. In each case the subject is the same: a child shelling peas whose parent watches smiling. The difference is that the child in the earlier has become the parent of Geraldine, aged 16 months, two decades on. Shelling peas was something Adrian was taught by Kit, a practice from her middle-class upbringing in Normanton Road, and was emblematic of their new-found freedom and self-regulation. His young Master status at Hintlesham would have debarred him from such a small, pleasurable task. Similarly 'digging for nuggets' (new potatoes) was garnered from Kit, passed on to all his children, a throwback to a rosy past.

Marriage to Peggy had been unconventionally enacted, as were his subsequent weddings. It took place on 14 January 1941, at Caxton Hall, all but nine months short of Adrian's twenty-first birthday. This necessitated his having to produce for the Registrar written permission from his parents for the marriage to go ahead. Kit point blank refused. Vivian, 'up in the clouds', as Peggy put it, wouldn't say no, but Kit was in this instance effective in preventing him from saying yes. A document signed with his name was nevertheless produced which allowed the marriage to take place without a hitch and with Slade tutor Peter Brooker[2] and faithful OE school friend Adrian Liddell-Hart present. The gold cufflinks once given by Lady Ryan *sans perruque* were pawned to advance the funds. The approving signature, later revealed to be a work of forgery by Adrian – always an admirer of faking – failed to cause the outcry from Kit as might have been expected. Probably she feared greater scandal from publicly proclaiming the deception. Her silent bids to divide their sleeping arrangements at Iden were no penance for fraud, offered hardly insurmountable obstacle and certainly fewer implications for Peg – converting to catholicism much later in life and a double-divorcee notwithstanding – than the Church's ultimate and inflexible assertion that she'd not been properly married to Adrian in the first place.

The Second World War precipitated marriages that would not otherwise have taken place, according to Guy Roddon, whose systematic espousing of those whom Adrian termed 'two of the most terrifying women in England' began to the accompaniment of bombs falling in 1944. As a serving officer (in the camouflage corps), Guy knew that, after the first night, he would not see his bride for many months, and felt 'driven by something greater than oneself to perpetuate the race in the face of destruction.' For Adrian the feeling was not much different, except that army life was something he managed to curtail. In January 1941 Peggy was already pregnant, but their boy-child was miscarried. Geraldine was conceived in August the following year and born on 1 May 1943 into a terrified world, her nightly shelter from doodle bugs being the under-stairs cupboard at 48 Tite Street, which housed her pram.

'Adrian's relationship with Peggy,' averred Guy, 'was founded in respect.' This is not altogether what Peggy felt at the time. She respected that Adrian was very much a youth who needed his space, especially, she said, when he had either 'a nude model or a pretty boy coming round' – whereupon she clocked up untold miles pushing the pram round the streets of Chelsea – and made no demands of her young husband. Guy's impression is not unfounded, however. That Adrian lastingly loved and respected her is undoubted, but as a young man, he had difficulty showing it. As the official 'guilty' party in their divorce, Adrian invoked Guy as witness to his infidelity. A trip to a Brighton hotel and a woman whose profession it then was to appear on demand as co-respondent in such matters, sealed it. Their case was presented at the Law Courts in the Strand by an able and spruce young barrister friend of Polly's, a

2. Whose first wife had lived with Leonard Woolf after Virginia's death. He later became Peggy's Catholic godfather

distinctive figure in round horned spectacles, whose prominent and immobile-looking bottom lip caused him to speak in an efficiently cynical drawl. This was John Mortimer acting in one of his first cases. Peggy's view of him then was that he was not at all the avuncular figure he became in later years. He was 'stern-looking, gaunt and hard; made no effort to put me at my ease when standing up in court, which I found difficult'. He also charged the immense sum of £500 as his fee – so much then that she never forgot it – which Adrian had to ask Willie Brass for so he could pay it. Polly's name was not brought into the proceedings. Guy gave nervous testimony. He was startled to behold yet another total stranger in the place of the unknown lady with whom he had supposedly surprised Adrian *in flagrante* in Brighton – these ambassadresses operated cross-country to save shillings on train fare – but his affirmation brought to a cordial conclusion less than a decade of marriage in which each had spent almost half the time living with other people. Not mentioned in court was the very modern gesture of Peggy and Adrian having spent the night together prior to divorce being granted.

The same cordiality did not pervade marriage number two to Barbara. His friends were astonished that he could have married her. Possibly he surprised himself. Barbara, at 17, was the youngest student at Goldsmiths'. She was not his pupil and the relationship only developed some time after her eighteenth birthday, fuelled by her taking six months out of college to go to Paris, paid for by her modelling for Anthony Devas for Aero chocolate bars. This Adrian took as a gauntlet thrown to him and took himself after her to Paris, making her return. It took Barbara no time to realise, upon marriage, what an impossible situation it was, claiming that Adrian suffered 'almost an inferiority complex wanting to prove that he could be loved.' Scarlett, conceived in August 1953, arrived the following May and was a mitigating influence on their burgeoning differences. Not much is recorded about Adrian's infidelities at this time, but within a year of the marriage, Polly was back on the scene as a result of Barbara's having sought her out – 'to get to know her' – and a ménage à trois ensued at Wood Farm, Fressingfield, a gesture which Barbara refers to as her 'being accommodating' and certainly one appreciated by her husband. It is difficult in hindsight not to reflect that Barbara was gaining marital respite by the situation, her interest being not enduringly in Adrian as a man but as a person, and in no man that followed. Had she been otherwise, she might have been more jealous or aware of those people, some more casually than others, with whom he was enjoying carnal liaisons at this time – Max Chapman, Keith Vaughan, Sir Edward de Stein, and the sexually voracious Elisabeth Frink among them. Frink met Adrian at Finch's wine bar in the Fulham Road, where she approached him wordlessly. After a while, she posed the question, seemingly rhetorical: 'Are you thinking what I'm thinking – good, then let's go back to my studio', which was handily placed in Fleming Close nearby.

The year 1955 was not inspirational for Adrian ensconced in the country at Wood Farm. Entries in his diary begin 'Paint for the first time in ages' and 'No work for a month', and the classic titles of the few paintings he refers to do not accord with the sort of subject matter that was most likely to appeal to the London galleries at that time, even if his handling of the subjects did: *Onions and sprouts*, *Apples and plums*, and his series of 'Four seasons' still lifes differently referencing an egg, bread, apples and a pheasant, and which did not sell in his lifetime. A 'very pleasant Easter' with only eating, drinking and gardening as frequently noted activities; losing on the Derby – mitigated by John Kilbracken, on form, simultaneously winning £520 – the calm enjoyment outdoors of reading Proust's volumes and *Animal Farm* during the long summer days; pleasant trips to Sadlers Wells with Desmond Shawe-Taylor to see *Cosi Fan Tutte* and *The Bartered Bride*; late autumn lunching with Eardley at Long Crichel and evenings drinking with Augustus. Days of pleasure but very little work. Soon came the onset of several storms.

Less than a month after 'B not well – pregnant?', Adrian's diary entry for 10 December 1955 flatly registers the fact upon which their relationship curdled: 'B loses Baby.' Depression got to him and he looked for comfort physically from Polly and spiritually from the humour of Max Miller, whose mastery of timing and the double entendre ('I met this young boy who inherited money from his father: What must I do to invest it? he asked – Put your little bit into rubber an' if it comes orf you can marry the girl!') was much loved by Adrian. On occasion he would treat himself and his friends to the entire front row of the Chelsea Palace to see the comic perform.

Evidently they tried again, to attempt to satisfy his desire for a boy, and succeeded some time between 7 January 1956 when in the diary: 'B gets her period' and 22 April when it coolly reveals: 'B miscarriage in hospital.' Barbara's recollection is of him blaming her 'for not looking after herself' and that it was as a result of losing this baby that 'the whole thing came unstuck.'

Less than a month later, Tite Street was lengthily tidied 'for [sub]letting', as once previously, to the two sisters of actor Errol Flynn, for the purpose of saving money by heading off to Wood Farm for the summer, which they did on 30 June. For neither can it have been much of a jolly period, not least because it was the wettest July for 100 years. An invitation for the evening before they removed to Fressingfield, and a name entered in his diary for the first time, presaged trouble ahead: 'Bottle party + Joan Gillchrest & B etc.' it was stated, and a little local difficulty was begun.

Joan was a Gilbert Scott before marriage (into the family of a prosperous Anglo-American tobacco manufacturer), great-granddaughter of the noted architect of St Pancras station, and niece of the creator of the red cast-iron telephone box, based on a design taken from the interior of the Dulwich Picture Gallery, and of the power station that is now Tate Modern. She was six years older than Adrian and eighteen years older than Barbara, and she lived in the flat immediately above them on the first floor of 48 Tite Street. Hers was a proper studio with huge windows. She had been brought up in a large house in Cookham, in a way similar to Adrian – nannies, boarding school, her brother went to Harrow – society with a little 's'. 'We talked the same language,' she said, 'we could recognise each other.' They both liked to drink 'a lot,' she added. Joan was in numerous ways the opposite of Barbara, who was penniless in her own right and therefore dependent – a material factor in her post-analysis of the sharp depreciation in her stock value after Joan appeared on the market.

Barbara received no allowance from Adrian, except once, when she was put to the test for one week. Her recollection is that she asked for too little and so failed, and that this was used as a reason not to continue the experiment. His imbalance over money has labelled him as both unstintingly generous and startlingly thrifty throughout his life. Barbara said that to an extent with drink and predictably under the influence of pentathol after visiting the dentist, he would be giving. What he could afford to give was in question. The eight paintings sold by Tooths in 1956 don't appear to have been augmented by other sales that year. There was outstanding money owing from the settlement by the French government for their requisition of Villa Santa Lucia at Cagnes, against which uncertain amount an evidently concerning – and enduring – drip, drip process of loaning money to Desmond had begun. The worldly Joan, back in London with independent means, meanwhile gained in attractiveness to Adrian during the divide of that dampest of summers.

In the middle of October the news that the National Gallery of New Zealand had bought a picture delighted and emboldened Adrian. Shortly before his diary of 26 October matter-of-factly records 'Joan evening', he writes: 'Drive over to see Augustus at Fordingbridge'. It seems inconceivable that he would not have spoken to him about difficulties with Barbara or of the management of some sort of affair with Joan, whom Augustus knew slightly. Also that the old philanderer would have done much else but encourage his protégé. Six days on and it's 'Cinema with J Gillchrest.' Two weeks later still and 'Home to Joan's 12.0.' and 'B. packs', which Barbara recalled was acting on his instructions and to get her out of the way. On 3 December he started a painting of Joan, varnishing the finished work on 29 December and spending various evenings in front of the television with Joan in between. Barbara remained at Wood Farm.

On 1 January 1957: 'Pub J and B etc.' (in that order) while the following entries for the month are so inflammatorily peppered with Joan's name that it constitutes mention-it-is. Painting her again, painting her tulips, staying at her flat (seeing Barbara once only for a midday appointment probably to give her some cash) then in late February painting a 'self portrait in my studio – rotten' which may have reflected an overall sense that what he was doing had a degree of the unacceptable attaching to it. For Barbara was again pregnant at this time (and would give birth on 14 August to a girl, Vivien Frances) while looking after three-year-old Scarlett on her own.

In March 1957 Adrian took on a responsibility from which no distraction could eventually save him. He underwrote the farming project with which Desmond was struggling at Barnes Farm, Stradbroke, meeting Margaret Ryan, his sister-in-law, at the bank on 27 March to sign the relevant papers. Joan went soon afterwards with Adrian to look over the farm and give her opinion on its chances of success. 'It had had it, it was a pathetic mess,' she said, adding that she 'felt very sorry for him over that.'

Adrian flew to Paris with Joan on 3 May 1957. They stayed in Edwin John's studio on the courtyard floor at 91 Rue de Vaugirard, near the Luxembourg Gardens. 'Drunk at the Dome' is all that his diary reports of ten carefree days in which he was evidently too hooked on hedonism to commit much else to record. Guy Roddon went to join them in Paris and arrived on 15 May. Never a Zen master of acting, he was able to hide neither his embarrassment nor surprise when he ascended the airport escalator and unexpectedly confronted Adrian with Barbara to meet him, not Joan. Her hairpins had been located in the bed by Barbara, chancing a visit to Tite Street. Fuelled by the righteous indignation of a wife six months pregnant and venturing by boat and train with all the advantage of surprise, she succeeded in dislodging her guilty rival from the compromising position in which she found her. Joan was obliged due to the exigencies of travel to stay for one more day, departing almost as the bewildered Guy arrived. It was not a party atmosphere, but in some ways Adrian was the least dissatisfied with the situation.

He continued working on a painting of Rue de Vaugirard he had begun on the very day of her dramatic denouement, shortly after returning home with her four days later, having promised – according to Barbara – 'to break with Joan and make a fresh start' with her. In hindsight this did not strike Barbara as ever being his real intention, but if it were of any consolation, Joan's view of the situation, decades later, admitted not only that she had 'behaved very badly' but made it plain that she had 'had to pay for it'.

The picture shows a solitary male figure walking to the left and cars heading chaotically towards the far horizon, where the most remote buildings are more defined and less faceless than many nearer ones. A street light stands like another lone figure, weakly yellow, buckling and giving no light. Right of that is a building defined with tints of rose colour and a car without passengers, whether moving or parked it is impossible to tell, for cars in Adrian's pictures are always either badly parked or being recklessly driven. Three possible directions to be taken are on offer: left where the figure walks, straight ahead to a remoter horizon, or sharp right behind the lamp post – the longest street in Paris never held so many lengthy possibilities; so many darkly anonymous, shuttered windows, or so few people on the streets failing to enjoy life. No café or shop open, just a lonely man in an empty street, no doorway inviting him in, and three distinct outcomes from which to choose.

With Barbara back at Wood Farm which, unsettlingly, was put up for sale, what Adrian chose was to spend the weekends there with her and Scarlett, having spent the week in London with Joan, but angrily denying it when questioned. Vivien's birth in mid-August 1957 at the West Norwich Hospital was of dubious satisfaction, billed in his diary as matter-of-factly as the Russians putting up a satellite thereafter. His affair with Joan became more openly expressed. Barbara claims she 'could not handle' it any more. Joan having no interest in her, although initially her friend, probably did not help. The disputed truth behind what occurred next is a matter of conjecture. What Barbara alleges is that 'Adrian came down from Joan's with the news that she was pregnant by him' and subsequently that she chose to abort it, after which 'Joan and Adrian had a terrible row' and furthermore 'that it went septic' – all denied by Joan.

On 3 November 1957, the day after Joan's birthday and a three-hour lunchtime drinking session with Francis Bacon, Adrian reports Joan being 'ill' and a week later to her being 'ill all week'; also to his looking after her. A week after that his diary tells that he too was unwell – initially the result of drinking to 5am – and again sick all the following day and for some days after, eventually leading to his staying upstairs at Joan's with Barbara pointedly in the flat below.

Parallel accounts accord of more disturbing events in play (the only work he executes over this period is, of all things, a Crucifixion) as evidence of his desperately unhappy state of mind. Barbara's version, recounted decades later at her comfortable home in Cape Town, is that she returned to Tite Street to find Adrian lying on the spare bed in the studio. He had been found drunk in the gutter having also overdosed on pills in a failed – and at that time illegal – attempted suicide. Oxygen was brought and he fought to stay alive. In a state of delirium and not even wanting to be touched by Barbara, he desired only Joan. On 30 November 1957, when he had recovered, he packed and quietly went upstairs to Joan's, merely pushing money thereafter for Barbara and the two children through the letterbox to meet their needs. Joan's latter-day account adds the detail that she 'wanted him to go back to Barbara' who 'had every right!'; she 'wanted to end it [between them] before the suicide attempt' but it was the doctor (Karly Precop, a friend and neighbour) who said to her she had to take him back or he'd kill himself, an emotional blackmailing line that she also claimed was taken up by Adrian. The threat concerned her enough to get her brother, a doctor, down to assist, as she felt she 'needed a witness.' Something she neglected to mention, however, was a short liaison she had conducted before Adrian came fully on the scene with Barbara who, somewhat perversely, was the other party concerned. Eclipsing his wife in the seduction of Joan seems to have been yet another game which Adrian had to win.

However unwilling, for seven years and eleven months Joan remained in relationship with Adrian. Her verdict on what she gained from it was that 'He was terribly funny. That's why I liked him. Very good conversation and company, especially at a party with his painting friends – he was marvellous amongst a crowd.' Although undeniable, this pales beside claims of her consequent privations, because with two children of her own and three of his, it was an impossible situation from the start. By the end, she 'loathed him' so much that she didn't want even to give house-room to a single one of his paintings – a principle on which she was to renege some 35 years later, keen to buy a painting showing Mousehole Harbour from the cottage they had shared together. Joan cited 'inability to be loyal, because he liked men… but loved the attention of women' and his 'cruel' refusal to let her paint, as well as hitting her when she 'wouldn't go to bed' among the litany of reasons behind her allusion to having had to 'pay.'

For Adrian's part, there seemed little in his life that rankled so much as the manner in which he was dismissed from the their relationship. Joan admitted that it was 'an awful thing' to have done to him, aided moreover by her 'toy boy replacement in his late twenties'. Before he died she had written to Adrian kindly on hearing via some source – they were not in touch otherwise – that his cancer had returned, and he graciously responded. The phrase 'forgive and forget' is often used, but in life the reality is that there is no forgetting and not much forgiving. There is, however, understanding. He had long understood what had happened, including his own part and his inability to bear being done to him what he did to others. Unhappiness was theirs as a matter of joint choosing. He may only not have examined the relationship fully in the context of its unpropitious beginnings.

Of failure there was his behaviour to Peg and all-but-marriage to Polly before Barbara, with whom he fought a bitter battle for custody over the children, a pyhrric victory ensuring the suffering of all parties, especially Adrian's, during school holidays. Sweet and inventive though he was with children

– so like a child himself – and so often playing games with them and their friends, nevertheless games were not games unless somebody could win at them. Furthermore, children and artistry do not inspire each other.[3] His difficulties with subject matter were more compromised by the constraints of having a family, let alone being free to paint at times when inspiration – echoing his favourite saying of Rodin's – would find him at work. However, the demise of any child was dolorous to him. (He was grief-stricken when, in September 1960, Anthony died, the young child of Peggy and her second husband Richard Alexander.) Even in today's enlightened society, the intensively grieving woman who miscarries often feels so damaged that there is little place for the damage done to the male. While he is required to be strong, that strength evaporates. The rejection by a baby of the father is scarcely considered, but parenting for both starts in the womb. Inadequacy, impotency and grief turn inwards too easily for the sensitive male, only to be acted out in other ways; for they will out. By miscarriage, Adrian had lost three, possibly four, children to a cruel emasculating fate. In Joan, more mature and by her own admission 'a strong woman, stronger than he', there seemed far more security than with – and quite possibly *for* – Barbara, who in truth had her sights very differently set. This was the security of the mother figure he lacked; not realising that no one can offer true mothering other than your mother – if she has it in her to give – and the human spirit must otherwise find it within.

Last but not least was the underwriting of Desmond's ailing farm. A diary memorandum less than two weeks after his move from the studio to Joan's flat upstairs simply states: 'Des going bankrupt – me also'. Bravely he wrote to Desmond at the end of the year, notwithstanding the consequences to himself, that he must go ahead with the bankruptcy. In the diary for 1 January 1958 he wrote: 'End of a bloody year.'

Joan, with her long hair, was painted by Adrian severally in the comparative honeymoon period of those early months: with it tied up, down, posing provocatively, semi-nude, and in the bath Bonnard-like. The most striking picture known to survive is *Kneeling Woman*, a large canvas with its sexy and scantily-clad subject resting on her elbows and knees, side profile on, viewed roundedly and voluptuously from above, rather like a still life and owing some influence to Matthew Smith, known to them both. The bed on which the figure is positioned ceases to be midway, its soft-cushioned markings

3. Unless you were Harry Thubron, Adrian's Goldsmiths' colleague, the celebrated collagist who worked on the floor surrounded by as many animals and children as possible 'on account of their always knocking things unselfconsciously into exactly the right position'

transform into hardened arrows raining down upon her exposed back and raised buttocks. On her knees, a sure sign of submission, a dark cavern of blue-black begins to absorb her foot, while she looks remotely and dully into the past, paying no attention to what goes on. Around her, what rose-pink there once was is all but turned to raw-red anger. It is a picture of palpable passion and strident suffering.

On 5 March 1958, after two recorded days of drunkenness and some ten years after the film was released, Adrian saw Vittorio de Sica's *Bicycle Thieves.* An Academy Award-winning movie, it is a fathers-and-sons beacon containing the classic elements of neo-realism: harsh cinematography, poverty of the principal characters, urban squalor and, of course, a lack of judgement at the central male character's predicament, who manages to find a job after months of unemployment that is dependent on his owning a bicycle. When it is stolen, his job is in jeopardy. The film is his search of the city for the culprit. Instead he ends up stealing a bicycle himself and his consequent disintegration of stature and self-respect is heart-rendingly witnessed by his tearful son, who nevertheless takes his father's hand to say 'I'm on your side,' and together they find dignity after a long day of humiliation. Adrian's diary does not comment on whether he enjoyed the film, but it is a poignant backdrop to his and Desmond's fracturing finances and a reminder of the self-destruction by drink of their father and of Adrian's own empathising.

On 15 March, Desmond left Barnes Farm for the last time, and on 1 April 1958, 'Desmond bankruptcy' is written in Adrian's diary, and on the following day: 'Completely broke Des owes me £6082!' At some point, sparing no one's feelings, he spoke the haunting phrase to 13-year-old Geraldine: 'There goes your inheritance…' It was also the end of Wood Farm for Adrian, which he managed to sell in early May to the composer Tristram Carey, son of the Irish writer Joyce Carey. It was (apart from Myrtle Cottage, Newlyn) the only property that he had ever owned in his life, which, considering his family background, seems an extraordinary testimony to improvidence. As for 48 Tite Street, after a creditors' meeting at Ipswich in mid-June, he could no longer afford the rent beyond the autumn, and his diary entry for 16 October, 'Tite St goes!' reads like the death of a beloved friend.[4] The necessary sale of his much polished MG, and its decidedly utilitarian replacement – an elderly London taxi, bought from Mary John – paled by comparison. The money Desmond owed him was never repaid.

4. He moved from there, after 17 years, into a semi-derelict studio in Camden Town at a rent of 27 shillings and 6d a week. This even proved too much for him and he had to share the place with his Goldsmiths' colleague, Harold Dow, whose death in 1969 gave space for Sue Curnow to move in and help with the rent

In *The Times* dated 8 May 1958, a brighter spot illumined the gloom. It was the announcement that a still life of flowers on a chair on exhibit at the RA had been bought by the Chantrey Bequest. The picture, in the Tate collection – specifically the stores near the Old Kent Road – shows a dark red background against which an equally dark chair-back stands, whose spindles suggest bars of imprisonment; pale irises reach upward and outward for inspiration and air. Lesser flowers, yellow emblems of courage, sit together in a glass vase of tapering clarity below the water's surface. It stands on a base which has all but lost the sturdiness of its legs, while the familiar dark elements of blues-depression gather, extending to the signature, lower left, which is distorted and pulled into abstraction.

Not a single mention is made in Adrian's 1958 diary of Vivien, whom he doubted with short-term indifference to be his daughter, preferring to think Barbara guilty of having an affair with Anthony Devas, for whom she had continued to act as part time model/secretary. With Barbara – who had written in her 1953 diary 'Happiest girl in the world!! sharing my life with the most wonderful person' – he was barely on speaking terms. Their communications increasingly occurred via lawyers or via third parties of whom Polly was one such. This added a peculiar twist, and for a fraught, short and next-to-impossible period, Barbara and the two children occupied Polly's smallholding at Fivehead, near Taunton, and also St Buryan in Cornwall.

Joan having acquired Old Hill Cottage, Love Lane, high up above Mousehole Harbour, where she repaired with her own, both older, children, Adrian was thus – from 16 July 1959, their first night staying there – in regular close proximity to make formal, hostage-like exchanges of Scarlett and Vivien. Custody was hard fought for and was duly awarded jointly. This decision was eventually altered to sole custody, a victory for Adrian – the court's response (putting her in the public 'wrong' thereafter) to a heartfelt move by Barbara who up-sticked it to South Africa on the heels of a lesbian love interest. The latter event was an outcome that Adrian was slow in not having foreseen. They remained connected, partly because of the children, and partly because there was some commonality that had brought them together in the first place. He liked to play down any fondness he retained for Barbara and his capacity for contrary – indeed impossible, double-binding – behaviour is reflected in a work on paper in her possession. On it he has inscribed: 'Stolen by Barbara – with my permission!'

With so much energy going into other things, it is hardly surprising that painting suffered. Work was enhanced by his building a studio in August 1959 in the garden of Old Hill Cottage where he managed to complete '41 oils, over 40 watercolours, 3 sketch books; 5 destroyed; 2 sold; 6 exhibited' inside a year. Meanwhile, forever up and down on the night train to Penzance, he continued to teach at Goldsmiths', and in the holidays to accommodate the children.

Good times with Joan are evidenced in his diaries. His 40th birthday was 'lovely', made special by presents from her. The two of them were that year asked to judge the floats at the Mousehole carnival, which they did in pouring rain. When her mother had a stroke and died, he was supportive and kind. Geraldine and Joan's daughter Mara got on well, and together with Mara's husband, went to Paris to see the Beatles perform, contriving via the bell boy and a somewhat formally written note to Ringo – 'Dear Mr Starr...' – to meet and spend time with the band afterwards at the Hotel George V, where they traded French translations in exchange for food and chauffeur-driven transport around the city till it was time to go home. Christmas 1964 was jolly with 'everyone up at Old Hill!' and the following May, before Adrian flew to Nigeria as an external examiner for the Ahmado Bello University, he made a new lawn and lily pond. There were artist friends such as Dod Procter, Mary Jewels, Peter Lanyon, Patrick Heron, Paul Feiler, Bryan Wynter, Jack Pender, Michael Canney, William Scott, Max Chapman and Josef Herman. This may have frustrated Joan more than inspired her as one of her great complaints was that Adrian didn't want her to paint, and her claim that she 'had to nag him like mad to get him to [paint] – he had no great passion for painting' for her turned the knife. Saying that he was lazy, as he did of himself, was in both cases uncharitable and to some extent untrue, as his large body of work confirms. He worked to save himself from himself and he drew on an enormous amount of inner resources preserving him from a far worse life than he could have had to endure. By this time, however, the passion and the ambition was either spent, or had turned in on itself, as passion literally can turn to suffering. At forty-five, he knew where his work lay on the world's ladder. He must have assumed he would always be, like his father before him, the second disinherited son. Adrian had a great need for power

– his breaking the bounds of fidelity was one manifestation of this. Another was having to win at every game he played – and the point was about to be reached where he knew he would never be number one, and he couldn't bear it.

Forever in the background of his time with Joan was the battle over his two children. From interim custody awarded on 30 November 1960, through joint custody to Adrian's sole responsibility, handed to him on 1 March 1965. Within almost no time and immediately following a rare – in this period – five-day visit to Cornwall from cousin Pam in August 1965, Adrian provides the first diary indication that all was not domestically well. 'STICKY TIME WITH J' is the banner headline. By mid-September, it's worse: 'Joan Hell'. Naturally 'no painting for weeks' is yet again evidenced. On 23 September he removed to London, staying at Guy Roddon's studio then in Roland Gardens. Adrian's Camden Town studio was being re-built by the council and was about to be liveable. This circumstance was not lost on Joan who, having once lost out on the basis of surprise being the best form of attack, now aided by the much younger lover she was secretly involved with, swiftly got all Adrian's things and sent them irrevocably by car to a furniture depository and a note saying 'Don't bother to come back'. Adrian's diarised devastation was as great as his astonishment. 25 September 1965: 'JOAN PACKED ME OFF!' 28 September: 'Letter from Joan. Everything gone.' 29 September: 'Misery.'

In his despair Adrian sought advice from Clive Gardiner, undoubted wise man and Principal of Goldsmiths', and told the sorry tale of what had befallen him. Clive's son Stephen Gardiner, the architect, recounted Adrian's surprise report of what ensued. 'The extraordinary thing was that your father roared with laughter! And I suddenly saw what it was all about.'

His diary entry for 30 September reflects his even-hearted acceptance of fate, like one receiving a chance card in a game of Monopoly: 'No Mousehole. Go to Marriage Bureau!' This was the man, the understanding person, the hugely circumspect individual, whose humour could override his sorrowing sense of being a victim. Nothing was simpler than this two-way signpost leading along a new path and culminating in a species of stability for which he yearned.

The Heather Jenner Marriage Bureau became as much of a success for Guy Roddon, still giving Adrian safe haven at

Roland Gardens. Half in a spirit of friendly rivalry, half wanting to compare notes, Guy went along too. Sheila Eyre worked for the proprietress – Lady Jackson – and Guy rather took to her and asked her on a date. She said to Lady Jackson, 'May I help myself to any of these lovely gentlemen?' and came the reply: 'Of course, if you work in a chocolate factory, you help yourself to the confections.' In the course of Guy's friendship with Sheila, he gained access to his own file, with reports given by those whom he had taken out. Chief amongst the comments was 'Eyes all over the place.' His rival's file was unreported.

Adrian's first date was with a 26-year-old barrister living in Thurloe Square whose particulars given him on a slip included religion, given as 'Tolerant'; income encouragingly 'Comfortable', which might have been enough to be getting on with, but were gratifyingly bolstered by interests consisting of: 'Reading, cl. music, riding, sailing, travel, the arts, country life, dancing, antiques'. His second one was with an Oxbridge don. Guy 'couldn't wait for him to come home and tell me all about it!' In stages, Adrian created an ultimately unsustainable timetable of a Monday girl, a Tuesday girl, a Wednesday and a Friday girl etc. and for some time was not dissatisfied.

In addition, as had long been the case, there were the dependable mother figures who to varying extents looked after him and vice versa. Coralie – 'Miss Hurd', Dot (Dorothy) Litherland (1916–2007), and the highly individualistic Jack (Jacqueline) Low, who came to study at Goldsmiths' having been Lucien Pissarro's gardener, and whose female persona was so subsumed that Clive Gardiner had said: 'We simply must have this woman, she'll be good for the students.' Better for them than for Adrian. She was dependably a bully to him, a source of loyalty and pain, for more than 50 merciless years, quite unable to stand up to her as he was. Far older than he, she pre-deceased him by only five months. Relieved of her physical presence she left him the substituted burden of her estate in July 1998. It consisted mainly of her practically uninhabitable cottage in Kent, untouched for 20 years, not so much as a used tin can thrown out, everything piled at room height with a narrow pathway through. Of summers past, being met by Jack at Canterbury station and of covering the distance to West Stourmouth sharing her only bicycle (each taking turns to cycle a couple of miles ahead while the other walked, then leaving the bike against a hedge) there remained only the memory. Dot, however, living in Callian adjacent to Montauroux, inland from the coast at Nice, was a lifesaver when it came to the long school holidays. In the summers of the 1960s she provided weeks' duration of accommodation for the Ryans *en famille,* while generating as inspiring a working environment for him as he had enjoyed with Polly when staying at the Pissarro villa Campagne Orovida, near Toulon, back in 1950.

Polly re-entered and again departed the scene in 1966, and from 1967 an even race between Susan Curnow – whom he met in a pub in Llanfrothen on 24 March – and Gillian Mounsey, ran fully until the early 1970s. Gillian then faded to an increasingly infrequent opera date and Susan gained unassailed position in his diary for the 26 remaining years of his life. His large body of work from this period, if relieved of earlier passion, is the result of commensurate freedom from financial pressure. Had Susan not been, many of these paintings, dating from the 1970s, would not have been either. A painting called *Montauroux: Joss walking* heralds the new phase. Joss was an old Dutchman living locally, with whom – visiting Callian in 1969 with the children and Gillian – Adrian had made friends. On 20 July 1969 they all watched the televised first moon-landing at Joss's house. Some time later, possibly the following year – revisiting this time with the children and Susan – Adrian proceeded to paint Joss apparently walking home from shopping and carrying a filled basket. The figure of Joss walks uncertainly. It is unclear whether he has walked from the road behind him or the gate to his left leading from the unusual little house on which he has turned his back. It has only a door and no other window on the ground floor. A few more yards and the road turns in a new direction. Part of the track – that which is described as a graceful curve – is lost. The wall bordering it makes a sharp turn in his projected path. Around the corner another gate leads to another opening to a contrasting house: less substantial yet with more possibilities for *living* room. The two houses, whilst very close together, are approached from far apart. Beyond the second house, the way is closed off. There are many and some very distant (memories of) houses dotted in the background. Despite the path which the lone figure appears to be taking, ie off-track altogether, the likelihood – given what we know – is that he will take the sharp corner and take refuge in the rose-pink house, from where the darker, red-coloured wall of its rival with its high up, out-of-reach window, will no longer face him.

Paris, Cornwall, Suffolk and Wales

Adrian's use of paint makes for an emphasis in his pictures of painterliness over anything they apparently have to say. Robert Savage, who ran an excellent gallery and framers in Brompton Road opposite the Oratory, observed early on to Paul Drury, a Principal of Goldsmiths', that 'Adrian turned his back on anything new or experimental, including Picasso, Bacon, and Sutherland.' The downside to doing so made it harder to find plausible wide-ranging subject matter without, at times, repetition. Which was inarguably less easy than experimenting with totally abstract themes and colours out of the landscape – as Ivon Hitchens or Patrick Heron – or reducing themes with the colours extracted, like William Scott.

Oscar Wilde's 'To rescue art and conceal the artist' and 'All art is quite useless' are prominent among several quotes (including 'My paintings are like the clippings of my toenails: they grow out of me and I have cut them off. That is all I know about it', by Walter Sickert) written in the front of Adrian's 1938 diary. Right at the back 'Art is the emotional utterance of life' and 'Art is universal, eternal, not parochial' close the brackets on his thoughts for the year, but not ultimately on the argument that the spectrum of his well-informed good taste in art verged upon the restricted.

'Ugly Uglow!' he remarked of Euan Uglow's work (1932–2000), citing as proof: 'Who'd want to go to bed with any of *his* women?' The Euston Road School fared no better, while Coldstream was 'the death of art'. Asked what he thought of a postcard showing a semi-figurative landscape by a painter in his first year at Winchester School of Art: 'Is that by a monkey or a cat?' he enquired. While of a greetings card from the Getty Museum showing a masterful German 15th-century etching of a forest scene: 'I don't see a little rabbit or a pheasant...' he said sorrowfully, his way of expressing the feeling that it was somehow lacking. He could be extremely cutting, and as Sven Berlin acutely observed to Guy Roddon: 'The knives in Adrian's paintings are always terribly sharp.' Never so damnably sharp though, as when turned sadistically upon himself. Although it is quite a natural thing for a good painter to feel from time to time that he's never going to be Goya, and quite British also, it was often carried to extremes in Adrian's case. In such moments it also lacked the humour that otherwise tempered even his bursts of supreme arrogance, as when Patrick Heron compared him in print to Constable: 'There you are!' he said to Guy Roddon, giving the article a positive slap of appreciation. He meant to self-deprecate. He jokingly used to claim, on the problem of signing a picture: 'Sometimes I sign the canvas at the *beginning* and build the whole bloody painting around it...' His frustration was very strong, as was his sense of worthlessness. He wanted and expected more of his work and was unfulfilled by it, hence the extensive destroying of (good) pictures when his ambition was intact (but not, later, of bad ones when all lingering ambition was negated).

Adrian's early difficulties with subject matter were another facet of self doubt. Self-styled John [Lord] Kilbracken (1920–2006) played host to Adrian several times in the beautiful back-of-beyond house he had inherited in Killegar, Ireland, after the war and when he was taking a year off from being a cub reporter on the *Daily Mirror.* He witnessed the problem at first hand. The locality, for a landscape painter, presents many possibilities. The countryside is beautiful, although it is without mountains, with the typical feature of Co Leitrim being drumlins: small green hills with many interspersed loughs and rivers. Many of the drumlins around the house were planted with hardwood trees of oak, ash, beech, elm and sycamore by an ancestor when he finished the house in 1813. In short, a delightful wilderness with much fine mature timber. The nearest mountains are along the border, twenty miles northward, faintly visible on the horizon. John Kilbracken described Adrian on his first visit heading off to find a subject worthy of paint, weighed down with the tools of his trade, and returning three or four hours later – to John's amazement, with all that scenery – saying that he was going into Killesandra 'to paint a side of beef in the butcher's shop there.' Pictures of goats' meat from this time include a canvas, 20" x 30" sold to the Contemporary Arts Society from Tooths in January 1956, now in Cheltenham Art Gallery. (One other butcher's shop painting, of Fressingfield, exists in reduced form, Adrian having cut it down to half its original size.) Other work executed on Christmas visits during the early 1950s to Killegar House – jolly occasions with Kitty Freud (née Epstein) who later married John's brother Professor Wynn Godley – was less bloodthirsty but took in very little of the wonderful surroundings. Ireland, which Adrian described as being 'always close to tears' and despite his native roots, did not provide lasting inspiration for this returning son.

Paris, unfailingly, did. His annual visits to the French capital were for him 'mandatory' and entirely fruitful and unlike London, which he scarcely painted at all: '...the moment the train pulls into the Gare du Nord my eyes open wider and out comes my pencil and sketch book. To me even the shabbiest Parisian hotel with a top floor room and no lift is as near to heaven as an artist can get. The view from the attic window of ridiculous roofs with their assorted chimney pots is nectar to my muse not given to me in London or Penzance!'[1] But in Mousehole, from Old Hill Cottage, on a level with the dizzy gradient of Raginnis Hill, Adrian had indeed found inspiration along very similar lines provided by the Paris attic window. His article continued: 'One part colour, two parts grey; so runs the painting dictum of Rubens. What is Paris if not that?' *Mousehole rooftops*, a series of pictures he executed in myriad sizes and mediums upon canvas, card and newspaper for the assistance of the textured greys it provided, practically accords with this dictum too. In whichever case, the complex and improbable-seeming structures and roof apexes dotted with occasional smoking chimneys, appealed both to the architect in him and, because of the imagined lives being led beneath them, to Adrian as an observer of humanity and respecter of privacy – his own and others'. Making paintings of people's homes, especially of humble-looking dwellings, viewed either near-to or from a distance, is something he did repeatedly. What you never find is his getting past the exterior. His own homes are no exception to this rule. There may be exterior scenes of Wood Farm, Hill House, Holbrook, of Seagulls Cottage, Mousehole, even of Myrtle Cottage and Villa Santa Lucia in Cagnes, but there are no interior views,

1. Article 'Painting in France' by Adrian Ryan, published School of Art CCAT, spring 1984

despite his interest in objects and furniture. There is in Adrian a place beyond which one does not get. In France, however, there comes to him the relaxed bonus in feeling the comfort of being a foreigner; as opposed to the not uncommon sense of isolation that many artists feel, even when they find themselves at home.

Thus Adrian's paintings of Mousehole roofs and narrow streets are sparsely peopled – dark and distant outlines of predominantly male figures most likely walking to or from the Ship Inn – whereas in French scenes, if dignified with a figure, it is more closely observed. Something relaxes and pulls him nearer in; such that his own presence to the subject he is observing is implicit. *The Village Street, Montauroux*, a scene of which a number of versions exist, is one example. It is also a system for projection; a closing in on himself while using others as illustration.

In a starlit Brittany night scene of circa 1980, the viewer is confronted with a vista without parameters of near and middle-distance rooftops with a church steeple beyond. Certain, but not all, windows of the homes sheltering beneath the coolly blue roofs are bright with warmth and light. Around the corner of the blank, less cosily lit right-hand wall and up high in an architectural nook, one tiny little window looks down from the highest point, excepting the greater glory of the church spire, upon the entire scene. It is a quirky, unusual vantage point – Adrian's own mode of noticing – of which the false perspective looking *down* on and simultaneously *up* at this window is proof. Far left, however, in the warm yellow of a level attic window stands a little man in a blue hat, watching the artist watching the scene. A reflection of self, at work while others unseen pass the time in sleep, or reading, or being alive. It is a very controlled way of revealing an intimate moment. A private one made public, unguarded, with window unbarred – not even a section of its frame showing – through which he contemplates life elevated from the ground and the twists and turns of the unseen streets below, seeking the world of the uttermost stars.

Adrian's French speaking was by some accounts good but unorthodox: conversational but lacking some conventions of grammar or vocabulary. Had it been better, he would have seemed a candidate for living there, either somewhere not too far from Paris, and taking working holidays to the northern coasts and in summer to the south, or else on the Riviera.

The influences of Bonnard, Soutine and the young Utrillo – his three preferred landscape artists of the nineteenth century – were so strong in him, it would have been comforting to inhabit their milieu on a more permanent basis. Instead, he made do with Cornish granite for supplying the greys found otherwise in French walls and shutters. He substituted colourful fishing boats in place of the coloured lettering and awnings above French shops and cafés, and remained long years a sort of foreigner in his own country, by staying in Mousehole and keeping at one remove from all the artists of St Ives. 'I just kept out of it,' he said, 'I wasn't interested in all that bickering.' Trips to France beyond Paris were for him 'pilgrimages' made annually, if possible, in addition to those visits to the capital. His familiarity with it, from the age of eight, via 'interminable channel crossings with school trunks', found him as much at home there as in the Suffolk countryside.

Considering all the time that he spent in Suffolk, excluding growing up at Hintlesham, Adrian painted it almost sparingly. Few of his Suffolk pictures, excepting church paintings – which are like portraits in their close-up scrutiny of lines, contours and expressive searching for identity – take anything other than distant and generalised views of places. Although there is no evidence that Adrian was following the advice given by Pierre-Auguste Renoir to his son Jean, the film-maker, that a truly gifted artist should try to paint the same tree over and over, there are repeated versions of one particular tree, an ancient elm, which stood at the end of his land at Wood Farm, consisting of pencil drawings, watercolours and oils. Regarding one such example and with that commonplace deprecation of self, Adrian remarked: 'I must have painted that tree a hundred times because I was too damned lazy to walk any further.' This literal statement does not ring true. That one tree claimed his repeated attention betrays a concern that has nothing to do with a lack of energy – confirmed by the circa 1956 painting, which is dramatic and symbolist. Close framed by the canvas, it portrays a tree whose 'face' is polarised into two distinct halves embodying sun and shade. On the left, space allows the low evening sun (constructed of thick impasto) to peer through the tree's branches like a huge, benign eye surveying the Suffolk landscape. Light illuminates with truth, but also cauterises: the future can be seen as the darkening landscape on the left and a pending move upon the somewhat brighter right-hand side of the picture, where the sky is still bluer and the grass greener. Contradictions are everywhere, but the message is of change and a clear link to the Suffolk that Adrian shared with his brother's ailing farm close by. The non-specific location of this symbolic tree fuses land with land. It also references the former acreage of their grandfather and the physical loss and social effect of all that had gone in 1937. Since which time (in 1996, under duress) Adrian only once returned to Hintlesham, a scene of bitter-sweet memories, despite living long years a handful of miles from the Hall. The painting, so closed off from the land on either side, declares his reluctance to look further afield. Subconsciously, it shows his perfect awareness – past and future, poised in the present – of his actual stake in the Suffolk landscape and that we own nothing in reality, for neither the land nor the sun have any regard for the short leases granted to man.

An earlier Suffolk village scene, painted with later reworking, represents another closed-in view of the locality. Hills – unusual for Suffolk, but around Fressingfield, they exist – decorate the horizon and two puffy clouds sit in a sky of inspirational blue and heavy with the possibility of birds calling. There is no one around. To the left, three windows of a church look un-churchlike and incidental without more of the building on show.[2] Three lush trees cross the middle of the picture; three cottages, two deep pink either side of one pale, stand together as one at the end of the pink-infused street; more separate, some indistinct, cottages further right create three more distinct entities of all the cottages, the furthest right of which front two windows opposing those of the church opposite. Threes and twos abound, and there are notable phallic shapes in the form of the street and the windows of the church that make reference to the period of Adrian's, Barbara's and Polly's Suffolk-spent ménage à trois during 1953.

Following the Queen's accession in 1952, a commission to design Fressingfield's new village sign was offered to Adrian by Ipswich Borough council. In profile against the light, his design showed a man leading a mule, which was executed by a local blacksmith in black metal. It stood in the village until the Queen's Golden Jubilee in 2002, when a new sign took over and the old one was erected outside the village school, which had long since adopted the emblem for the children's uniform. The blacksmith followed very literally Adrian's loose manner of drawing – paired objects – for example: hands and feet had a tendency to variation, following the dictum of his Goldsmiths' friend Kenneth 'Watch your shapes' Martin – and created a

2. Adrian's attitude to religion was freethinking. In his final hours, he was asked by a nurse for his religious views and he replied that he 'would like to be able to believe in something' because he'd had a good life and would like to thank someone for it

figure with one foot larger than the other. At one fell stroke of myth-making, the Clubfooted Pilgrim, a proud figure triumphing over his adversity, entered local legend and has so far not been displaced.

Wales, by contrast, was site-specific in providing inspiration for Adrian to paint. Litigating with Polly, he had encountered and befriended the solicitor Cyril Cobbett, who had tenure of an uninhabited cottage in Merioneth (later Gwynedd), a short distance north of Snowdonia National Park. Called Garreg Fawr (meaning 'large stone'), it stood among the scattered range of mountains known as the Moelwyns all around Llanfrothen, west of Ffestiniog. On the last day of May 1952, Adrian and Barbara paid their first weekend visit to Wales and stayed in bordering Llangollen while reconnoitring for an extended visit to Cyril's place that summer. 'Very good week end – wonderful country' he wrote in his diary.

On 7 July 1952 his financial case against Polly was settled in the law courts and Adrian's relief that justice and fair play had been served was immense. On 16 July 1952 passed the first anniversary of his distressing parting from Polly the previous year. On the 13th he left with Barbara and Cyril bound for Llanfrothen, staying overnight at the Randolph Hotel in Oxford and arriving on the evening of the next day. It was a new beginning in a Polly-free zone. Not least in subject matter, which would be seen in his Redfern show in January 1953 (alongside Paul Feiler, Frederick Gore and Hilde Stieler), where 16 of 45 pictures exhibited were of Welsh subjects. He painted on the first day, even before they had begun the process of, as he put it, 'Tidying up Garreg Fawr' and moving in furniture, while staying nearby until 20 July when, with Cyril, they took up residence, getting 'very drunk!' in celebration of their general satisfaction. Drinking at the pub in Llanfrothen, the Brondanw Arms, was commonplace, as was the consequence of having to be pulled out of ditches on the interconnecting path home. Garreg Fawr was halfway up a steep mountain. Too steep to have Adrian wandering far in search of things to paint. Like certain of his Cornish subjects, he worked and reworked images of the low, stone dwelling with its outbuildings and the countryside around it: in different seasons, weathers, by day or under the moon, during visits over many subsequent years.

That first visit, punctuated by nine-year-old Geraldine arriving on 1 August, seems to have been a happy mix of working, walking, bathing, sunbathing nude and helping with the harvest for John Jones, who owned the farm higher up the mountain. The farmer provided eggs and milk and kept cows which he is said to have much resembled and which, disregarding Matthew Smith's advice that 'Cows are *unreliable* Adrian', he painted without much success. Mr Jones also kept a horse called Big Jim, through whose field Geraldine had to pass when entrusted with collecting the provisions. Forty years later it would still reduce Adrian to great mirth to recall his daughter returning from a solo encounter with Big Jim, who had helped himself to her tasty wicker basket, leaving only the munched-at handle which she continued to grip, tearfully repeating the blindingly obvious explanation of her failed mission. It marred Geraldine's holiday, but not more so than the evidence of her father's growing involvement with Barbara, a girl not ten years her senior, which culminated in their marriage less than a week after returning to Tite Street on 29 August. Adrian's diary entries for that date and for the previous day mention difficulties which could mean Barbara exerting pressure, that he later claimed was her proposal of marriage: 'B. hell' it states in both cases. In any event, he went ahead with the union.

After one day in London spent shopping at Harrods and in the evening drinking with Caspar John, Adrian took Geraldine down to Cornwall to reunite her with Peggy on 31 August. Arriving at 7pm, he drank until late (going to bed at 2am) at the Ship Inn, Mousehole, and nearly as late again with Sven Berlin on the following night. He returned via Redruth picking up Michael Canney, arriving in London at 8.30pm on 2 September, with only one day clear in which to prepare for the melange of wedding, 'Mad Party' and flight to Paris on the 4th.

Polly and acrimony had taken Adrian by indirect route to Wales, which rendered a surfeit of drink and the beauty of its mountain landscape. It also led him into liberty and out of it again so fast that it was as if he did not value it. Or was his life, as his father's, so devoid of freedom already that he didn't recognise it when it came – as a bird fails to fly when its cage door is opened? Or maybe the excitement and novelty of a teenage bride was a way to get back at, or expunge the memory of Polly. If so, as a means to secure freedom from enchainment, it was a curious path to have chosen and it wasn't any fault of Garreg Fawr's, which for Adrian remained a place of enduring beauty.

Newlyn and St Ives

The Newlyn Art Gallery, used by the Newlyn Society of Painters and operated by committee under a chairman to organise their exhibitions, has provided a forum for locally produced contemporary art since its founding in 1895. In the late 1940s when Adrian visited it with Polly to see about exhibiting his work there, the custodian and general factotum husband of the then curator, Renée Nichols, turned them away on the grounds that Adrian was 'visiting' Mousehole, although he allegedly promised to 'put the matter before the committee'. Being turned away by Wallace Nichols was a new experience for both of them. For Adrian, because most doors professional and personal were then open to him (he was included in the Third Crypt exhibition in St Ives, 1948); and for Polly, because she as a teenager knew and had had lessons – in a class of seven private pupils – with Mr Nichols, during which she had frequently had to experience his persistently wandering hands as he put his arm around her to explore her output of work.

The two of them repaired to the Tolcarne pub close by and the result of the committee's deliberations is not known, but it may be the case that Adrian did not exhibit at the Newlyn Gallery until as late as 1960, when Peter Lanyon served two years as Chairman. There followed Charles Breaker who was previously known – with his companion Eric Hiller and with Marjorie Mort, while living in what later became Terry Frost's home overlooking the town – for starting the Newlyn Holiday

Sketching Group, an arts school for old ladies of type. His 'thick and colourful paintings, one up from chocolate boxes' may, Polly recalled, have been frowned upon by established artists, but his skill as a craft worker and a knitter of jerseys was much admired. His memorial exhibition in Newlyn's Lower Galleries, June to July 1985, and reported in the gallery newsletter the following spring, comprised 'Some fifty water-colours and a selection of knitted jackets'. Polly's verdict on Charles Breaker was: 'He was a lovely old dear.'

Halfway through Breaker's stint as the Newlyn Chairman, he fell ill and the position was filled *pro tem* by electing the unexpected candidate Adrian Ryan. Being chairman of anything was not Adrian's scene. Nevertheless on 19 January 1962 he was, as records show, 'elected for one month' and late in February also sat in the chair for an 'Extraordinary Meeting to consider applications for membership.' In September that year, another Chairman was temporarily elected – Charles Breaker remaining unwell – and Denys Law filled the post. No minutes or records of meetings contain any reference to controversy over these appointments. The painter Margo Maeckelberghe,[1] a committee member in this period, could recall no difficulty either. Adrian, however, recounted with pride the fact of having been 'asked to step down as President [sic] of the Newlyn painters for wanting to adjourn their boring meetings to the pub' – a request to which he was only too delighted to accede. Far more of a triumph for him to be removed from office than elected in the first place. To Polly, Margo remembered Adrian as 'always a charming, polite and rather quiet person, pleasant and never rude.' She added: 'Most of us were bored to tears towards the end of those meetings... most of us wanted to decamp to the Tolcarne.' It is likely that Adrian was proposed for continued *pro tem* chairmanship during that September meeting; and it is only conjecture, by elimination, that Eileen Hunt – a pushy *pro tem* curator bearing a reputation as a man-eater with the gift of the gab, and evocatively recalled by Polly as 'bitchy and dreary' – may have had it in for Adrian, not realising her mischief was doing him long-term service by toppling him. If so, he stayed chivalrous and as silent about the precise mechanism of his fall as he was vocal and satisfied with the act of it.

Under Michael Canney's late curatorship (1956–64), Adrian's representation at Newlyn increased. He and Michael were friends. The *Manchester Guardian*, 1 August 1961, reported Canney's writing about the NSA summer exhibition, containing:

1. One-time studio assistant to William Scott

> *work by Peter Lanyon, John Tunnard, Adrian Ryan, Paul Feiler and Dod Procter, all of whom have reputations outside the Cornish circle. But the exhibition is interesting for the absence of any bias towards any particular school or style... and there are exciting examples of the younger figurative artists who are perhaps reacting against the cool abstraction that dominated Art in Cornwall through the influence of Nicholson, Gabo and Hepworth.*

At nearly forty-one, was Adrian one of the 'younger figurative artists' referred to? Was he 'reacting' to anything, or just carrying on with his habitual method of painting and increasingly literal and anachronistic titling as the tide of Abstract Expressionism rose up against him? Although continuing to teach at Goldsmiths', he was virtually living full time in Cornwall and committed to its inhabitants, not just the many artists whose now distinguished names are archived in the pages of his diaries. Adrian was often out in the boats with the fishermen, including when it was rough, or watching the boats return in the early morning. In this, amongst the artists, he was an exception. And if a boat was wrecked, as in March 1962, it mattered to him. He had moved on from Chelsea and was growing more remote from the artistic community of Camden Town, especially when his studio there was demolished and before the new one was built. Living by the sea suited him. A less dramatic separation from Joan, when their time together was up, could have created a very different outcome. Physically he might not have left Cornwall. According to Sven Berlin (in a letter written in 1994 to Polly) Cornwall was Adrian's 'mystical love... He longs for [it]... but we each get misplaced... and Cornwall is now a dream, part of the floating world which cannot be relived.' Adrian could have remained more in the circle and consequently been more prominently and properly featured in its 1985 Tate Gallery homage exhibition: 'St Ives 1939–64'. Spiritually, Cornwall was indeed his home, but his ambition to make it so was more abruptly and bitterly knocked out of him by his humiliating ejection than any gradual erosion. Adrian's extraordinary achievement, during long years spent on the fringe of St Ives and with the infighting that accompanied its artistic endeavours, had been to conjoin with its artistry and keep free of its enmity. And yet it was bickering, albeit domestic, that had bruisingly extricated and sent him sprawling from the geography of Penwith, removing its inspiring surround of 'prussian blue, chunky sea which is somehow watery and solid at the same time'[2] and drastically

2. Patrick Heron reviewing Adrian Ryan, *New Statesman*

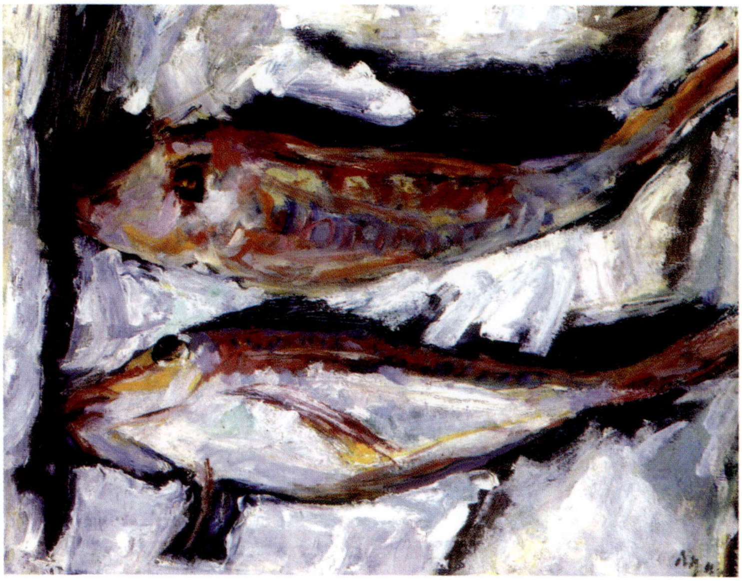

Gurnard and red mullet
oil on canvas, c. 1949

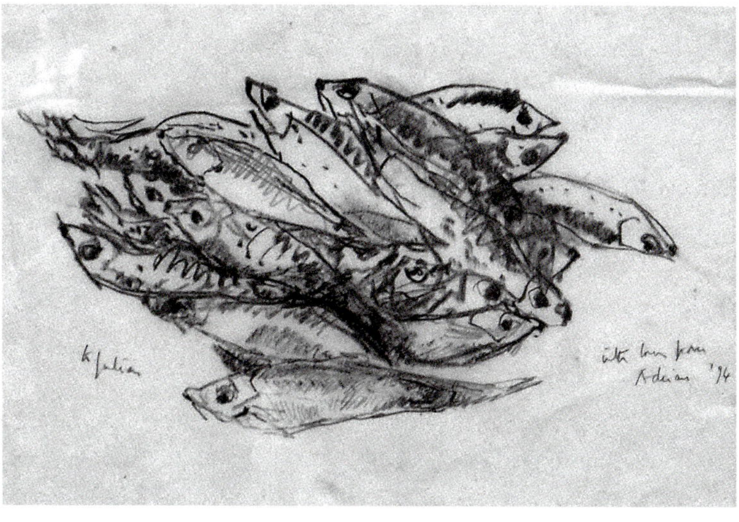

Sprats
charcoal on paper, 1994

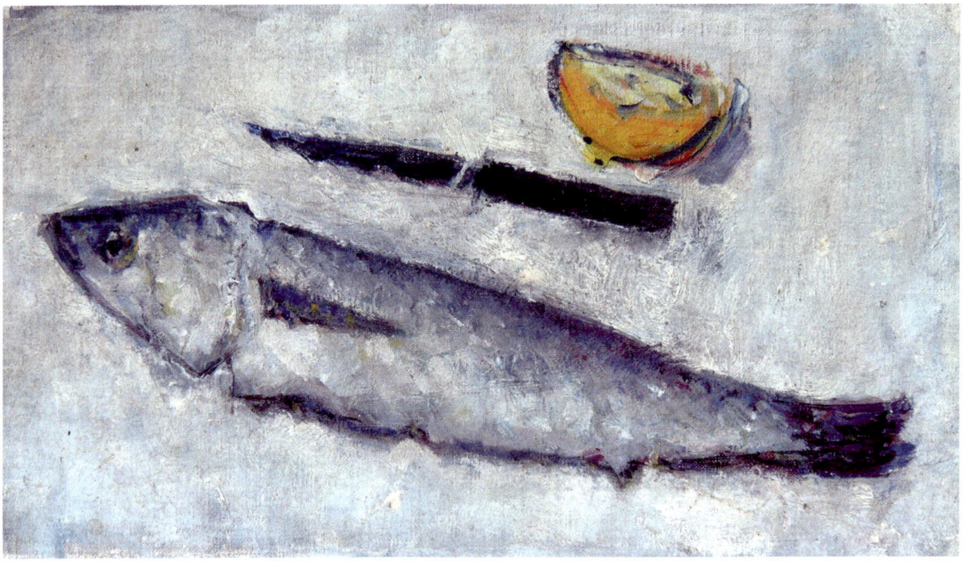

Still life with trout, lemon and knife
oil on canvas, c. 1960

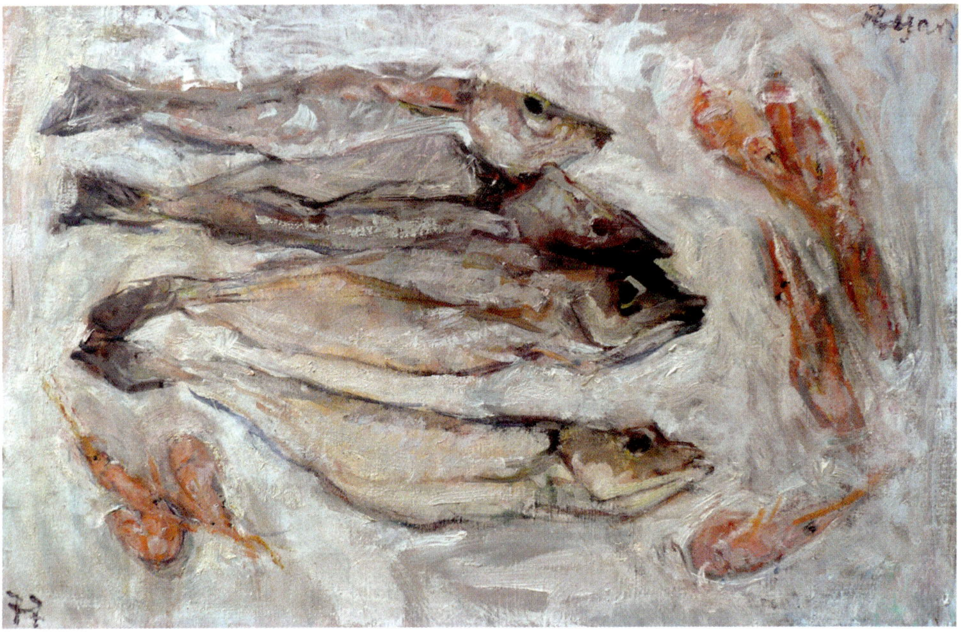

Whiting and shrimps
oil on canvas, 1977

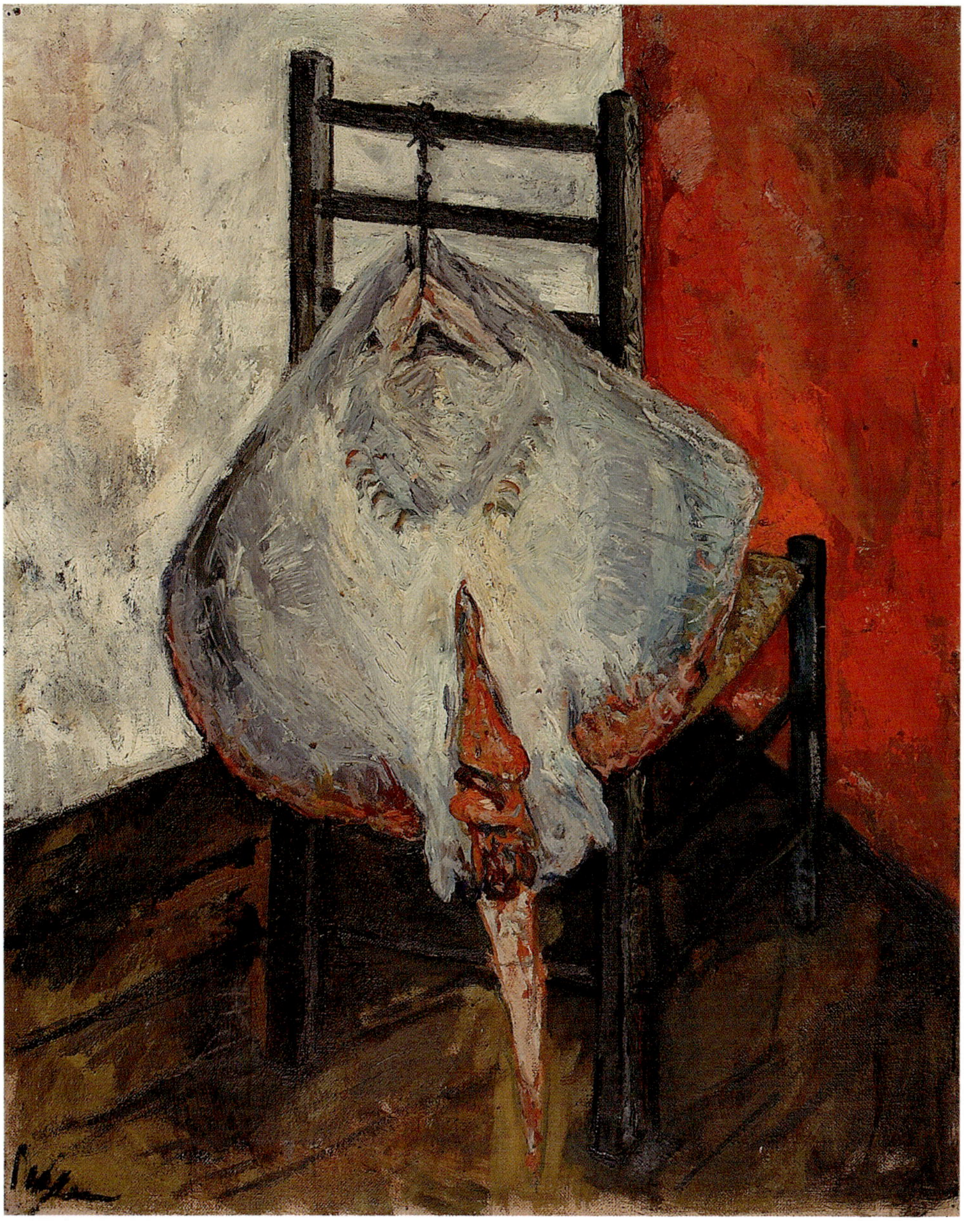

Skate
oil on canvas, 1945
courtesy of Gulbenkian Foundation

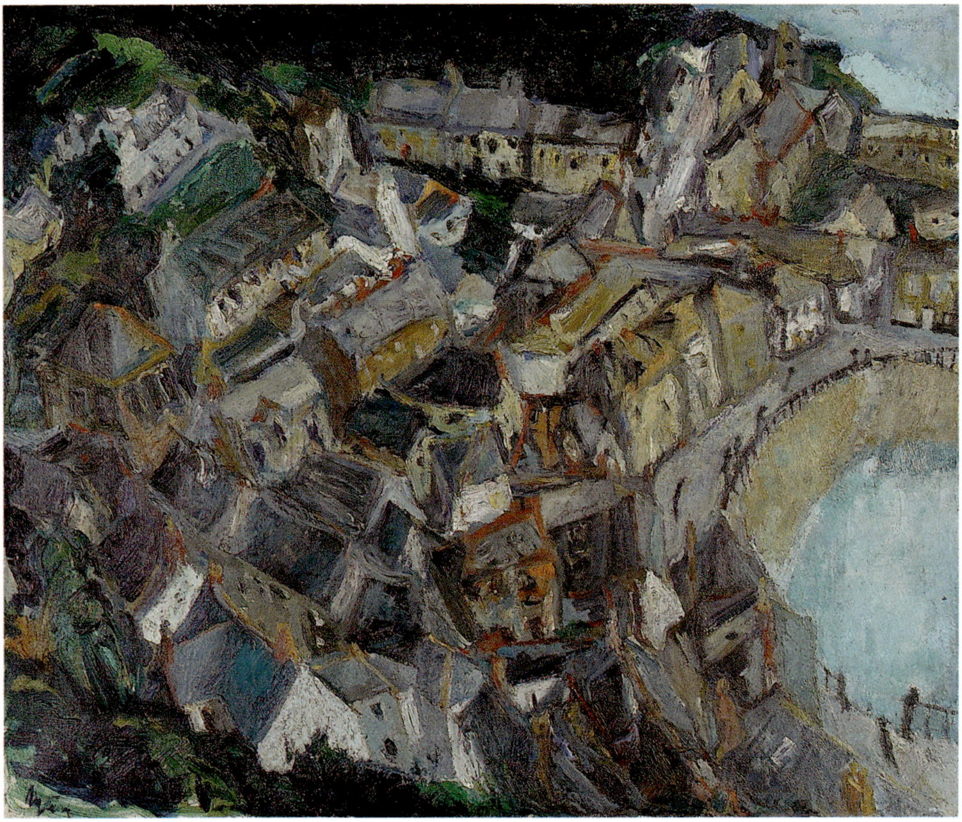

Mousehole harbour
oil on canvas, 1960
courtesy of Gulbenkian Foundation

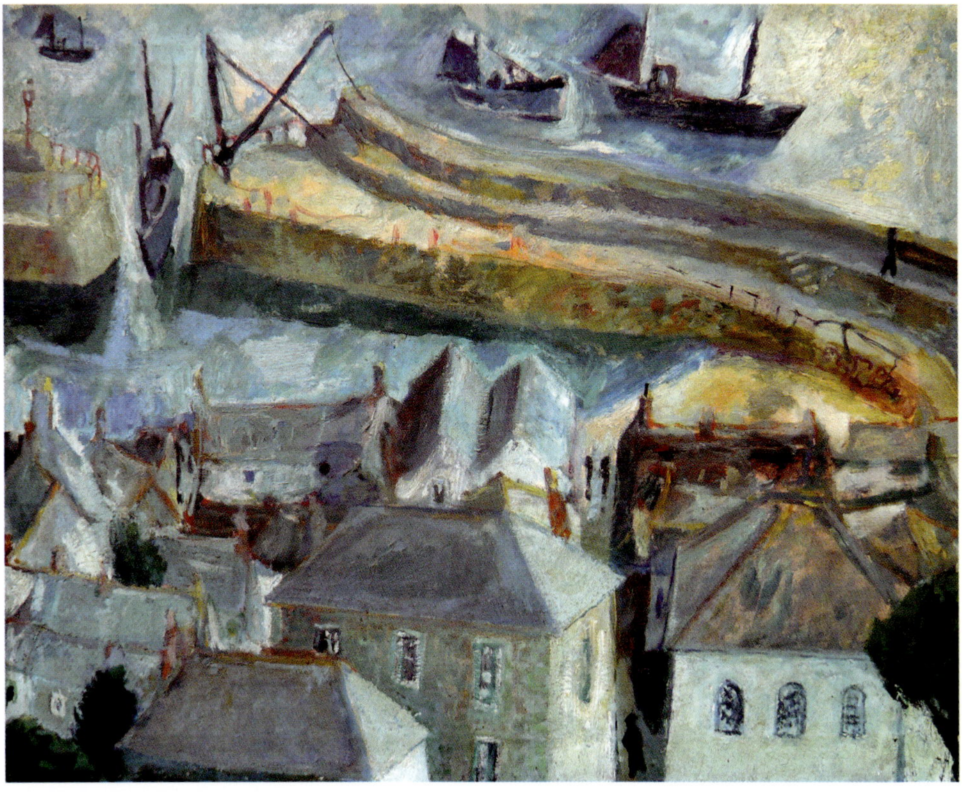

The Old Quay, Mousehole
oil on canvas, c. 1960

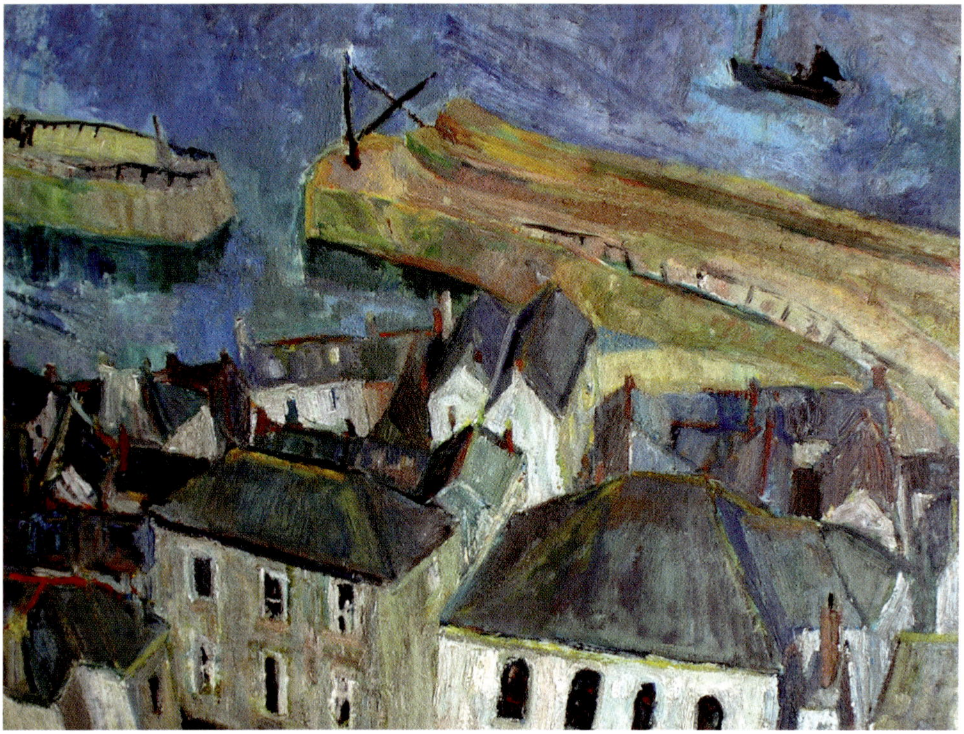

Mousehole harbour
oil on canvas, 1964

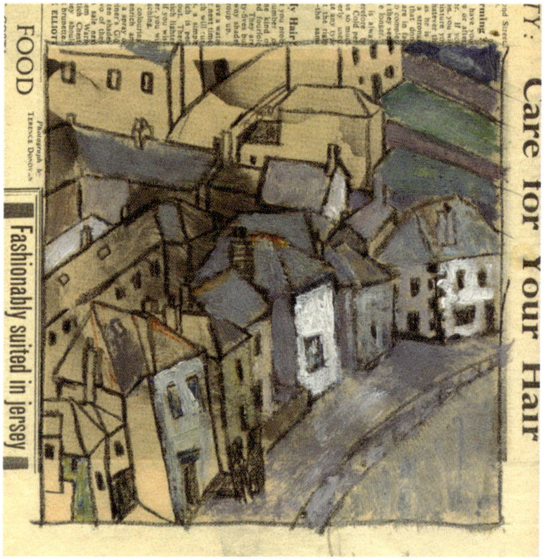

Mousehole Harbour
mixed media on newspaper, c. 1960

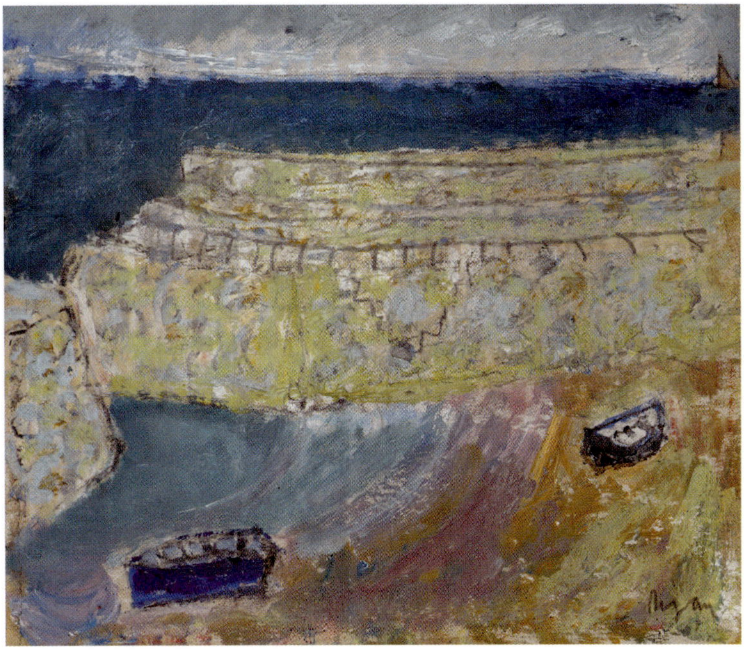

Prams, Mousehole
oil on cardboard, 1988

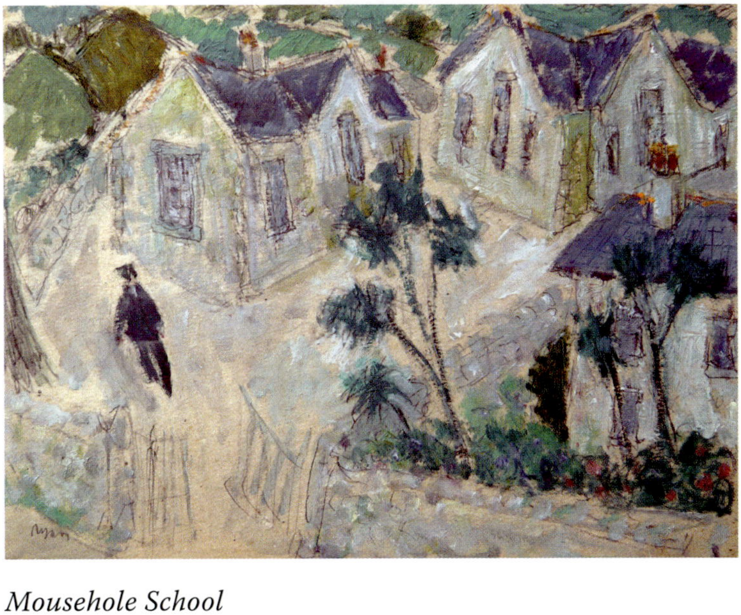

Mousehole School
watercolour with bodycolour, c. 1962

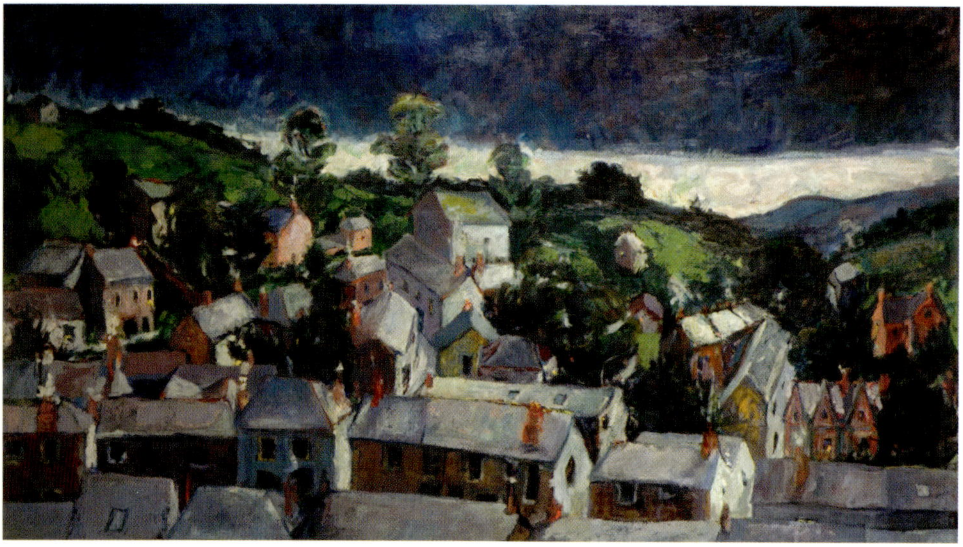

Dawn over Newlyn: view from Myrtle Cottage
oil on canvas, 1951
courtesy of the Potteries Museum & Art Gallery

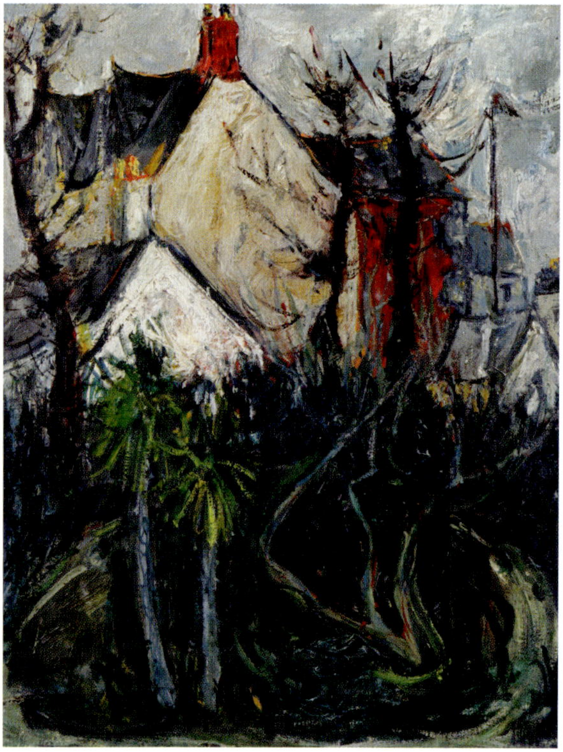

Myrtle Cottage garden
oil on canvas, c.1950
courtesy of Penlee House Gallery and Museum

reshaping his artistic reputation. Years later, Joan Gillchrest was quite public about what Adrian had done to her by preventing her from painting, but that was artistically less devastating than her banishment of him from Cornwall, about which he said not a word.

The summer of 1962 was pleasant. Judging once again the Mousehole Carnival was much more up Adrian's street than meetings of the Newlyn Artists. He had sent three pictures to the RA and was very pleased that all three were hung on the line. Six further pictures were exhibited, according to his diary, in St Ives. Meanwhile divorce papers came through from Barbara late in May, auguring resolution. Also promising was the advent of the Gulbenkian Committee, comprising the painter William Scott, who already knew Adrian and, from the British Council Fine Arts Committee steering the Gulbenkian's coffers, Alan Bowness, who did not. The state of Adrian's acquaintanceship with William Scott is unchronicled in the intervening years between their late August-scheduled Gulbenkian encounter in 1962 and their first meeting over a decade previously in the White Hart in Chelsea – to be precise, sometime after 6.30 pm on Saturday 16 June 1951. It is also confused by the fact of Adrian's friend Asgeir Scott being so often referred to as 'Scott...' in the diaries. 'Met W. Scott' makes it clear upon that date; as does, on the following Monday, the pencilled statement 'William Scott came round [to 48 Tite Street]' and in brackets and in blue biro underneath: 'I kissed Mrs S!!!' and underneath that again, underlined – 'Row'. Par for the course, maybe, but nevertheless memorable for Polly, who was preparing a meal for all four of them when William Scott entered the kitchen and, in response to carryings-on in the living room, attempted to force himself upon her. Scott was reluctant to take no for an answer, resulting in Polly's undiminished memory of him as a 'persistent little stinker'. She escaped him on moral grounds, she recalled, by pointing out that the curtainless kitchen windows allowed people to see in from the buildings backing onto Tite Street. These houses were, and remain, low-built by comparison with few windows through which to view. Exposure to remote strangers was a feeble excuse, and the meal that followed might well have been embarrassing, but Polly felt that oddly enough it wasn't, as neither she nor Adrian much took to Scott and didn't trouble about his feelings. Mrs Scott may have been content anyway. Polly regarded him as 'an obnoxious, self-important little man having to be mightily praised' for his achievements in painting that neither of them rated, while

Adrian muttered deprecatingly afterwards: 'All he can do is poached eggs,' which in fairness to Scott he was, in 1951, in the process of giving up. Norbert Lynton, Scott's biographer, confirms that William, despite being 'neither Hollywood, nor a person one would at first warm to' was notwithstanding 'a bit of a one for trying it on with women' and rather kept on trying 'although he may not have been as successful as he'd like to have been.' The two painters therefore had little in common apart from a strand of Irishness and the act of spending summers in Mousehole. By a trick of alphabet, the two of them sit juxtaposed on the very same page of the biographical section of Dr David Brown's enduring 'St Ives 1939–64' exhibition catalogue (page 140/41); the one pictured self-consciously awkward against an anachronistic carriage, the other warm and engaging.

However they met, or didn't, in between, William Scott came as assistant to Alan Bowness in his advisory and buying role for the British Council – who benefited from Gulbenkian funds to display pictures which the Foundation would end up owning – and they arrived at 4.30 pm on 3 September 1962 at Old Hill Cottage, Love Lane. Also to inspect the work came the painter Mary Jewels (1886–1977), a friend of Adrian's from at least two years previously – when she had swapped pictures with him to mark their mutual admiration of one another – and at 7 pm they all went over to view her in-house studio in Newlyn. Much later, it was not clear in the memory of Sir Alan Bowness why William came too, unless it was because 'He said he knew Adrian already' and that William could drive them, which he could not. Alan Bowness said he had known Adrian's pictures for years and 'had always admired them', but short of, on occasion, running into him at the Chelsea Arts Club, knew him scarcely before this friendly meeting. He further recalled 'a feeling of the house in Mousehole being very attractive' and the impression of Adrian having private money behind him, which would by then have been Joan's. Four pictures were chosen: *Skate, Cornish Landscape, Mousehole Harbour,* and *Bird Sanctuary, Mousehole.* The two latter pictures were roughly contemporary at that time; the first were not, although Adrian may not have emphasised this to his visitors if he thought that new work was what they were after. The landscape he describes as 'early' in a diary note. The large-scale skate (40" x 32") is known to have been one of two, differentiated as *Skate* and *The Ray.*[3] Both were exhibited in 1949 at the Academy and were indirectly referred to by the critic of the *Daily Telegraph* whose focus was firmly on the

3. A mere convenience of titling as the genus *raia batis* is termed in English only as 'skate'

painting they flanked, described as '...unfortunately hung between two pictures of a revolting fish.' Thirteen years on, the Gulbenkian purchase vindicated Adrian in regard to this unappreciative comment (which, continuing to quote it in after-years, seemed to amuse and yet not quite to have amused him). Eardley Knollys, in the 8 October 1949 *Art News and Review* article, wrote of 'a fine painting... of some hateful rotting skate,' a complement to the ray being drawn from the sea on a fisherman's line – which for Adrian was to be viewed as a symbol of victory, not of defeat. Both works are thought to have been painted some time before 1949 – the year in which he was hospitalised with pneumonia, and the same year in which he gave up the rental of Seagulls Cottage, Mousehole, and with it the life there that he had embarked upon with Peggy. Polly recalls a skate picture already existing before they got together in 1946, although they had first met some time in November 1945,[4] the other being perhaps circa 1947. Both were painted at Seagulls, although the background of the Gulbenkian picture shows an approximation of the interior walls of 48 Tite Street (with the bare boards of Owl's Nest studio, as opposed to the stone floors of Seagulls), where the skate never was. In the year of the Gulbenkian acquisitions, Adrian was again living with a woman not his wife, while litigating with the mother of two of his children pending a hearing for alimony.[5] Not much had changed in his situation or, in some respects, his subject matter though the paintings themselves appear differently charged. In early middle age he was as pleasure-loving – at times as irresponsibly so – and childlike as ever. He delighted in his birthday gift from Joan that year of a tape recorder, which he used to broadcast stories for the children in the exaggerated tones of a BBC announcer with excessive Received Pronunciation. He loved the look and sound of the sea as it moved in all weathers in and out of the tiny harbour. He took pleasure in the activity of boats and their shapes, each one as similar and yet as different as their catch of fish. *The Old Quay, Mousehole* (24" x 30") was one of his three pictures shown at the Academy in 1962, and contrasts with a version of the same view (17" x 23") both as through a window of Old Hill Cottage. The first painting is much about movement; the town is animated with light and evening shadows as after tea three boats graduating in size[6] set out – except for one maverick – the mid-sized pilchard-catchers having worked through the night to return the next morning. There are figures in the streets and on the harbour, which seems just a stepping stone away from the sea. The horizontal shape of the harbour and its sandy beach is conspicuously

4. AR diary entry 11 December 1945, 'Painted Ray'; 12 December 1945, 'Painted Ray. ate Ray'
5. Interim custody was awarded to Barbara on 30 November 1962 requiring him to pay her £8 a week
6. 'Toshers' up to 30", 'Half & halfers' and 50" 'Long liners' would not normally accompany one another

phallic. The second painting shows the stillness of early morning; its single boat is the only moving thing, distant and remote. Where the town, the harbour, the quay and the sea seemed as one in the first painting, now they are all separated. The lone tosher is heading leftward as though into the past; the sea is the only freedom but seems out of reach, and the body of the town suggests a prone figure with a flat, gingerbread arm, passionless, caressing nothing. The whites of the painting – representing the outer self – stand out. A simple window and chimney count reveals stark differences in the realities depicted. The date of the second painting is thought to be 1964, the year before the bitter and irrevocable split with Joan.

Sir Alan Bowness recalled both Patrick Heron and William Scott, as others before, having at some time spoken of Adrian as 'never developing'. But Eardley Knollys had more accurately noted him as 'a painter remarkably free from contemporary obsessions...' and as 'directed to' familiar forms and landscapes '...more concerned with their reality than the reality of his own responses to them.' Eardley went on to make the point, valid now as then, that the viewer soon realises: '...that [Adrian] likes what he sees, he likes a contrast of pure colour, he likes the feel of paint. When he is most successful his pleasure in the visual world becomes infectious...' The reality of the two giant ray paintings, the one rising from the infinite greeny glory of the sea, the other hooked from a chair back in an acute corner of a room's interior, is perhaps that for Adrian intellectually their very different states covered every base. Only increased stability in his home life might have engendered any more so-called development other than by natural evolution.

The Gulbenkian skate, as tortuous as anything of Soutine's against red and white walls, impacted on the abstract painter Albert Irvin while exhibited at the Academy when he was a student of Adrian's at Goldsmiths'. Somewhere among the many art reviews, not at the time kept by the RA – and more extensive in those days than now, with almost 30 British press admitted – Bert Irvin absorbed and remembered a phrase that the picture elicited: '[It was] Like the Rock of Ages being cleft...' (this was apposite, because the hymn of that name was so often sung by the Cornish folk in pubs when drunk at the end of the evening). Bert's lasting opinion is that in terms of development, Adrian came a long way by refining the 'wild' work of his youth.[7] Bert remarked that Adrian always had 'to

7. The peintre maudit into something more fun-loving, as Eardley noted

have something in front of him, like Matisse, to paint from', and expressed a wish that he could do the same.

Whatever was made of the Gulbenkian skate at the time, certain things stand out in hindsight. The muddied surface of clean white wall, left, bleary with dark, unrelenting blues that impose themselves on the stark plank floor. Blue-black heavily infects the white of the skate, which also glows fiery red at the bottom. The grotesquely hooked fish is unevenly balanced on the top rail of the chair, precarious, poised to slide as though by the unseen hand of fate as easily as moving an abacus bead. Behind the skate, the background is a little clearer. Caught open-mouthed, its face stares out of the canvas, its tail drooped toward the floor, presenting an unequal triangle echoed by the three legs of the chair, which, pushed oddly into a corner with only a slither of yellow seat is turned offering no support except for the rail. Lines are drawn and crossed, vertical and horizontal posts and strengthening spindles pointedly number twos and threes. The line where the white wall meets the inflamed passion of crimson red – with just a dash of rose-pink – is all but separated by one side of the chair back. All the while the skate's part-gutted liver is raised red raw and angry, caught in the middle of the picture plane.

What's depicted is a humanly contrived situation and a fish-wreck. The significance of the skate being in Cornwall called 'the upstairs fish' is because, to quote Mousehole's Harbour Master, 'It does married life the world of good.' Aphrodisiac it may be, another historical peculiarity pertains to the skate: of not, since Victorian times, being brought to the shore whole – hence skate wings – because sailors spending long periods at sea would engage with a skate's sympathetically formed parts and copulate with them. In common idiom, the psychological equivalent of the mouth as a body part equates with readiness to accept. Whereas the liver – and skate liver is much prized – equates with discrimination, philosophy and religion.[8] Given what has been said about some of the recurring themes in Adrian's life, it is not such a surprise to consider them being subconsciously addressed so pertinently in this remarkable Gulbenkian acquisition.

Mousehole, as a start and end point for Adrian, was almost perfect. Its moods and guises in strict relationship to its sea and sky balanced the often contradictory elements of his own nature: beautiful, mischievous, naughty, cruel. But the distinctive little harbour alone was not enough truly to

8. *The Healing Power of Illness*, Thorwald Dethlefsen and Ruediger Dahlke c. 1983

develop, as those such as Alan Bowness and William Scott might have had Adrian do. There is a little painting called *Prams, Mousehole* – prams being rowing boats – parked casually on the sand above the low tide. Oil over pencil, measuring 6½" x 7½", and following Bonnard's habit, painted on cardboard. By his own ingenious discovery, Adrian used this as a painting surface before systematically floating the finished works, including watercolours, in a warm bath or sink for 20 minutes, allowing easy removal of the top layer. *Prams* was painted in Camden Town when Adrian was 68 and entering the last decade of his life. The picture reveals a subtly understated passion. The weight of the mighty Atlantic – much as Jim Ede of Kettle's Yard, Cambridge observed of water washing against the vessels of Alfred Wallis – detectably brushes against the horizon of the wind-stirred sky, against the stone quays, the strand, the boat sitting calmly at the water's edge; treatment of the water of the harbour and the waters of the ocean differs in deference to its depth and capacity to move. Old and new quays meet almost as one but are clearly delineated, allowing the tide to flow leftward – from and into the past – permeating the watery deeps of private emotions. Nothing stirs, and yet... Soon after it was painted, Adrian, responded to the question – '*Is* that a sailing boat on the horizon?' [top right] – and already holding a pencil ready for signing, with one deft outline of the shape of a triangle, chuckling: 'It is now!' Otherwise the scene is one in which the crowd has departed. The busy harbour is deserted, not a person on either quay. It is a tranquil moment of immortality, a contemplation built around small boats as separate entities. Brushstrokes lower left show water defining the shore, the communion of earth with sea: today calm, but in the past... and there is still tomorrow. Two separate, alone but not lonely 'prams,' one larger-seeming than the other, will reunite at the return of the high tide; like twin hearts, timelessly beating. Distant love in the sailing boat heads off on the horizon.

In the stillness of this retrospective narrative is an inspired document of his life both in Cornwall and beyond, and of what, at its most simple, it could represent. It seems unlikely, from its basic pencil mark-makings and from the absence of any comparable, focused view of this spot by him, that Adrian deployed so much as a photograph or postcard of Mousehole to assist him in the creation of this small evocation. As Bert Irwin pointed out, this would be an exception to his normal practice. For this reason, Mousehole by itself was not enough fodder from which Adrian could work generally. Newlyn, rather than St Ives, was a necessary extension of the vitality he needed in order to find subject matter. Paul, Sennen, Sancreed and Porthcurno were as adjuncts forming a loose inspirational web, with virtually everything else in between and around curiously omitted. Forcibly removed from it all, he could only lack for material inspiration, although this did not stop him, long years after leaving, from re-creating old Mousehole scenes[9] including as modified, improved subject matter, but from integrity painted on cardboard rather than on canvas. An affinity with the place remained. Despite which, of his place in Mousehole, it can be said that he was as much a maverick figure not fully integrated when living there, as he remains to the St Ives movement overall today. Had he remained in Cornwall, the observation of Guy Roddon's that 'he was in the group and yet he wasn't' contains more than a hint of truth. The Mousehole Harbour Master, questioned about the term 'prams', refuted its usage by true-bred locals and was adamant that true Cornish spoke of them only as 'rowing-boats.' Like that hero in the novel by Camus, Adrian has retained the self-imposed status of the outsider wondering, but not expecting, if he might ever be invited in.

9. But not retrospective scenes of Suffolk, Ireland, Wales or France, or anything to do with growing up

Art schools

Consigned to London, with escalating domestic and artistic concerns, Adrian had more time – because less spent travelling – to reflect on the matter of his having to teach. Teaching requires patience, of which Adrian had little. Of the years he worked at Goldsmiths' from 1948 to 1983 (until 1985 at Cambridge College of Art), it has been said that he was a good teacher, but it would be more accurate to describe him as an individualistic one. John Bolam, the Head of Cambridge College of Art, once took John Norris-Wood aside to thank him for introducing Adrian to the college, confiding that: 'I notice he does an awful lot of teaching in the bar of The Locomotive', adding that he was such a good influence on students, telling them about music, poetry and opera, that it was worth it. The painter Haidee Becker was a devoted student of 'Professor Pesci' – a reference to their each making fish paintings – and feels that teaching, except on a one-to-one basis with students he truly liked, was not something that he really cared for or from which he derived much benefit. At Goldsmiths' she said he seemed to get lonelier and lonelier and spent more time drinking in the pub. Increasingly few were interested in what he was teaching, reflecting the contemporary direction that the college was taking, hostile to disciplines such as 'The three p's: paper, pencil and paint', or when drawing from life, 'pose, proportion and personality'.

When Clive Gardiner[1] died in 1960, Andrew Forge, Graham Sutherland and Adrian wrote recollections of him which were published in the catalogue to a memorial exhibition at the South London Art Gallery in the summer of 1967. Sutherland refers to this 'master teacher of integrity' and of owing Clive 'a debt which I can never repay', although the reason is not given. Graham Sutherland, whose father had once been tutor to Slade Professor John Richardson, in the academic's eyes lacked integrity for filching imagery from Francis Bacon and giving no credit.[2] Sutherland's written compliments about Clive Gardiner come by his own admission with a lack of authority and somewhat late in the day: 'How blind I was to resist for one moment the message of this real painter, this man of education...'

Adrian's shot at appraisal is sure of itself, comprehensive and was much appreciated by Lilian Gardiner and the family. He begins with the fact of this 'man of great culture' devoting nearly forty years of his life to 'creating and fostering a school of art that came to stand for all an academy should be – free and noble.' He writes of the Summer Carnival which always had a theme 'such as a medieval tournament, a bullfight, a vintage car rally' being 'one of the most important aspects of the students' training,' because in the great activity of creating floats, costumes and taking part, imaginations were stirred. Similarly, he tells of the long-gone Toy Theatre, of the Christmas Dance, and of the retirement of Clive being for the college 'an irreparable loss'.

Adrian's view of art school was that it should not be an education having exclusively to do with art, but a means to discovering talent without having to end up as an artist. He said that in 35 years of teaching at Goldsmiths', he knew only one student who had potential as a true painter, adding that 'lots, such as Mary Quant, had potential of a different sort.' Of others whom he taught there, such as Bridget Riley, he said disapprovingly little.

What he most valued in teaching, perhaps, was culture, liberalism and the basic discipline of drawing. When Clive Gardiner retired and the mood increased in favour of non-representational, non-objective art – the Abstract Expressionists led by the action painters (Pollock, de Kooning) and the colour field painters (Rothko, Noland) – it left Adrian as a lonely voice, feeling without audience as painter, teacher, humanitarian. In his growing isolation, the world of the strawberry tea party

1. Principal of Goldsmiths' from 1929 to 1958
2. cf the famous Churchill portrait and Bacon's 1945 *Figure in a Landscape*: Richardson's *The Sorcerer's Apprentice*, p.167

in the fields behind Goldsmiths', where Clive gave his annual speech and concluded with a story written specially for the event characterised by 'a magical, childlike quality', could not have seemed more removed. The world was moving on, leaving abstraction in its place, whose lack of human content it was not in Adrian's nature either to respect or accept.

The next Principal of the college was Patrick Millard, who, according to Stephen Gardiner, was neither his father's first choice nor a very interesting man. Clive had selected the highly regarded and influential Kenneth Rowntree (1915–97) as a sympathetic follow-up, who was teaching at the Royal College of Art. To this end, Clive wrote to Robin Darwin (RCA Principal 1948–71 and formerly Assistant Drawing Master at Eton, 1933–38) and received in reply a peculiarly disagreeable letter, throwing, as Stephen Gardiner described it, 'a very dark and disgraceful shadow' over Rowntree's suitability. Adam Rowntree, Kenneth's son, who from childhood experienced its author as 'an amazing and charming man', knew nothing of the offending letter – although it was declared by Stephen Gardiner to have horribly upset Kenneth's wife Diana, the architectural critic of *The Guardian*. Adam was aware that latterly the daggers were out for his father – who wasn't exhibiting enough to please Darwin, whom he called 'that benevolent bully, too much practised in standing against whole governments.' The naturally cautious Clive was dissuaded and Millard was hired from 1958 instead, whilst Rowntree in the following year removed to Northumberland to become Professor of Fine Art at Newcastle University. The loss in distinction seems only to have been Goldsmiths'.

Adrian was not at all alone in feeling isolated in the aftermath of Clive Gardiner's departure. Others, cited by Professor John Norris-Wood – a former pupil then colleague of Adrian's – included Sam Rabin, sculptor Harold Dow, Bernard Hailstone, and the curious and authoritarian figure of fashion, needlework and embroidery that was Constance Parker. Mrs Parker, an already singular figure who dyed her hair viridian green long before it was *de rigueur*, commanded Adrian's definite respect, he perhaps finding in her somewhat removed manner something akin to motherliness. She was, said John Norris-Wood, a very good friend to him, religiously having her students take his life drawing classes.

The most isolated stalwart of the old school and most graphically critical about their developing sense of confinement was the graphic artist Betty Swanwick RA (1915–89). Betty vocalised her pain in letters sent to Adrian over several years, in which she vilifies the 'HELLHOLE' that Goldsmiths' became for her under Millard, whom she confirms as a 'very kindly but ...misguided idiot.' Writing from her home at 36 Gloucester Circus, Greenwich on 10 July 1965, and responding to an 'engaging epistle' Adrian sent while examining in Nigeria, she is unequivocal:

> *As you mentioned what a fearful vulgar horrific heap of satanic shite the [end of year degree show] exhibition proved to be. I shudder and suppurate with misery when I remember it. Fortunately I am gradually driving it out of my mind. I am humbly grateful that Jack Low and yourself found the minute contribution of my diminutive group more to your liking. What a prospect next year is!*

In advance of the arrival of the Principal to replace Millard, she detected that mistrust should prevail: 'I gather Paul Drury has already told Michael Rothenstein that he is not the SQUARE that <u>some</u> of his friends (YOU JOHN & MESELF) are. So beWARE dear Addypater.'

Paul Drury (1903–87), a contemporary of Sutherland's, was a kindly and avuncular presence, more distinguished than his predecessor, but his reign was short-lived, and there followed from 1969 to 1972 the politically-charged figure of Peter de Francia. On 2 April 1970, Betty wrote during the spring recess, apologising for 'what will turn out to be the world's worst typing, with possibly the exception of de Francia' and requesting Adrian's advice on how to respond to a letter from the Principal which she reproduces, typewritten, within her own:

> *Dear Betty Swanwick,*
> *...I must tell you how much I regret your decision to resign. When I came to the school I very quickly got to know the various complications and difficulties that existed there. But I was determined to try to unravel them, and one of the things I set out to do was to block my ears to all the ancient quarrels and disputes. I thought the best thing to do was to simply refuse to listen to them, or at least to ignore their existence. I was hoping in this way one could start afresh. Of course this can't ever be entirely successful, but even an 80% success might, I thought, be worth the effort. One of the main problems concerned what I felt was your own isolation within your own department.*

> *I fully realise that the fault did not necessarily lie with you. The news of the folding up of your class came as a complete surprise to me, and my idea of your doing block teaching seemed to me a reasonable one as I thought it would reduce personal friction to a minimum, make arrangements simpler, and give you more free time. I'm most sorry that that you did not like the idea, though I did think that you had tentatively agreed to this when we had last talked together. I also assure you that my remarks to you were meant most kindly, simply that I felt morale was very low, and I wanted you to understand that I valued your independence and originality. Nothing else was intended, I assure you. I am most reluctant to accept your resignation as final, and… I would be very sorry to see you go, though it seems to me that whatever is decided something pretty firm must be arrived at concerning your role as a teacher in the Graphic Department. For if I am determined on one thing it is that the place should not be riddled with disputes and what seems to me sterile arguments. Once more I feel it necessary to emphasise that I would not dream of suggesting that these are your own fault… Very sincerely Peter de Francia.*

Done with quoting, she resumes as herself:

> *Well Adrian what a marathon task this typing has been, I gasp faintly at the mechanical aid, worn to a frazzle. What do you make of PdeF's letter de misunderstanding? Well I certainly am far too drunk with the joy of waving my big toe at the damned Hole to dream of considering a return to its sludgery, death and cold wet embrace. I feel that de F. is mad to think that it is best to take into NO account the injustices of the past few years. Do you ignore the suffering of the downtrodden and the crude ruthless way in which the arrogant master race has taken advantage of that poor weak principal so taken in by their grins and wooing? I think the whole place stinks of confused thinking and hoping to get away with it. Hope you are not too irritated by my bothering you in the holidays… Love from all here, Betty.*

Adrian's response is unknown, but de Francia was without doubt – for his communist, dictatorial politics and for his views on art – his least favourite of all the six Goldsmiths' Principals he worked under. According to John Norris-Wood, Adrian regarded de Francia as 'a total shit' and yet that, as with all of the institutional heads, he managed skilfully and with libran diplomacy to get along publicly and without giving offence, no matter what he thought in private. When asked about Adrian in after years, Peter de Francia had a clear recollection of what he looked like and also how he spoke, but nothing more. The name 'Betty Swanwick' he could not even remember.

Adrian liked Pat Millard, who was well meaning in his enthusiasm for Adrian's tribute to Clive Gardiner, writing to him, dated 19 March 1966:

> *Dear Adrian a lump came into my throat while reading your notes on Clive Gardiner. I did not know him well, but met him several times at County Hall... It was noticeable that all the Heads of London Schools listened to what he had to say with great respect. Dear Adrian you have written so sincerely and so well, that what you have written is a work of art that Clive Gardiner would have been very very proud to have read, and his friends to keep with them always.*

Paul Drury's cordiality and understanding made itself felt to Adrian throughout their professional association. Once, at the end of the summer term, when Paul had embarked on one of his customarily long and reflective speeches to the college, the audience could see that on the table in front of him there was an alarm clock ticking away. After much time spent summing up this and that somewhat comprehensively, the alarm eventually sounded and the audience sighed with relief. 'That *isn't*,' said Paul Drury, surveying the crowd sternly, 'to tell me that it's time to finish...' – here he paused – 'that's to let Adrian know that The Rosemary is open.'

The Rosemary, the local pub, had become the place where Adrian did much of his teaching and a fair amount of his seducing. His style of educating was understated, but was classified, by senior staff and pupils alike, as curiously enlightening. Haidee Becker maintains that for him to say anything very much about her work she really had to have painted something awful; in which event he would stand beside her and regard the offending canvas, hold his head on one side and simply say: 'You *are* a funny girl'. John Norris-Wood agreed that if he really wanted help, he would have forcefully to ask for it; otherwise Adrian would merely come along, mutter a few things and sidle off.

Of his role as an educator and not without pride or some irony would Adrian remark that, in addition to 'surviving six principals' he was able to record that 'in over thirty-five years' teaching I managed to avoid having to deliver any form of public lecture.' For a man who held such enduring convictions about art – amongst other things – it was a facet of his contradictory capabilities that he abhorred the idea of lecturing *en masse*, due to the inherent danger of exposing his very private nature. Adrian as a rule felt institutionally challenged: Eton, the army, the RA, Goldsmiths'. His response was in all cases to recede from all possible conflict, along with the potential for self-development. Gentle self-expulsion was better than exclusion, though where the divide lay was in his case not always clear. Exclusion correlated with the disabilities of his father, Vivian. In assisting the growth of this state, however deeply unconsciously, Adrian marinated in his father's self-worthlessness and frustration, and drank damagingly from the same well.

There were, of course, gains accruing to Adrian from nearly four decades of teaching. Money was not one of them. Structure was. The New York School painter Richard Diebenkorn (1922–93), whose dogged integrity in reverting as early as 1955 from abstract expressionism to naturalistic painting led to a dust storm of analysis that forever marked his trail, knew the difficulty inherent in getting any kind of painting started: 'I used to hang around bus-stops near my Ocean Park studio envying impatient people who had some important place to go.'[3] Teaching is to a timetable, and in whatever different situations and continents it helps any number of diffident painters as a means to an end. Chiefly, for Adrian, it brought him forever into the company of young people, in front of whom he got to exercise his delinquent youthfulness uninhibited by adult restraint. His behaviour was at times frowned upon then and would be unlikely to be tolerated today. But, as Professor Norris-Wood explained, having encountered Adrian as a student aged 17, and going on to teach alongside him: 'He was incredibly clever as a diplomat and with officialdom was very, very good at changing the subject.' He recalled that once, having been out all night with a student, Adrian was called to account by Pat Millard responding to enquiries by the girl's mother (whose first frantic telephone call to the College had fortunately been intercepted by Betty Swanwick, a convincing antidote to parental anxiety flooding the sleep-deprived mind). Betty and John Norris-Wood were then entertained as Adrian was

3. Final interview with Richard Diebenkorn by Julian Machin, *San Francisco Chronicle*, 17 November 1992

cornered in the refectory by the flustered Principal, who asked him pointedly what he knew of the girl in question. Adrian calmly paused. He then admitted that she might once or, possibly, twice, even have been in his class, but naturally he couldn't be certain. Insouciantly, he next took out his cigarette case and calmly rearranged its contents. 'It was,' concluded John Norris-Wood, 'the coolest performance you ever saw.'

Getting to be with young people with whom he got to be mischievous necessarily meant that Adrian avoided a commitment of having to be so often at home. Taking the long overnight sleeper journey from Cornwall was therefore no hardship. Train travel he liked, never knowing with what stranger he would be sharing the double-couchette. Once it was a uniformed sailor on leave who took the lower berth, and Adrian watched in fascination as the man knelt down and uttered lengthy prayers aloud, wholly unself-conscious of having an audience.

Teaching gave much needed support to the uncertain elements forming the structure of Adrian's existence. In that it was work and provided money, which was becoming increasingly difficult to obtain via sales, it assisted greatly (hence the acceptance of one day at Cambridge College of Art, then handily placed for the journey when living at Hill House) although as a part-timer without holiday pay, it was never enough.

The first phase of Adrian's teaching must have seemed a wonderful pathway, in no sense its gradual decline and disappointment being foreseeable. The rot set in, as Betty Swanwick saw it, when Pat Millard became Principal, that kindly but slightly dull man, an epileptic whose periodic fits served to undermine the necessary strength required to govern. He was alleged to be suspicious of Adrian, not without some cause, and yet as letters testify and especially by the time of Millard's retirement, there was fondness and respect between them. Adrian gave him an oil still life of sardines and prawns, which Millard hung in his bedroom at Charity Farm, Cranbrook, and also a work on paper of Mousehole School, which Geraldine, Scarlett and Vivien had attended. Adrian later called it his favourite of all his own watercolours and it was typical of his random ability to act generously that he should have given something so prized. Later, and indirectly, it was returned to him after Millard's death. Millard brought in Andrew Forge in his stead as a sort of international genius, which led to the contemporary swing and the beginning of the unrelieved isolation felt by Adrian and Betty Swanwick alike as Goldsmiths' was taken over more and more by conceptual bowls of vomit and abstraction. The passions of the old guard became derided, and even Betty's most dire predictions, admitted John Norris-Wood, 'having once seemed especially extreme, have all come true and been exceeded.'

Andrew Forge (1923–2002) teacher, critic, influential figure and ultimately Head of Yale Art Department, came a bit like Adrian from traditional English stock. Having removed himself from it, following a coming to grips with abstraction on his first trip to the US in 1963, he moved there permanently in 1973 but later underwent something of a reversion to old values – not least in returning to be buried in the family plot in Kent. The extent of Adrian's aversion to him and his work may not have been known to Andrew Forge, whose abstract work deployed a system of dots accruing, he wrote, into 'pathways, constellations, geometries' seeking to emphasise the sensory effects of colour. Adrian would have preferred the critic Maureen Mullarkey's opening summary reviewing Forge's posthumous contribution to a mixed show in New York's Kouros Gallery in 2003: 'Elegant and spare, his work has struck me as having an air of the podium about it – a distillation of style-conscious theories with little blood in them.' Definitely opposed in their attitudes to teaching, there was forged no friendship between them, unlike the many he did befriend from the staff of Goldsmiths'. But at Adrian's memorial service at St James's Piccadilly, Andrew Forge turned up and was seen to be moved to tears by the sight of Adrian's easel-propped painting of *Whiting and Shrimps* (dated 1977) at the front of the church. He told Bert Irvin how moved he was just to see the process of a human being taking what he'd seen and translating it into little bits of paint, which Adrian would have appreciated.

Generally, the Goldsmiths' staffs were in all phases congenial company, the Gardiner years being the most relaxed. Bert Irvin remembers Adrian in the late 1940s opening the staff bar, where members recorded their own drinks, and automatically signing 'Bernard Hailstone'. The academic Bernard and Adrian were close friends and of their travels to Toulon together with Polly and Bernard's wife, more later. Guy Roddon, already known to Desmond Ryan from having been pupils at Bryanston together, was on the staff in 1949. He and Adrian indulged in plentiful rivalries: among them, collecting matchboxes and playing chess in between teaching. With wallet-sized chess sets, having worked on opening gambits, play would begin in earnest just before ten o'clock when the life class started. More moves would follow in between tutoring someone or other, and this would go on for hours. In sport, as in rivalry over women, Adrian sought to win. Once they played off and on from morning till late evening, including on the train they took to Victoria, where Guy would change to get home to Brighton. The presence of the Crazy Gang, having been playing at the Victoria Palace, added to a sense of comic timing. The carriage lurched threateningly and from the platform, Adrian handed the chess-wallet back through the window and annihilatingly pronounced 'Check mate' as the train rolled out of the station.

Adrian's mental agility did not much decrease when imbibing either. (Nor did it when dying: Frances Fyfield recalls the near-terminal Adrian, when asked by a nurse what he would like for a Christmas present, contemplate before replying: 'I'd like a jolly good fuck', uttered with the wistfulness of knowing it was sadly not going to happen. The nurse laughed appreciatively.) But when the balance had shifted and it took over from the teaching, there were fewer of his peers who appreciated the wit, which like charm requires an audience. Sam Rabin, a wonderful draughtsman and teacher, was the first to retire. Most of the old guard followed, like Harry Thubron (1915–85), the distinguished collagist whose OBE awarded for his teaching was, in Adrian's view, an honourable misapplication heralding the shift in values to which he so objected. 'It should,' he emphasised, 'have been given him for his art.'

A judicious opportunity for Adrian to take an anti-establishment stand came with his invitation to become peripheral to the Tom Keating affair. A letter dated 15 August 1978 was sent him at Goldsmiths' written by John Ford, of the civil liberties firm of Bindman and Partners, Solicitors. 'We act for Tom Keating, an artist, who is currently awaiting trial at the Old Bailey upon charges of dishonesty arising from the copying of works of art... We are anxious to establish certain facts concerning the history and practice of imitation and making of pastiches which we feel ought to be presented to the Court at trial.'

Tom Keating having been a scholarship pupil at Goldsmiths' from 1948 to 1952 (though he left having failed an examination and without qualifications) and a friend of Barbara's, Bindmans had sought out Adrian, hoping to find him a sympathetic advocate of traditional teaching values, not least in drawing and painting from the Antique. They were not disappointed by his response. Adrian replied on 5 September evidently offering his assistance, and Geoffrey Bindman, later celebrated for his human rights work and famous for representing Amnesty International in the fight to extradite General Pinochet to Spain amongst many other cases, gratefully responded two days later. The firm's records do not show the extent of the help Adrian provided. All that survives is a series of correspondence from Tom Keating to Adrian, increasing in warmth as the trial drew near. Also his newspaper cuttings of court reporting, often hilarious, prior to the eventual collapse of the case, halted by the judge on the grounds of Keating's health problems brought on by a lifetime of cigarette smoking and inhaling toxic chemicals used in art restoration. Adrian and Tom Keating had in common a love of practical jokes – which in Keating's case, through greed not his own, had gone disastrously wrong – and came to live with women significantly their juniors not far distant from one another, respectively in Suffolk and Dedham, Essex. Keating's 'Sexton Blakes' – fakes – were annotated with joke clues and anachronisms as antidote to fraud, using lead white under surface paint that would be revealed by x-ray, such as 'Big Bertha' written on a Goya nude, or more obviously the water in a Samuel Palmer pastiche *The Wonderful Providence of God* that ran uphill. Those who were unlikely to be fooled by Adrian's 'copies of Matthew Smith' might not have been taken in by Keating's work, but for the profit they sought to make from selling it on. As Brian Sewell pointed out at the trial, the work spoke for itself.

The first, undated, letter Adrian appears to have received from Tom Keating thanks him for his help, having 'today received a photostat copy of your kind letter to John Ford...' It continues: '...not that I am overworried bearing a clear conscience, but I suppose if one upsets the establishment one gets the old bum smacked! More importantly they should shoot the bastards who blatantly over clean our masters!! It was only after I filmed at the N.G. last year exposing this and other sordid matters, they "arrested" me.'

People who fake artworks, a practice going back to Roman times, are asking recognition for their work (even in the case of Jean-Baptiste-Camille Corot (1796–1875) who, having painted

700 works himself, also signed imitations made by others in his name because he felt honoured to be copied). According to Geraldine Norman, who first exposed Keating's name in *The Times* and with her husband Frank wrote the book, *The Fakes Progress* (Hutchinson, 1977) with the artist's cooperation, Tom finally achieved his plaudits, albeit by an unusual route, dying beloved by the public and his skills appreciated, having brilliantly managed the media in court and with two Channel 4 television series to his credit afterwards. This despite what she added was a 'strong self-destruct element in his personality', which seems to have worked posthumously against him, since there is only a small market for his paintings more than twenty years after his death in 1984. Adrian also desired recognition for his paintings, but a gentlemanly reticence – contrasting with Keating's brash demeanour – would not have had him bask in it publicly. Combined with a wilful itchiness about his work and painful levels of expectation of what it should be, there is no sense in which public appreciation, other than at a dignified and more local level, would ever satisfy him. Thus was one-to-one teaching only of any possible interest to him, depending on who the other one happened to be.

Relations and property

Ownership of property was a luxury in which Adrian indulged twice. The purchase of Myrtle Cottage, Newlyn, and of Wood Farm, Fressingfield, was each time mortgage free, an enviable state of affairs which, ironically, ended in loveless litigation and ruination respectively.

Myrtle Cottage was a small eighteenth-century house reputedly built by the Adam brothers for their own use while working in the West Country. It had simple, beautifully proportioned rooms and a lovely garden sheltered by a belt of pine trees and a granite wall. Kay Walker, Polly's mother, had lived in it since her divorce from Alec, but lacked income to maintain it. In May 1951, within an extended summer period in which Adrian was writing 'HAPPY' and 'Very happy with Pol' etc. in his diary, a more wistful observation also appears: 'a sad life that Kay lives' following a visit by her to dinner with them (4 May). Kindness prevailing, Adrian offered to buy Myrtle Cottage and allow Kay to live in the downstairs while he and Polly would, when in Cornwall, make use of the rooms above. He loved the house, and appeared to get on well with Kay, whose financial difficulties it would immediately solve. It troubled Polly, whose vision was to escape her mother as much as possible, knowing her to be 'near impossible to live with' and likely to regard Myrtle with self-centred disregard for anyone's well-being other than her own. A warning light denoting Polly's unease manifests in June: 'Painted fish but

Polly NOT INTERESTED', which was unusual, as she was both critic and muse consistently. The plan proceeded as summer unfolded; of bathing at Porthcurno, Geraldine visiting, bathing at Sennen, at Marazion, seeing the Carnival Queen crowned etc; and duly two thousand pounds was paid to Kay for the property. For no obvious reason other than at Kay's suggestion legal ownership of it was put into Polly's sole name. Kay and Polly dined with Adrian on the eve of his divorce (when he and Peggy spent the night together) and the idea of Polly's possession of Myrtle was put forward then. Peggy remembers Adrian telling her of Kay exhorting them to 'Celebrate!' and Adrian saying: 'I don't think it's anything to celebrate.' They seemed each to be referring to the divorce. Thereafter clouds gather, there is evidence of growing bad tempers and resentments and by 10 July 1951, underlined in the diary 'Polly doesn't love me!' is followed by an end-of-week memorandum: 'Pol cross with me – sleep downstairs after telling me to go.' He went, taking the next night train with Geraldine to London and on to Desmond's farm at Stradbroke. 'Very Sad,' but growing defiant, 'don't care a damn about Polly,' he wrote on consecutive days, in which sadness clearly dominated. Pencil annotations sur-title the next two weeks as 'the blackest days' and 'lost days' were spent in Suffolk with an aggressive toothache raging throughout.

'Want to go back to Polly but too proud to ask' he wrote inauspiciously at the end of July. Thereafter not one fall, but a series of them, starting with the first of several 'not nice' letters arriving from Polly, rattling her right to ownership of Myrtle Cottage. More days were lost in London, exchanging nasty letters with Polly and nice ones with Kay, with Adrian's mood remaining hellish; drunk and on some species of unprescribed drugs. London palling, he decided to go to Paris, where being 'drunk in Montmartre,' 'drunk all day' accounted for most of the nine days he spent there, calling them the 'unhappiest ever'. All the while expecting a forwarded letter from Polly, but receiving nothing. On Sunday 26 August, having returned to London and to his friend Asgeir Scott's in Walpole Street, a telephone call from Jack Low alerted him to the sale of Myrtle Cottage by auction on Thursday of the following week. The sense of something irrevocable about to happen seized him. He wrote a memorandum saying: 'feeling awful about Pol but decide to SUE her if she takes my money'. Of all that splits loved ones, money and property are what drives the wedge deepest. What Adrian wanted was to have Polly back, but without his having to ask. A lawsuit fought in public would surely expose and humiliate her. The threat of it could also compel Polly to change her mind, realise her love for him and return. On Monday 27 August, 'feeling bloody', he instigated the issue of a writ claiming proceeds in the event of the sale going ahead, then sought the stoic presence of Peggy, thereafter getting drunk while awaiting delivery of a letter from Polly that did not come, because it was never written. The next day he met solicitor Cyril Cobbett to proceed with the summons, and got drunk again. The writ was served the day after, on the eve of the auction, at which Myrtle Cottage was sold for £3,000, giving a 50% profit on what he'd paid for it. There was no time to savour this potential windfall. The following day, which he described as the worst of all, he heard (from Pino Barnes, whose film historian husband John ran the St Ives cinema museum) the devastating news that Polly had married Jess Martin. This was a man she knew from her Camberwell pottery class (her counter to Barbara being by now on the scene, the two newcomers being the source of Polly's and Adrian's original argument) and who had arrived in Mousehole in July at her invitation. Now the humiliation was Adrian's. It detonated more unhappy drinking, unproductive days, and energy directed towards the legal battle. It was three months before he felt able to paint again and nearly twelve months before the case was settled, throughout which, although installing Barbara, he missed Polly miserably, while decrying his own vanity. One exceptional painting he made at this time was unusual in its direct response to events. He called it *The Snake in the Grass* and it showed Polly, Jess and himself as the victim of their conniving. Only a fragment of it survives – his own likeness; a dark but recognisable silhouette – as he destroyed the remainder with scissors. Polly's hasty marriage to Jess disintegrated without intervention.

In regard to Myrtle Cottage, the case ended in the first week of July 1952 in response to a settlement proposed by Adrian and accepted by the other side. Proceeds were divided into equal third shares for Kay, Polly and for himself, with £100 for costs, which it seems that he paid. 'V. Happy' he wrote of this result, a curious response given what he'd lost by flattering Kay with more money. The reality was that Kay was 'the other side' and had played Adrian for what he was worth. Something in her sad mothering state blinded him to her true colours. Polly had not wanted to own Myrtle, she wanted to break free of it, which, with Adrian all too readily despatched and without evidence that he wanted her back, was why she married Jess. Kay benefiting from both house sales, which she had herself instigated, and having to steer her daughter just once to a solicitor in Penzance to sign documents making the auction a reality, are facts upon which Adrian would not have cared to look closely. Easier to find fault with Polly, whom he had wronged as much as he did any of his women, and having declined to marry her in law, to spare no use of its enmity when taking his reluctant leave of her.

The loss to both of them was profound and yet befuddled by each getting involved with other people. Brought together by Kay, who had spotted Adrian in the Fisherman's Arms, Newlyn, and was keen to inveigle her daughter into his life as child carer to Geraldine, she also parted them. Kay's role was intrusive as Adrian's mother's had been, but his connection with Polly long survived her and other considerable obstacles.

In its first phase, their relationship charts from June 1946, with Polly staying the night four days after the opening on 10 June of the Perranporth Theatre,[1] which is what had brought Peg and therefore Adrian down to Mousehole in the first place. Her only previous inclusion in Adrian's diary is of having painted her one day in April, the same week in which he began sleeping with her sister Pip – of which Polly knew nothing until later – boxed between affairs with Pino Barnes and Shirley Maiden – of which she knew everything. Six years and one week younger than Adrian, she was four months short of her twenty-first birthday, an unworldly adolescent unable for the next five years to resist the combination of his sense of fun, good looks and charm.

There is a painting of the mountains behind Toulon (*Landscape near Toulon*, exhibited at the Redfern, 1951, 40 guineas) where they stayed in the summer of 1950, in which Polly is partly integrated with the landscape, as though in his mind she were a permanent feature of it. There is also a photograph taken by Adrian of her in the rough garden of Villa Campagne Orovida where they stayed. In the glare of the sun, one eye guarded by shadow, she stands naked with all her weight on one leg, poised to take an uncertain step, a sculptural figure set in the landscape, but not of it. This is the real woman, exposed to the pleasures and pains of their coexistence. The painting is a representation of the woman in his mind, using the mountain backdrop, the path and olive trees to suggest female anatomy, for the most part caressed by the sun. It evokes mother Earth, too, and a longing for unconditional motherly love. Polly gave a great deal of love unconditionally, but even this holiday in

1. Sponsored by Hans Lasson, the art dealer mentioned earlier

remote and peaceful surroundings was not proof against tremors to her equilibrium. On returning from a trip to the village sooner than she was expected, she disturbed Adrian and the wife of their postman in the 'well-room' that provided the house with its sole supply of delicious icy water. Righteous indignation overspilled into a scene of outright bad manners. Adrian's response was to tell Polly *she* shouldn't be behaving like that. She hurriedly packed her bag and took flight down the mountain. It only resulted, after an hour, in Adrian nonchalantly appearing before her, saying as he often did that he was 'only having some fun' and 'not to be so silly' and their returning together to go to bed. It was the only upset of the trip, which lasted nearly six weeks from 24 July, taken in the company of Bernard Hailstone (1910–87) 'whom God preserved' as Adrian referred to him, and his wife Joan. Bernard was well known as a portraitist whose sitters included Olivier, Churchill and Sir John Barbirolli, and by invitation of Kenneth Clark as an official war artist to the Ministry of Transport, and was regarded by Polly as 'such a lovely, gentle person'. They drove down in Bernard's old Alvis, mostly in darkness and in a state of grim-jawed tension, taking far longer than they had imagined. On many of the mountain bends leading up from the Rhone valley there were monuments to all the vehicles that ran off the road and crashed onto the rocks below. Campagne Orovida was a pleasant little house enjoying a soft breeze that came in from the distant coast. It had windows over the valley behind and a view of the mountains rising beyond. It was basic, but comfortable and clean. Polly could recall no lavatory but said there must have been a bearable approximation of one or Adrian 'could not have survived'. The garden had a flat section overlooking the valley and some steep sloping ground with olive trees and a mulberry alive with tasty fruits and irritable hornets. A narrow, rocky ravine led via a cheerful gauntlet of stone-throwing communist youths to a primitive village far below. Breakfast was at seven, outside, before it became too hot, followed by a trip to the village for provisions – with coffee and pernod for Adrian and sometimes a little *boules* with amused, impenetrably accented locals.

Thereafter, to work sketching or painting, Adrian wanting Polly to go with him to find a spot he was happy with and stick around in case he wanted her to comment. When it became too hot, they returned to the house for drinks, followed by lunch made by Polly and washed up by Joan, before siesta. They drove to picnic and swim in deserted coves where pine trees grew to the water's edge. There was shopping at Hyères, there were trips to nearby Le Revest, further amusement at Toulon, and there was always plenty of wine. Meanwhile Adrian finished a total of ten paintings on canvas, all of which, with some touching up, were exhibited the following spring at the Redfern[2] together with 11 related watercolours.[3] They motored home less perilously than they had come, stopping one night at Valence, on the Rhone, and for two days in Paris, returning on 2 September to Tite Street with no wish for the trip to have ended. A bonus was the substantial core of work produced, assisted by the ambience of the Pissarros, convivial company, proximity to the sea, and most important of all, a dependable domesticity.

Wood Farm, near Fressingfield, set beside a pond, was really two ancient cottages made into one around a central chimney, as beloved for the land as for its low-beamed self. There was no electricity, only a rayburn and myriad paraffin lamps, and no room inside to paint, so he built a studio next to the house.[4] The surrounding landscape still seems ancient and unchanged, but the garden Adrian lovingly planted reads very differently today, all its varied fruit trees gone apart from one gnarled pear tree, although the avenue of poplars remains. Jack Low advised him in the planning. Her pencil notes end in the worthwhile caveat: 'REMEMBER GARDEN WILL OUTLIVE YOU SO DON'T LET IT KILL YOU TOO SOON'. From rolling the lawns to every type of planting, seeding and forking, a schedule of work to be done week by week was written into a garden diary of 1953. Precise diagrams, similar to an artist setting out his palette, were included. Adrian's love of the landscape[5] echoed his grandfather's, and his own hard work in reshaping it, nurturing it, helped to balance his male and female sides, between which there was so often a battle. He was so unable to integrate the female side properly that it came out in the form of unkindness to women, whom he either idealised or disliked. His maleness was never simply expressed and he grew terrified of women's power because he could never balance his own. This accounts for his resistance to commitment with women and the necessity of connecting with them at every opportunity. It accounts also for his overcompensating in committing to Polly and to Kay by unnecessarily signing over Myrtle Cottage. Having two homes later on, but without ownership of them, echoed this resistance, and he succeeded in this policy for most of his adult life. Possibly he could be as infatuated and excited, then bored and unfeeling, about finding and creating a new home as with any of his significant relationships with women.

2. 3 April–28 April 1951 with Rowland Suddaby and Matthew Smith *et al.* priced at up to 80 guineas
3. 8–16 guineas each
4. Later Tristram Carey, the electronics pioneer, wrote much of the incidental music for *Dr Who* there
5. Asked what he would have been if not a painter, he once replied 'professional golfer' in order to be outdoors as much as possible

If there was a favourite amongst his homes, it was felt privately, although the extent to which he painted them – if at all – may give clues. *Welcome Home* shows Seagulls Cottage, Mousehole, on V.J. Day, 15 August 1945, which he would have painted in his then 'studio' – the outside lavatory at the back, sitting on the wc, facing out with the easel beyond. Adrian with Peggy and Geraldine had been in Mousehole for one month exactly, Tite Street having been let to his cousin Pam. Seagulls is shown second from the left in the foreground with a blue door, behind a low wall. The painting is finely balanced between stillness and movement. The light tells us that it is late afternoon or early evening. Bunting is the only clue to there being a celebration. Smoking chimneys suggest a general baking of Starry Gazey pie, a Mousehole celebration dish made of seven fish, including pilchards rising vertically through the crust, in memory of fisherman Tom Bawcock, who bravely brought back a catch in a lull between storms to feed the hungry villagers. Lanes leading left and right invite us to wander the village within the canvas. The composition is based on a diagonal and triangle in a quartered rectangle, but unusually it has no false perspective. Instead we occupy his viewpoint head on. The abounding greys reflect the long war years whose official ending is marked by the colourful, but discreet, bunting. The celebrations themselves are significantly out of view. Adrian is unlikely to have regarded them conventionally, bearing in mind his war service and the correctly held belief that it is braver *not* to take part in war unless you try to cover it up.[6] Now that the conflict was over, Adrian could consider the appalling tragedy of it all. The two figures who have absented themselves from the party appear isolated and unaware of one other. The three windows of the Methodist Chapel preside over the scene, but on the horizon is an estate higher and more honourable than mere churches, its window glass glinting and with a better view all round. That he had occupied Seagulls for a month assists in understanding the title *Welcome Home*, which works on more than one level, though there appears to be little personal attachment to the cottage as yet. Later versions, small ones, of this scene, contain a greater warmth, as affection developed. Meantime, right of Seagulls, beyond what was a set back, uninhabited store, a startling cottage wall evokes what Clive Gardiner said of Adrian being 'the only painter of white' while reflecting the underlying concern of the day – the white flag of surrender. It is possible that his moderated response was informed by the sudden news, just nine days after Victory Day, of 'Uncle' Willie Brass's death on 24 August, a painful surrender of a different kind.

6. Adrian politely withdrew from a high profile exhibition at the Camden Arts Centre curated by the painter Keith Grant and themed with the war in Vietnam, because he didn't want any political capital made out of his work

Although there are no oils of Hill House, Holbrook, there are numerous works on paper and it is probably the house he painted most of all, in a phase of his life which was most trouble free. Tite Street, Old Hill Cottage and Camden Street where he died were never rendered in paint, although more views from the windows of Old Hill Cottage, Mousehole, exist than all of the other houses added together (Joan was latterly unwilling to share her studio, so he used the house). At least two oils of Myrtle Cottage are known and possibly the same number of Wood Farm, but these are not close-to and cannot be classified as house-portraits.

Houses are separate from what goes on in them. Discounting Tite Street and Camden Street – London was never good subject matter for Adrian – the answer to which country home did he like most, for its fantastic sea views and comforting past associations with the village below, may well have been Old Hill Cottage. Hill House, less elevated but within walking distance of the Holbrook estuary, where his ashes were scattered, might reach the finishing line as Adrian's chosen runner-up. Peggy, however, opted for Hill House, recalling that he had told her how well it suited him – the rhythm of being alone and then not. Canvassing Barbara, Sue, and not forgetting Polly, Hill House comes in as three to one favourite, yet without Peggy's conviction, with Barbara dissenting in favour of Wood Farm. Which still doesn't answer whether treating as subject matter something as personal as a house denotes affection or not.

Adrian once remarked to Guy Roddon: 'I've been a friend of Whats-his-Name's for twenty-five years and I'm only *just* beginning to like him'. Sensitive, loyal and with shifting depths to his friendships – rather like his painting style – and generous. Mindful of Polonius's speech from *Hamlet,* money lent was money not expected to be returned, which it mostly wasn't. Adrian always treated Sven Berlin with great generosity, for example when his first wife Helga left him[7] and he had no money and was drinking heavily. Sven fell out with just about everybody at one time or another, but he didn't with Adrian, and habitually sent compliments about his work scripted in purple prose accentuated by the hieroglyphics which served him for handwriting.

7. Sven and Helga had been professional Adagio dancers, which due to understanding balance later helped Sven create sculpture. Adrian tended to refer to it as 'Apache dancing'

Asgeir Scott, in the spring of 1968, by probable suicide in a Dublin boarding house he could no longer afford, closed another great friendship for Adrian, for whom it was a tragedy. They had long lived close to each other in Chelsea; Asgier in Walpole Street, inhabiting rooms remembered by Geraldine as having 'an air of opulence – a sort of shabby gentility and Wilde-esqueness.' Asgeir's instability was chronic. Adrian had written to him, enclosing money, and received a reply mere days before his death by barbiturate poisoning. Asgeir's letter dwells on unwanted changes to the hostelries of Dublin they'd frequented together. It twice mentions death, including that of a Major O'Hare 'late of the Indian army, now late of this world', who returned from work saying he felt 'slightly ill.' Requesting a cup of tea, he went upstairs where his daughter found him shortly thereafter 'sitting up in bed – dead.' There is a sense of his envying the major. Although he goes on to write that he foresees 'no joy in living', for Asgeir such language would not be unusual, neither would his being in a state of insolvency, which the letter sadly details. In hindsight, the message is clear. From the bereaved father, Adrian received acknowledgement of his own letter of sympathy, beginning: 'If there could be anything heartening at this time it would be the spirit of the letter you have written to us. There must have been some great virtue in Asgeir for him to have deserved such a friendship.' Like attracts like. Virtue exemplifies much of what Adrian was about in his dealings with people generally. He could tolerate and give time, money and hospitality to people who came seeking hours to kill, instead of hours to live – some whose society those closest to him frankly found impossible. As there was virtue in his life, so were there many contradictions to oppose it, but overall, as in his work, there was both poetry and consistency throughout.

Late showing

In March 1985, 86 works forming a retrospective period of 42 years, went on show at The Minories, Colchester. Adrian was almost 65 years old, and was in the last year of working as an art teacher, within a new epoch very different in mood and confidence from how he had first exhibited at the Redfern, also in March, more than four decades previously. The Minories' curator, Jeremy Theophilus, wrote in a catalogue note of him: 'He has endured a long period of being ignored by public and critics – ever since the sudden advent of abstract expressionism... and for many years it was as if he had never existed... This exhibition... aims to set the record straight and pull him back into the limelight where an artist of his calibre truly belongs.' To be achieved within the Ides of March it was a noble aim. That it didn't quite succeed has more perhaps to do with that interesting line *for many years it was as if he had never existed,* which was written on the basis of conversations with Adrian and approved by him. Over twenty years later, Jeremy Theophilus recalls that the remark, meant in the context of an art world point of view, was what Adrian seemed to think of himself. Also that in terms of motivation, it struck him that Adrian was one of those who did seem to want to have a profile, events notwithstanding, over artistic invisibility.

The exhibition, although not the sought-after turning point, was no failure either. It comprised 59 oils and 27 works on paper, card or newsprint. Thirteen were from the 1940s, only four of them not being of Mousehole. The largest was called *Pollarded Trees, Moret* which was dated 1948 and measured 36" x 28". The smallest was *Mousehole from the Old Fish Store,* 7½" x 8½", dated 1947. The most recent were 1984 scenes of Montauroux or elsewhere in Var, or of Provence. France accounted for 25 subjects. Of still lifes there were 16. Of Suffolk, of portraits and of Wales, there were ten, seven and three pictures respectively. It was a representative selection of his oeuvre.

The original Redfern show (11 March to 3 April 1943) reads very differently. Listed on the first page of the catalogue opposite 24 works by Andre Masson were an equal number of early Ryans. Travel had not yet fuelled the repertoire of the young painter. Not a single landscape was among them. There was a high proportion of still lifes (ten) and one fish painting (plus the *Crayfish* lent by Edward Le Bas). There was one self-portrait and another called *The Artist As a Butcher,* which at 45 guineas, together with *Dogs Playing,* were the most expensive. Several others with esoteric titling were included: *Arab, Child With a Camera* and *Newspaper Boy,* of which only the latter's whereabouts is known today.

One thing that had shifted significantly over the years was the audience. The Minories in 1985 had a very different ambience to the Redfern's rarified walls of commerce. A manifestation of this came unfortunately in the form of a comment in the gallery visitors' book. Jeremy Theophilus was neither aware of it at the time, nor of the reaction it detonated in Adrian. Nor, in the matter of coping with criticism, was he privy to a tendency in Adrian, needful of reassurance, to be generally far too shattered by negative input. He was however not surprised 'because the remark is very Colchester' to hear that someone had viewed the paintings and had carelessly written: 'My eight year child could do better.' It was hardly coruscating art criticism, but for Adrian it hit home, as though there were a measure of reality not in the comment but in his psyche. The self-exposure of showing was never easy for him, which ran roughly commensurate with how much extra he had to do to bring about a result; framing, promotion and publicity to him being uninteresting activities. He could never get into the razzmatazz of selling, preferring to regard as cheap what others would see purely as good salesmanship. Thus was his ability to withstand a negative comment, in a childlike way, at odds with the majority of other people's reality.

March 1985, as the diary makes clear, is a dark period for him without one alleviating factor, but it is not a darkness that is anything other than held within. It is not shouted from the rooftops, but his tone is distinctly un-olympian in what might otherwise have been a milestone of triumph and celebration. Diary references to pictures being collected, to the hanging, the private view and party, are invested with little ardour and no enthusiam from a man whose life's work and worth was very much in question. More feeling is evidenced in his myriad references to the beastly cold weather. Contained, too, is the note dated 7 March 'Prepare list for Redfern of lost watercolours' where privately he was angry that his work could be so dismissable as to be lost and be silenced, but hardly compensated, by receiving £1,050 in lieu. It was another assault on his artistry which he was powerless against. More judgment and exclusion followed: in June, the RA rejected the paintings he sent for the Summer Exhibition. This gesture he did not expect. It had never happened before. It didn't recur either, for he gestured back – by never sending in again. The last pictures Adrian showed in the RA were therefore in 1984: no. 20, *Luneville Church, Normandy,* and no. 824, *Harbour Wall, Barfleur.* So ended in ignominy 35 years of exhibiting at the Academy, having begun in 1949 with his paintings of *The Skate* and *The Ray.*

An intrinsically final judgement next occurred. Between 30 July and 24 August, restrained little notes in his diary chronicle the demise of cousin Pam, the lynchpin of the Ryan family as it had once been; from feeling 'unwell' through 'Pam operation' two days later, 'Pam v. ill' and on 22 August 'Pam asleep all day'. Two days later 'Pam died' he flatly records, yet '...these rotten days' is the only reference made to his deep feelings in this period.

To say there was no allevation is omitting one instance. There was jubilation on Saturday 30 March 1985, which marked the end of The Minories show. Following a rallying lunch with ten people, including Sue and Peggy, Pam and her husband, writ large in capitals in his diary, contrasting with his almost mute handling of previously painful, professional developments is proclaimed: 'GRAND NATIONAL I WON!!' The horse he chose, ironically named and triumphing at odds seemingly inauspicious, is also given: 'Last Suspect 50–1!' Its welcome win was the agent of relief to his silent suffering of worthlessness. Indicative of which was Adrian's virtual abstinence from exhibiting for a period of nine and a half years following. That break in the pattern came not of his own making, but in spite of it, presented as a *fait accompli* with an unothodoxy of care and preparation.

It was 1994, Adrian's 75th year. The month was October. *A Kettle of Fish – A Loan Exhibition of Paintings* ran from the 7th until the 30th of the month at the National Trust's Tudor mansion, Sutton House, in London's East End, with a party on 6 October, three days after his 74th birthday. Care was invested in his party to make it tasteful, on which the success of the project depended, but in an understated way for a person who deserved it.

Sprats is a charcoal drawing which wasn't included in the show (it featured in the successor, 'A Different Kettle of Fish', at Penzance in 2002) but which existed at the outset of it. Cut down slightly from the original, what manifests is a sketch of sixteen very individual fishes (this preparatory drawing was used to make a subsequent oil painting). It makes for a curious pile. Almost all lie gill by jowl. The drawing is quick and unhesitating. All ten of Leonardo's attributes of sight are expressed: lightness and darkness, form and place, remoteness and nearness, movement and rest, substance and colour (suggested by line). The tangle of fishes – bought for Adrian from Sainsburys for little more than a pound – against the transluscent off-white paper is dramatic, and their numbers seem to vary as though they were still moving. One stands out from the crowd, the nearest one to the viewer, the remotest one to the rest and the least abstracted and tangled up. 'He was in the group and yet he wasn't' – the astuteness of Guy Roddon comes again to mind, whose remark extends metaphorically to Adrian's relationship with the St Ives movement and its eagerness to invent modernity within it. The lone charcoal fish at the bottom suddenly resembles a prop on which the aggregate rests like a bowl. It is as fundamental as much as it is also that the sketch balances the whole polemic between abstraction and figuration.

'A Kettle of Fish' at Sutton House was, as the first of a number of themed exhibitions, a bit of a capitulation because it ended up including harbour paintings, the original concept to exhibit fish paintings alone seeming too bold to bring about. There were constraints enough. No picture could be for sale. The timing could not be delayed because of the possible return of Adrian's cancer. The selection had to be representative and not repetitious, the party fun but dignified. Around 100 of 150

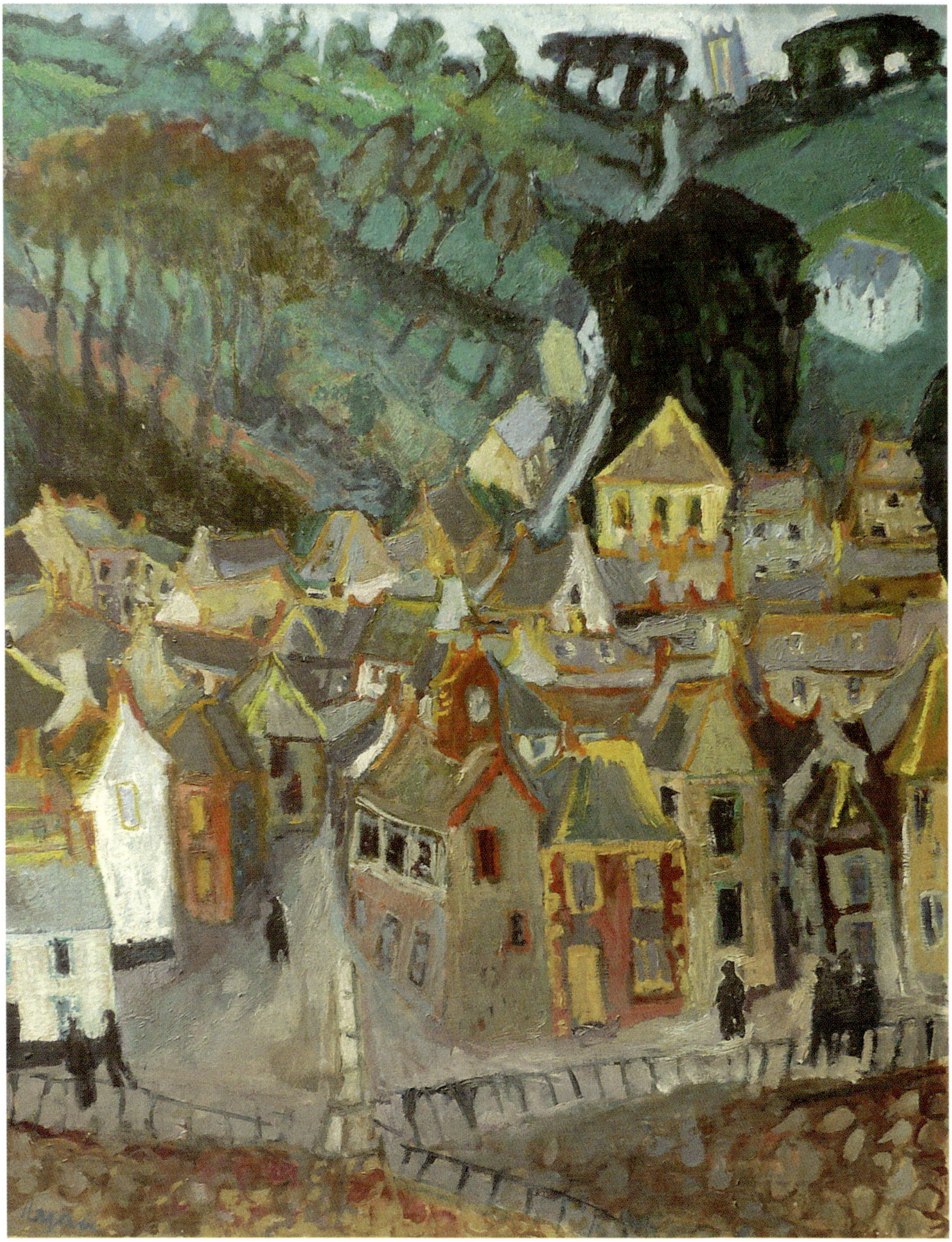

The road to Paul
oil on canvas, c. 1960

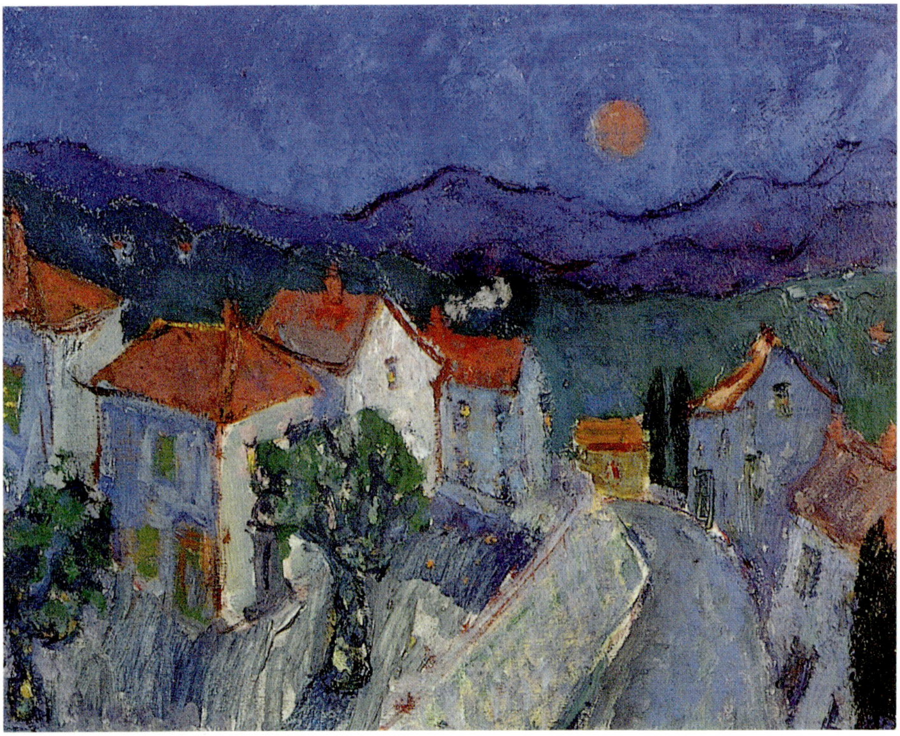

Montauroux red moon
oil on canvas, 1971

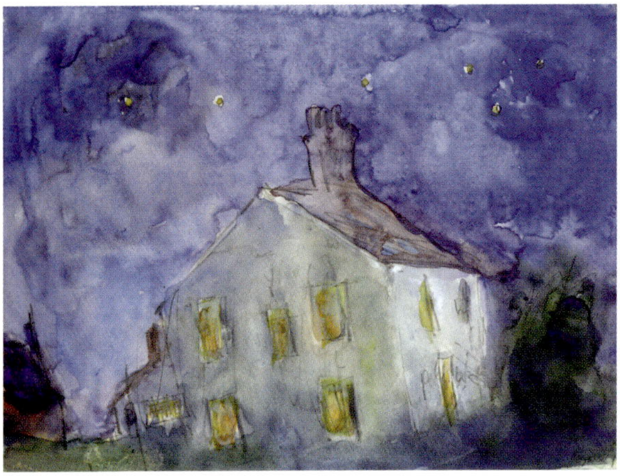

Hill House, Holbrook, under stars
watercolour, 1973

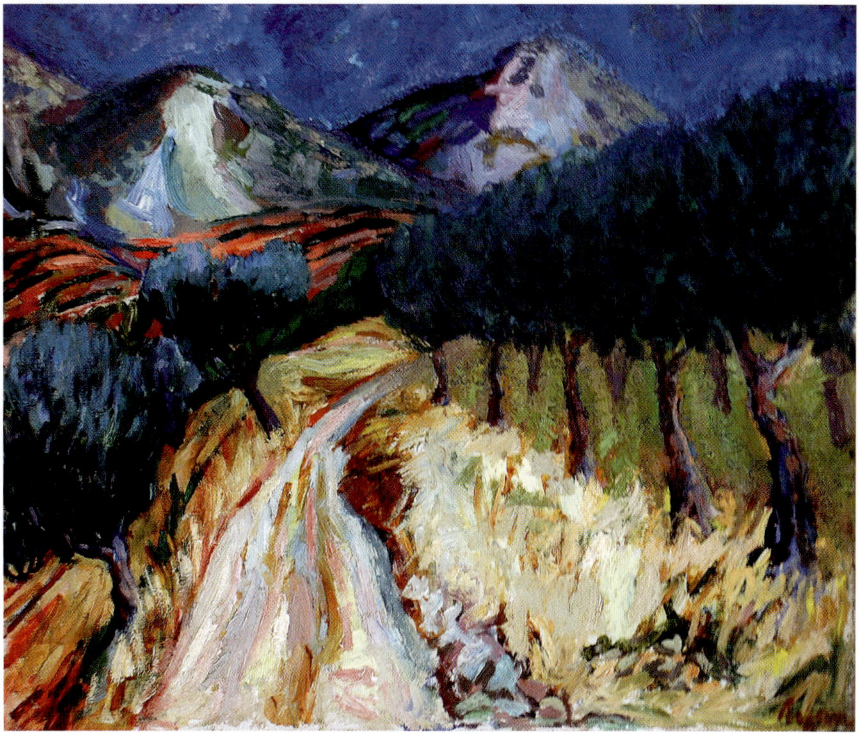

Mountains behind Toulon (Campagne Orovida)
oil on canvas, 1950

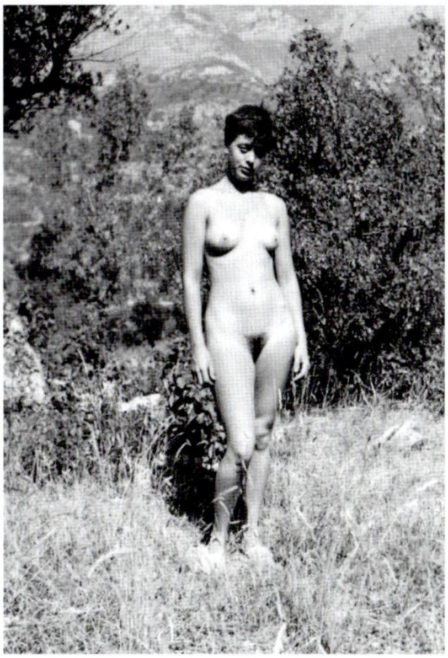

Polly Walker at Campagne Orovida, 1950 (photograph by Adrian)

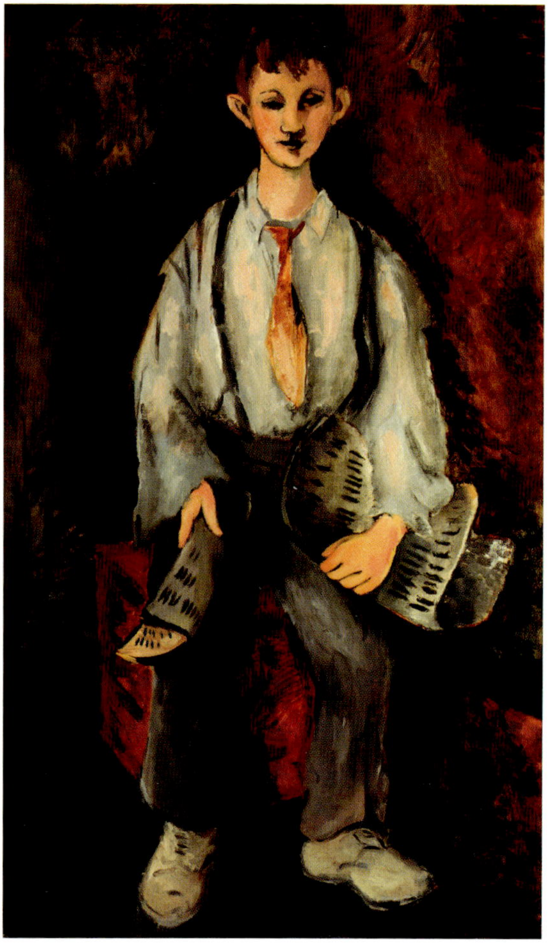

Newspaper boy
oil on canvas, 1942
courtesy of Redfern Gallery

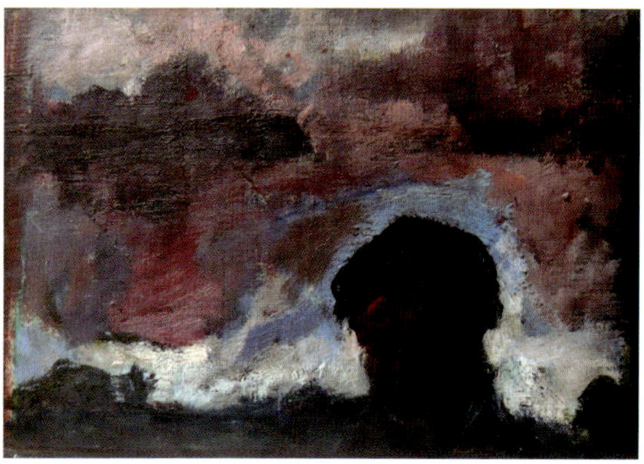

The snake in the grass [fragment]
oil on canvas, 1951

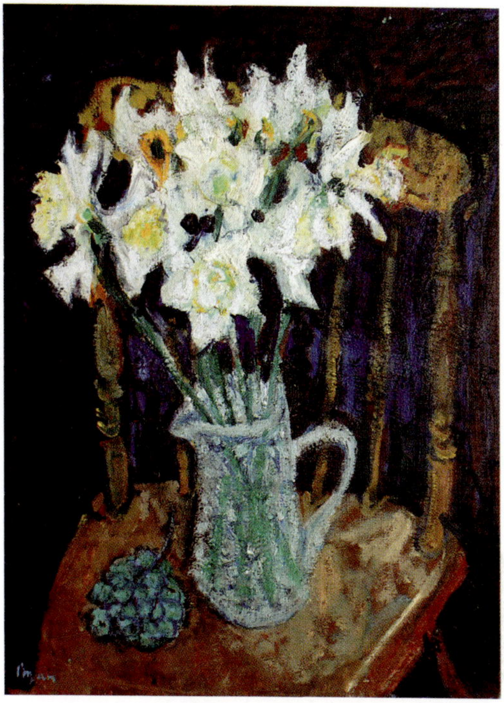

Still life of daffodils with grapes
oil on canvas, c. 1958

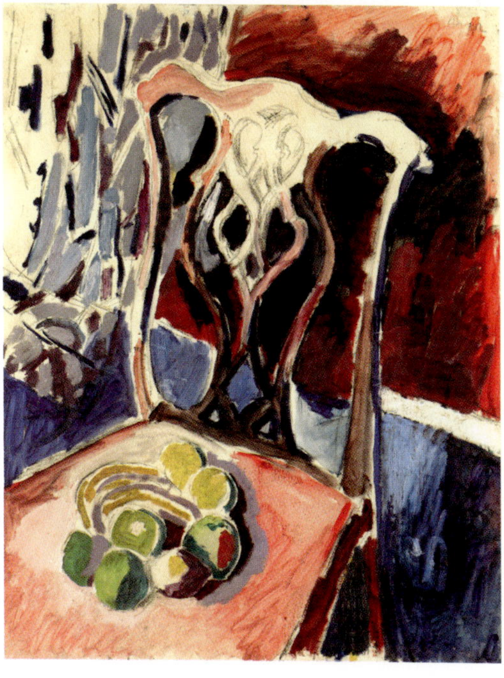

Still life with fruit on chair [unfinished]
oil on canvas, 1948

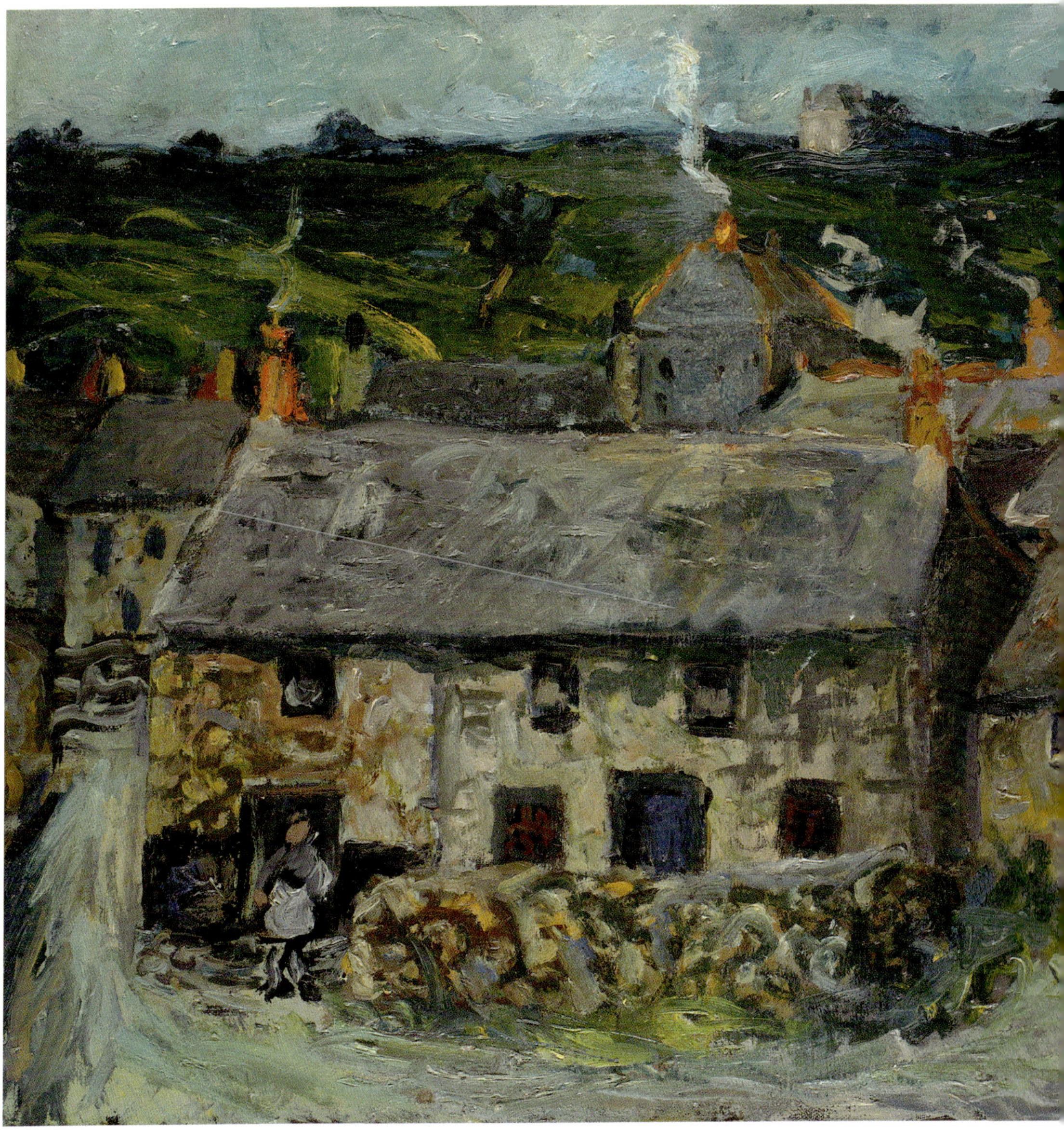

Welcome home V.J. Day
oil on canvas, 1945

courtesy of Redfern Gallery

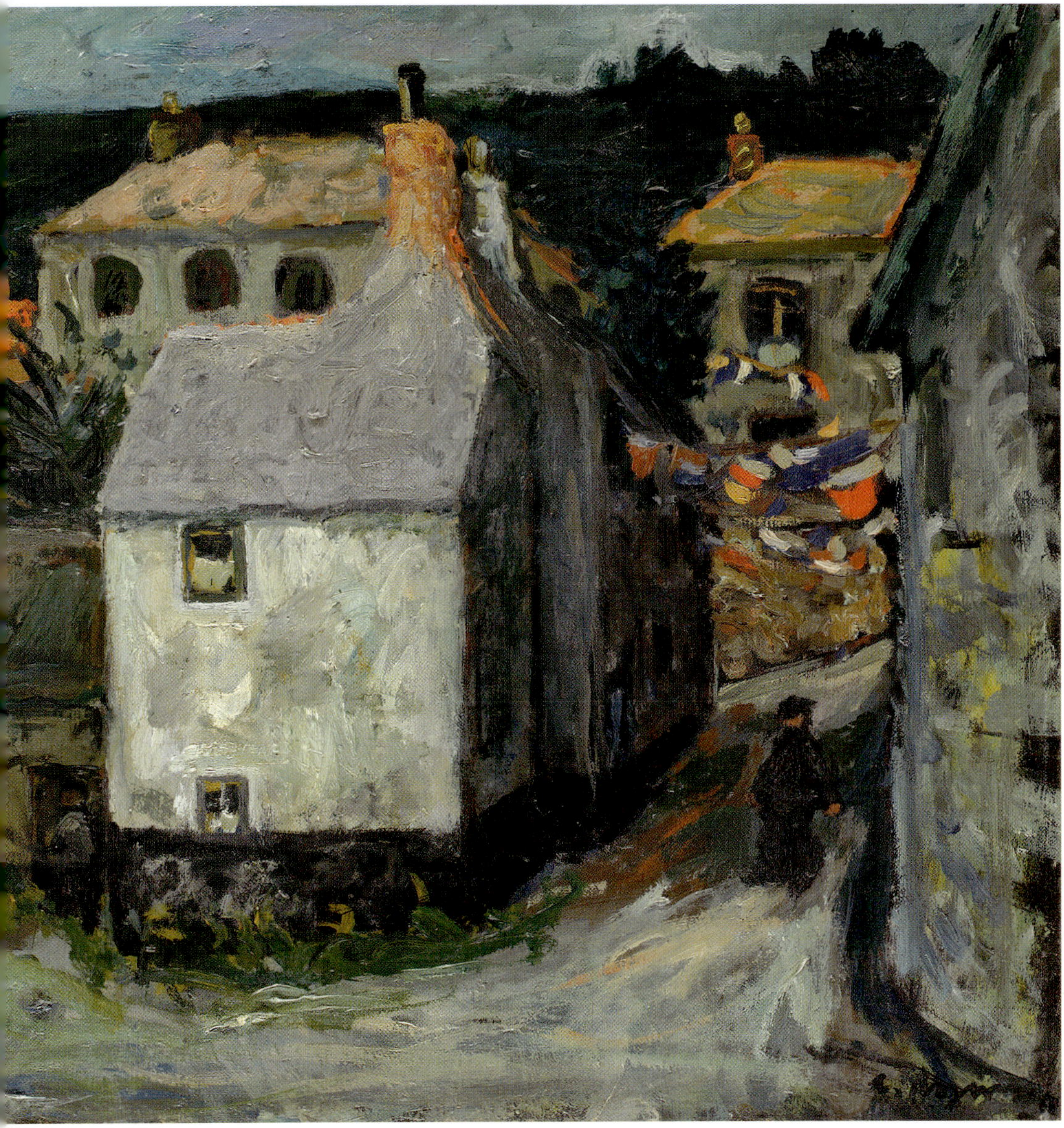

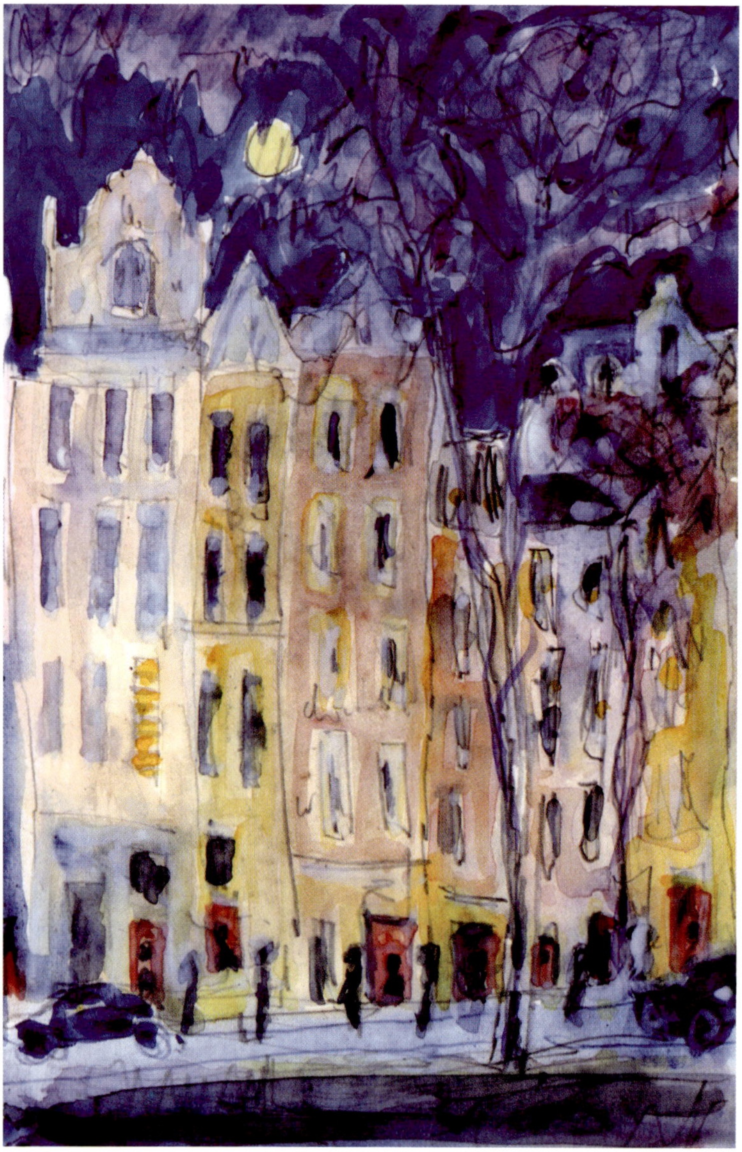

Amsterdam moon
watercolour, c. 1961

invited guests filled the gallery and spilled into the beautiful panelled rooms where a harpsichord played. The actress Prunella Scales had pre-recorded a reading – it was National Poetry Day – on a Cornish theme: *Trebetherick* by John Betjeman. There was plenty of wine. The 43 selected paintings glistened under halogen lights against new panels and ancient, distressed walls. They were insured by the Trust for a figure exceeding £80,000, a point of some gratification to Adrian. One thing beyond expectations it achieved: aided by the artist's neatly worded script, it created a niche market out of fishes previously stagnating.

> *WHY I PAINT FISH*
>
> *When times change, the landscape changes and the urban scene changes, and the fashions and appearances of people change, but fish remain the same. The same as the Romans painted at Pompeii, as the Dutch painted many centuries later, and as Courbet painted in his prison cell at Chalon later still.*
>
> *Fish lie before the artist with their sad eyes and fading colours, but in death – as in life – fish are beautiful. No two herring or whiting, however humble, are identical and each has its own character, as shown by the placing of two or more together. It is the poetry inherent in their uniqueness and agelessness that the artist hopes to portray, driven to follow along the path of his illustrious forebears. He does not have the passing clouds and the waving trees of the landscape to excite him, nor the fashionable look or posture of portrait sitters to help his composition. His painting must be simple and unadorned. He is painting the face of his own fate, from which he learns that death has a beauty of its own.*

Themed shows seeming to be the way to go, 'Four Seasons' followed a year later, from 17 to 29 October 1995, to coincide with the opening of the old kitchens at Petworth House, Sussex.

The remit was therefore pictures of food, and the title came from Adrian's suite of allegorical pictures referencing the harvests of the year. Petworth, because of its association with Turner, seemed likely to attract visitors engaged in appreciating paintings, but this did not apparently extend to the exhibitions beyond the finer rooms of the vast house. Certainly not to Adrian, who was downcast by the general response when he first visited. He did not appreciate the effort that had gone into making the exhibition, which admittedly lacked immediacy and atmosphere. He wrote on 26 October to excuse his embarrassed response: '...looking at my paintings in [my] studio is like sucking my thumb – very comforting – but seeing them exposed to an indifferent Public is like being tipped out of my pram!' He went on: 'I shall be more helpful I think over the Eton enterprise as I fancy my "architectural endeavours" (I'm sure that would sound better in French!) more than my food and drink.' Taking responsibility for the public's low-key reaction by denigrating his pictures was generous, but not called for.

'Dwelling Places' the following March did prove Eton to be a happier, more intimate venue, even though it was a selling exhibition. There was a modicum of tension because, for the first time in the College's history, it was opening its gallery for displaying anything other than its own works of art and antiquities. There was a lot of emphasis on things being by kind permission of the Provost, who only once and belatedly appeared. It was the then Vice-Provost, Tim Card, who was the front man, and the barrel-chested front he presented was sufficient to alarm Adrian. With kind sponsorship by three leading supermarkets there was an impressive amount of wine. The tension abated.

Sixty-one pictures relating to houses or cottages were on display, 31 framed around the walls, the rest mounted inside four central cabinets, or in a wall case. The majority (38) were of France. Venice, Greece and Guernsey were added to the canon. Watercolours 10" x 8" started at prices of £675. This represented much less good value than at the Redfern at that time. Oil paintings were on average double that, with the two most expensive being £3,750. It felt like some pecuniary progress was being made, although Mr Card's prognosis – 'I don't think many boys will buy anything' – turned out to have been correct.

The picture selected for the invitation and poster was *Montauroux Red Moon* – 'Sounds like a prize-winning cow,' said Adrian – measuring 14" x 18". A copper red moon glints eerily above the terracotta roof tiles of the village street. The reality is that the moon had not changed colour. During a total eclipse, when the moon is in Earth's shadow, some sunlight still passes through our atmosphere and is refracted inward towards the moon. Then it is reflected back, so during totality we experience the moon as glowing red. Colours seeming to be other than they are, is a fitting occasion for a colourist. In *Montauroux Red Moon*, the scene is palpably of night. From the Nautical Almanac Office comes the knowledge of an infrequent total eclipse of the sun, visible in the South of France, on 6 August 1971. Totality occurred at 21:43 hours local time. Adrian's diary shows that he was in France from 2–17 August that year, when he would have made his original sketch of the moon's position low over the distant mountains, with colour notes, for the oil painting to be completed later in the studio. The picture seems therefore to represent his interpretation of the event at that hour. Seven separate dwellings – Adrian's lucky number – occupy the foreground, which is deserted, as though the power of the eclipse had sent everyone inside (whereas as he once described it, many people in Montauroux were out watching) and seemingly to their beds judging from the softly lit windows. Each individual house receives the effect of moonlight or shadow differently, according to hue, value, chroma and transparency of colours expressed in every surface detail. One central wall glows stark white under the glare of moonly scrutiny. It is a searching scene, angled sharply into the future, whereas the road curves abruptly leftwards into the past as though for the moon's eyes only, eclipsed behind the principal three cottages. The painting captures a tender, emotional yearning represented by blues, contrasting with the coppery orange. Adrian was 50 years old and had experienced enough chaos to be able to know where continuing down that road would lead. Change, relinquishing that which has gone before, is after all the business of a powerful eclipse (from the Greek *ekleipsis – a forsaking*). The painting was large in its content, if not in actuality. Mostly smaller paintings followed, easier to frame, easier to sell. Enough large, early works still lay unsold in the stack in the studio. The fading presence of Gillian Mounsey during the following year left the nascent establishment of a stabler domesticity in the hands of one strong contender. It would be different in that it would be lasting. It would be the finale.

'All my best pictures,' said Adrian more than once, 'are in America.' Their conduit to getting there was Gallery 10, in Grosvenor Street, London W1, which gave him a one-man show coinciding with his 60th birthday in October 1980, and a mixed show in 1988. They also sold for him in between, but it is not recorded which pictures he meant. All that survives is an exhibition card showing a colouristic canvas 24" x 18" called *Path Through The Pine-Wood* and the diary entry mentions the gallery choosing '29 oils + 10 watercolours' but little more.

Gallery 10, run by a wealthy Greek family named Marcou, has been closed for many years.

Increased allure of America came not long after. The painter Haidee Becker effected an introduction in December 1990 between her 'Professor Pesci' and gallerist Timothy Tew from Atlanta, who gave him a show, 'Paintings and Watercolours 1948 to Present', in late October 1991. For Adrian, showing so far away mercifully signified not having to attend. Not having to frame things, which were shipped out for him, or else in the case of watercolours which were un-preciously posted by him between the pages of a National Gallery exhibition catalogue, was even more satisfactory. That the work sold was best of all; de-materialising out of sight and mind, not to be seen again except occasionally as illustrations, eventually being converted into dollars. The mixed shows that followed (1993, 1994, 1996) showed commitment and continuity. Sales were increasing on all fronts and looked set to continue. The outward pain of exhibiting was subsiding, but inwardly a debilitating cancer was advancing.

Last years

Immersed in labouring over his book *Still Life Painting Techniques* (Batsford, 1978) in late November 1976, Adrian wrote a note in his diary to go to the Camden Registry Office 'for 20th December!' On that very date, his diary amplifies: 'Wedding Bells 3.30! Party – 50 people 51 Bottles!' It was his third marriage, to Susan Curnow. The entry admits three pre-occupations of the time: social commitments (including having a burgeoning generation of grandchildren), a supply of drink and the entailment of being married again.

Regular working holidays, 'happy holiday snaps' – his euphemism for drawings done on the spot to be expanded later – and selling pictures wherever possible, were also on his list of life's vanguard. His great delight in watching sport, Laurel and Hardy and cowboy movies on television continued. He retired fully from teaching in June 1985. The years passed and were full and busy ones. By and large they were un-tumultuous. Many pictures were painted, on a scale less ambitious than before. Physically, he was changed from his youth; his hair was white and there was less of it than formerly. Haidee Becker has said that she has learned by his example (and from her other teacher Ulli Nimptsh) in these last years, how a painter who doesn't make the first grade can yet hope with dignity, while seeing a decline due to changes in taste, in the placing of their work.

Haidee correctly saw Adrian as so painfully modest in his successes, and equally that he regarded himself a failure as an artist. To her he showed great dignity in the notion. He needed courage to gainsay criticism; he didn't lack courage to keep silent about much of his pain.

He might be surprised by the renewed interest in his work since his death, and would be pleased as well as unconfounded if there were more. He might not have expectations about its lasting. He might not see himself as having a place in the shifting art firmament of tomorrow, but the last thing he or his paintings should be mistaken for is conventional, when in fact he is a velvet revolutionary. That he thought of himself as a figurative painter is true, but the abstraction in his painting is there, inbuilt for anyone to see. For which reason he saw no need to attempt to reinvent any abstract phase for himself, unlike his Cornish contemporaries. It might have served his artistic reputation better if he had, but it wouldn't have enhanced his integrity. That rests intact.

True to himself he remains, for the time being, in and yet not in the group, the last suspect in the modern movement.

Appendix

Julian Machin's journal

Note: My first meeting with Adrian Ryan took place at 10.30 am on Tuesday 12 April 1988, when I visited 8 Camden Studios, Camden Street, London NW1, and left with pictures which I took to sell on his behalf. I kept no regular journal until October 1989; thereafter I have continuously, urged to do so while in Los Angeles by Don Bachardy, who had in turn been advised to do the same by his partner Christopher Isherwood, saying 'You'll never regret it'. Adrian does not appear in the journal until December 1990. He is then mentioned with increasing frequency amounting to 118 entries, on a range of subjects and of varying lengths, until his dying time, although references do not in fact cease then.

---

16 | 5 | 1991

Yesterday had lunch with Adrian, intending to collect the two pictures I'd 'commissioned' from him – a still life of cherries, which came out as grapes, and another of playing cards which, in four variants, additionally featured dice, dominoes and a glass of white wine! The grapes are beautiful. They took him half an hour to do. I was impressed. It is a real gift… yet he does not realise. Yet his pleasure at my pleasure is evident. …Tho' we'd promised Sue not to over-indulge due to their packing for going to Paris today, we did in fact get rather pissed. But I felt in control; he looked to be in control, and we said our fond goodbyes and I came away happy as anything.

Today I went with grapes to the framer to have a linen mount, mushroom with gold bevel, made to fit. I hope it will be pale enough.

---

18 | 5 | 91

As a result of seeing Adrian a few days ago, a thought comes to me: the 2 frames I asked him to fill with pictures were such a pleasure to him... and that day he also mentioned that the 2 splendid frames he used for the Eton catalogue were given him by Haidee Becker. So he did the lovely picture on the cover to fill one of these. This is the answer; this makes him work... and gives him a purpose which may also result in him using his thinking processes more eg worrying about which cherries or grapes, buying the ones he wanted (and no more, he spent just a few pence on my grapes, even broke them off a pre-priced bunch... even the trip to Tesco is part of the work). It's the whole process that he enjoys and it helps make the painting exercise worthwhile. This strikes me as quite a discovery! We are getting closer all the time he & I.

---

27 | 6 | 91

Yesterday Adrian and I had a long lunch – a nice talk, maybe tinged with a little sadness as he mentioned dying and Viv. But he laughed wonderfully too and regaled me with a story about the nightclub in the snow [in Mousehole], Joan Gillchrest and Guy's terrifying wife – and in that little drunken piping voice of his: 'Don't be disrespectable towards your betters!' And 'What's that word, not Mephistopheles?' – 'Metaphysical?' I offered. 'That's it!' in triumph. But what was he describing anyway? Francis Bacon, I believe... using the unprimed reverse side of the canvas.

---

11 | 9 | 91

Lunch yesterday with Adrian (we began at 12.30 and drank till 8pm) and he opened with: 'Do you know who's died?' I didn't. It turned out to be Eardley Knollys who had, and the news made me sad, for I was fond of him... but we drank his health repeatedly and thus thought of him as going cheerfully on his way. But I ask myself what happens when Adrian dies? Where will I be without our lunches, without his companionship?

Meanwhile met Adrian, Guy [Roddon], Sue and Max Chapman tonight at the memorial show for Zdislav Ruskowski, who died in February. When he came in [to the Gillian Jason Gallery] he went wandering straight away through the passage to the next room, as distractedly as Lord Emsworth... and moved like a boat drifting in a gentle current. What did he say yesterday? – 'It's amazing what little one's parents know…'

---

3 | 10 | 91

Today is Adrian's birthday. And I went middayish to Camden, with an original copy of Sven's Wallis book and bottle of Graves Superieur (his favourite grape). He showed me a photo of Seagulls Cottage – so unlike his pictures of it, which are infinitely preferable – 'That's the point!'

I bought a picture of boules players, Montauroux. It's very spare, but the colours are beautiful and I think it will frame superbly.

---

25 | 10 | 91

Yesterday visited Adrian in his Suffolk gingerbread house [Hill House, Holbrook] – my first visit – arriving before 1 o'clock, some 45 minutes late, but not bad for me. He seemed pleased to show me round what turned out to be a four-up, four-down, with a central connecting section, so you can walk all the way around the downstairs – 'Children love it'. But he has to leave there by Sept 30th next year and is clearly very sad about it. Clearly he would have liked to see himself expiring peacefully there, one day but not yet, and I hear him saying as much to Joyce the charlady, whom he entertains… for an hour when I am upstairs looking through watercolours. He is aware death may touch him on the shoulder at any time: 'I ring Sue at 7.30 every morning, and she rings me at 5.00, just to make sure.'

His Pascin etchings line the living room and adjacent dining room. Some of his nudes, inc. one of Harry Thrubron, are in the passage. Upstairs his watercolours are along the landing and elsewhere. And books everywhere. 'I can't play my gramophone, because I can't get to it' for books take precedence. And he reads aloud to me from the Modigliani book, and from… a book on Matisse by Gertrude Stein…and finally from Sven's book on Wallis – 'It really is very good, except at times you have to remember that it is Sven…' and he reads a bit which he thinks Gertrude Stein would have loved to have written.

The space he works in is divided up as follows: downstairs at the back (next to larder) is for oils; painted standing up, at an easel – there is a crazy Venice scene in progress…all the boats that ever pass up the Grand Canal – surrounded by odd frames, tubes and general clutter… there wasn't really anywhere to put your feet.

Upstairs – watercolours in a little bedroom. A single bed is repository for works in varying stages of progression, a little table at the window is where the action takes place. Piles everywhere else, pictures of all descriptions, including two ancient oils, still lifes, that I tell him he's to reserve for me until such time as he should be willing to part with them.

Separate rooms for separate activities, but each one is minute, cramped, dark, cold, and you would think awkward. Thos. Hardy... with 2nd wife... has his image prominently displayed.

He showed me his picture of Sven's tower [in St Ives, since pulled down] – 'Have I shown you this?' and I replied that the lobster pot had disappeared since the 1st time I saw it. 'Well, you didn't like the lobster pot,' he responded, 'That's how much I listen to what you say.' Actually I only asked what it was... a query as to its nature...

I have first sighting of his erotica/porno etchings which are beautiful, very sensitive and subtle. Some of the rudest are good for titillating anyone, gay, straight, bi or anything else. Rather autobiographical (eg Sue hangs in the passage) it's funny when he makes a comment like: 'He seems to have missed his mark there' to which I reply 'But I think he'll find it in the end,' which is... a way of describing Adrian... in overall art history terms.

---

13 | 11 | 91

Post lunch with A.R. from 1pm to nearly 6.00. 'In the candlelight of old age...' he quoted Walt Whitman [before] we brought up Scott Fitzgerald...

He read me Sven's letter replying to his own re: the Wallis book – my gift. Sven calls me a 'smear' or something... intended as a compliment – I can't recall how.

Adrian had gone earlier to the Lautrec; 'It takes you down a peg or two,' he said sorrowfully, 'When you see his draughtsmanship, it's depressing to think of your own. But you can pick up a thing here and there. For instance, I noticed that when he draws a female figure he does an outline in red; over that he puts blue so he gets the warmth of the flesh and the moulding of the form where it turns the corner. You're going to notice a transformation in my things from now on, only <u>I'll</u> do it red for flesh over blue...'

We had... fun and laughter... including on religion inspired by some fellow lunch guest on Sunday who had said to him:

'Our prayers help; think how much worse it would be without them!'
AR: 'Worse than Hitler?'

And, AR: 'I get depressed just looking around at all my books, thinking I've read them all and in spite of it, don't seem to have picked up anything, not even to make a jot of difference to what I paint.'
Guest: 'Think how you would have painted without our prayers!'
AR: 'That's certainly taking an optimistic view.'

[He also told me]
'I've got plans for your frame, many and great plans! All in my head of course, for a tabletop with knobbly legs and <u>anything</u> might be on it… Infinite! So, with the help of the good Lord, I'll do something stupendous by the time I see you again – only somehow I don't think He listens…'

---

11 | 2 | 94

Adrian… has been painting exquisitely again, only 6 weeks after major surgery. He doesn't know he's painting so well, but the fish and the mushrooms which I took away are both delightful…

Also the grapes which I left for adjustment. No one would do… what I ask of him, so graciously, arduously or so modestly. Each of us knows this, tho' he maintains that he just likes being told what to do. His humour is back, too, as when we are about to say goodbye: 'I don't know that I want to kiss that,' he says of my goatee, and as he does so he gives a little squeal and skip.

We looked at the Soutine catalogue & I marvelled at the volume of work – unknown to me – as he had done, and we exchanged views. Yet Soutine and Adrian have painted so similarly – it is uncanny. And it was something to reflect that in Cagnes, the two of them were there at the same time; Adrian as a little boy, Soutine as a man of 35.

---

24 | 3 | 94

Lunch with Adrian. We sat out in the spring sunshine till the chill of the wind sent us inside, but he'd enjoyed those few minutes and I could see peace shown in his face reflected in the plate glass window, so I hadn't to look directly at such a terminal scene. His eyes were closed as we savoured the sun, which tasted of summers past and pleased and vexed him for that same reason. Still, he is painting more and that must be good… a racehorse that does not know how to give up. The watercolour of Harkstead Church, done last month, is surreal and pleasant. The broad strand of green in the foreground is unnaturally bold and effective. 'That's because there were ducks and geese there originally,' he explained, 'And if there is one thing I cannot paint it is ducks and geese.'

---

28 | 4 | 94

Adrian is prancing like a young horse in a meadow, eyes bright and sparkling, full of Wodehouse-like humour from the moment the door is opened.

'My dictum is: if you don't know much, don't say much.' He adds: 'I thought it up this morning.' Then he shows me 2 pictures of boats which he feels may be 'Perfection' and which I then manage to fault… a line of green along the side in each is too much one colour. They will be perfect after this is corrected.

---

6 | 5 | 94

Adrian was funny yesterday about his figures in the paintings of boats which I took away. On the back of one I have written in pencil his remark 'I can't tell you how many times they went in and out, trying to get them to look casual – I'm not Goya.'

---

11 | 11 | 94

On Tuesday we went to Haidee's private view where Adrian was charming under the influence of white wine and a woman client of mine who winked at him and said it was 'an honour' to meet him. Afterwards we strolled down Regent St where we were struck by the sight of two business men in near identical Burberrys. He turned round to gaze: 'Do you see that?' he exclaimed, 'They're identical. I couldn't paint that.' I pointed out that a line in the material crossed the back differently and that the shoulder straps were different. 'Oh well, then maybe I could,' he beamed, suddenly with hope.

---

27 | 1 | 95

Adrian was funny when I described meeting one of Pam's friends at the art fair as fifty-five-ish, probably used to come round on Sunday after the shoot – after a pause – 'There's something rather attractive about comfortably-off women of that age,' he said.

On Leonardo's 10 attributes of sight: 'Nearness and farness…' – pause – 'It's so difficult to remember all the attributes, but they're in my book, described in an apple' – he draws an apple quickly – 'If you look at a Pat Heron you've got about 4 of them. OK for a scarf, but...'

---

18 | 7 | 95 I told Adrian about Alan Hollinghurst wittingly or unwittingly pinching an original line from Hardy ('The unseen waters' ejaculations awe me') that I'd spotted in The Line of Beauty. 'Everybody does it... tho' it should have been more changed... and homage paid. Painters are at it all the time. I swipe everything,' he added, 'You can smell it. There's a smell about some of my pictures of someone else's work. Though every now and then I come up with something of my own. So you could say: 'Ohh Jim! That's you!' I don't know why, or <u>how</u> it happens, but occasionally it does.'

---

10 | 9 | 98 Adrian worries me. There is little to keep his spirit around for much longer. It's had so much in this incarnation. His eyes are bright still. They are the signature of his spirit. Looking at the blood transfusing into him from the reservoir [while in hospital] I wondered aloud who it might have come from. 'Well, the last lot was definitely an athlete's,' he replied.

---

15 | 9 | 98 Adrian was funny in hospital today, about the quote he was asked for – for Tim Tew – in conjunction with a large ink copy of his signature: 'I've done any amount of them – none of them looks like mine.' Then the quote 'in quotation marks!' he stressed: "Americans buy paintings for love not profits. God bless them – Adrian Ryan," he repeated. 'Who wrote that?' I asked. 'Adrian Ryan!' he replied, 'It's a slap on the back but they'll love it.'

---

18 | 9 | 98 Adrian. Cancer back and an ulcer. As he said, he's had 5 years since the last cancer. If he's allowed, he says, he'll go for no. 1 option of doing nothing but taking painkillers. No chemo, no op.

---

10 | 10 | 98 Yesterday lunch with Adrian. Some discussion over his will and his reluctance to decide. How I empathise. I told him what Reina James had said about him being a 'very, very, very, very, very intelligent man.' Immediately: 'She said that about <u>me</u> when I've spent my life being such a fool!'

28 | 10 | 98 Adrian: 'I'm bowing gracefully out,' said with much humour and as it was pointed out to me by someone with greater experience of patients dying, with much bravery.

---

13 | 11 | 98 Adrian: as ill as I have seen him, but still humorous and being brave. He was painting my portrait, but it looked like him, as Sue also remarked. The part where 'At last, I've got to a button' – a charcoal button he subsequently lost to paint – revealing 'Francis Bacon's secrets', and referring to recent portraits of me in LA by Don Bachardy he said: 'No doubt he had the impudence to paint you as you are...' Yes he is a very intelligent man and I was all too aware of how much he triumphed over physical pain as he drew.

---

11 | 12 | 98 Adrian today painting a little more of my portrait, just so he could say he'd done a little work and was still 'useful'. I almost thought I heard the beginnings of his death rattle, but perhaps I'm mistaken. I don't know what else to write about him other than that he was his usual correct self, thanking me for visiting, and that we had a good time before I popped him into bed as usual, waited downstairs till after he had fallen asleep, and left.

---

15 | 12 | 98 East Dulwich, evening

What I did, I did because I could. In response to Sue's telephone call, by train I made haste slowly to Adrian's deathbed, perceiving that I would get there in time because my presence was welcomed. I walked the last few streets under a soft December rain, remembering the first time that I found my way there to the studio, over ten years ago. Much of the good times we have enjoyed together fused with the rain and collected into one pool.

'This is it', said Sue, as she opened the door.

I went upstairs to see him. Death rattled upon his throat. I felt there was so little time and took his right hand gently. I communicated some important things: how much he'd helped me, taught me, how special he was, his love, ours, how I wished I'd done more, who would be there to greet him – Jack [Low], B.G., his Dad, Asgeir – and I stroked either his back or his hand with a soft, clockwise motion to help his spirit leave. Twice in that hour he removed his hand, twice I found my hand again. Once as he turned over to his right side, just before dying, he flashed me a look which I can only try to interpret. Just before the end, I had the nurse call Sue and together we experienced his spirit passing. The process was beautiful, almost more beautiful than anything I have seen.

The nurse asked me to help lay him out. We restored his demeanour, smoothing his hair, folding his beautiful hands and fingers, to make him ready for the family.

I remember the way he turned onto his side for comfort, how this stilled immediately the impertinent rattle of death, calmed his breathing and slowed his generous heart till the hand of his soul finally stilled it, like it was the pendulum of a clock. And now life is to go on with diminished fear and some strange enrichment.

The last thing he painted, last Friday, was me – a portrait that more resembled him than me – and which sits there on his easel and on my mind now as I go to make my own way upstairs to rest.

Adrian James Ryan died 15 December 1998 at 12.25pm at 8 Camden Studios, Camden Street, London NW1. His obituary in The Times *appeared immediately (16 December) followed by obits in other newspapers calling him 'The painter Art forgot'. He was cremated and his ashes were later scattered at Holbrook Creek.*

Letters from Adrian

There are 115 extant letters written by Adrian Ryan to Julian Machin. The last letter to arrive did so somewhat startlingly, reaching J.M. only in September 2000, at the time of the first posthumous Ryan exhibition at the Redfern Gallery, having been sent to his old address in California. It had been written and posted over eight years previously and was received almost two years after Adrian had died. It is the final one to be reproduced in the selection which follows:

---

15 | 3 | 88

8 CAMDEN STUDIOS CAMDEN STREET NW1 0LG | 387 8872

Dear Julian Machin

Thank you for your letter – Perhaps you could ring me sometime. I am however not v. often in London. My country address is Hill House, Holbrook, nr. Ipswich – Suffolk – Tel 0473 327 132 let me know what you have in mind & the sizes dates prices etc. Meanwhile I am interested to hear you have a painting of a Cornish fisherman dated 1943! That must be one of my earliest west country pictures. Can you give me any details? Where did you find it? etc! I can't remember it tho' I know I was staying at Constantine Bay in Aug 43 – near Padstow.

With best wishes yrs sincerely
Adrian Ryan

9 | 5 | 89 8 CAMDEN STUDIOS

Dear Julian

Hope all is well etc. Any cheque yet from Sotheby's –? would be welcome!

Meanwhile have a few golden oldies we could flog perhaps. An ancient mistress put an equally ancient flower picture of mine into LAYS auction room in PZ & reaped £800 – should keep her in her midday brandy & dry ginger for a while. I have several dozen more of the same – what can we do about it? My friend John Bellany goes from hundreds to thousands... when should I flog his mammoth canvas & get my daughters off my back? I am in your hands.

Sue & I are off to Pembrokeshire June 24–July 8 but am here or in Suffolk till then.

More querky news. My darling american cousin Jenny Ryan (now Newall...) rang to tell me a friend of hers bought many pics at Christies S. Ken. including a cornish Harbour[1] by Adrian Ryan dedicated to Sven Berlin with love & kisses & who were those old queers etc? I hope she put the record straight not that I'm fussy but Sven was an Apache Dancer...!

My half brother turned up with a trunk load of nostalgia that had been to Mexico & back in the fifties with his mother, recently deceased, & never unpacked. My father bless him had bought some ghastly paintings from me – thank God no one has seen them since!

We saw the Gauguin in Paris. Silly old Pat Heron thinks he wasn't much good. But he couldn't half draw!

Love Adrian

1. April 1946

---

3 | 4 | 90 HILL HOUSE

Dear Julian

Many thanks for yr letter & cheque towards the Parisien expenses – were we lucky! 4 days of sunshine & picnics in the Luxembourg & Tuilleries. You should expect a great improvement in my work after the hours we spent in the

Marmottan (a new collection added of impressionists) the Louvre 'management' inspected the bookshop & vast improvements (again) expected shortly when the Sainsbury wing (not a food store which disappointed one of Sue's customers!) opens at the Nat Gal. Complaints pour in regularly about the lack of Till Girls. We at last visited the Picasso gallery (closed for Madam Gobokov[2] & a strike previously). Beautifully restored building & wonderfully laid out exhibition. Pity such a talented artist was such a poor painter.

What was the Belgravia asking for my little (?) Cornish scene? The Marcous don't give up! Look forward to seeing you again – love Adrian

2. Gorbachev

---

4 | 10 | 90 8 CAMDEN STUDIOS

My dear Julian

Here among the endless seeming dirty glasses I write at once to thank you for yr magnificent presents. Will you kindly let me know the date of yr next birthday!! I have just received yet another present – a tape of Telemann Recorder Sonatas Der Getreue Music Meister & Essercizii Musici!

I don't think its puffing & popping is doing much good for my head. Sue I'm glad to say kept her head till all had gone then she tended to fall about. I found it difficult to have more than a few words with some guests & too many with some others but at least I did have some time with you & I thank you very much indeed! Embarrassingly I've discovered a bottle of whisky & no idea who brought it along! Your delicious Bottle of Margaux is safe & will remain so til an auspicious (?) moment!

See you when we get back from Wales (Sunday evening Oct 14) Then my up & down life recommences.

With much love Adrian

---

27 | 3 | 91 HILL HOUSE

My dear Julian

What a magical person you are! And who can they be that buy pictures these days?! Very many thanks for your letter

& handsome cheque. Will look forward to seeing you again. Hope you could help Guy at all… ?

We spent the weekend in Haarlem & Amsterdam – glorious weather – smooth crossings from Harwich – lovely paintings in the Frans Hals, Rijksmuseum & V. Gogh… Drank & ate too much. The Dutch are worse that the Yorkshiremen!

Popping up to London on Tuesday for Eardley's opening at the Parkin. See you there? My collage comes up at Sotheby's today – No 194 – if you feel like finding out how much it didn't go for.

Happy Easter & very many thanks again
love Adrian

---

24 | 4 | 91 8 CAMDEN STUDIOS

My dear Julian

Very many thanks for the three handsome cheques. I made a somewhat tipsy list of things you took – but not of the cafe scenes. Prices I leave to you. Will fill yr two frames next week! You forgot to take yr goodies with you but Fatso will do them justice.

love Adrian

---

4 | 9 | 91 HILL HOUSE

My dear Julian

Many thanks for yr letter. Glad you enjoyed meeting Max. I am coming up to London on Monday & would really like to see you Tuesday (12 ish) if possible – Reasons:– Nicola Shane from CAS is coming at 10 am on Tuesday – & Terry Burgess – who does my framing – is coming to take away her choices at 7.30 that evening. I would like you to see what she has chosen but if it's not convenient for you – Wednesday at 1.0 would be quite OK. I must get to the Constable again Wed am but if I go at 10 I'll be back in time.

Sue has been on holiday here for a week & we went to Dedham & walked to Flatford & back along the Tow Path. On Friday we went to Felixtowe & pic-nicked on the beach as I used to as a child. But when we got back someone had broken in & stolen Sue's Handbag – with everything in it (except the baby). The local bobby stayed an hour, told us his life story & drank prodigiously. See you.

let me know please! Love Adrian

Forgive me for forgetting – How is your mother?

---

2 | 11 | 91 HILL HOUSE

My dear Julian

V. many thanks for your letter – & the news of the CAS – and your PR work as they call it… The Welsh water-colour must be almost unique – being the earliest I did – & the others mostly burnt in my brother's housefire. Of that date I mean – there are thousands of later ones getting on my nerves.

Haidee Becker phoned Tim Tew who told her my ex. was 'a great success' – 5 or 6 sold. Funny use of the word!

Richard Cobbold called & walked off with 5 water-colours – cunning bugger brought his wine list with him – offering a crate of champagne for the little early apples – ! I refused – but accepted a case of claret for a minute pastel – & bargained with the pauper for the other 4 – with reasonable outcome.

I will bring the Sven up on the 11th or 12th when I aim to break the Holbrook – London speed record – 1 hr 35 mins last week – Bit dicey. Please photo the pic in Toto – or situ – the framing is Sven!

I've written to tell him of yr great generosity – ie the gift of his remarkable book – which I dearly love. The purple passages are beyond belief, but the story is well told – & I bet it's never been bettered.

Have just read DH Lawrence on Cezanne. Makes one think – I hope you didn't expect the leaves of grass was a travel book – Sue did – Good luck in the U.S.

lots of love
Adrian

14 | 11 | 91 HILL HOUSE

My dear Julian

V. many thanks for the cheque for the fish & for the lovely bottle of wine.

Sue accused me of being stupid again & sent me to bed early – I missed a good boxing match The Times tells me! But I had a pleasant surprise when I got here (just outside the record – works – 'sorry for the delay') – a cheque from Atlanta for 5 oils & 8 water-colours. Viv can rest in peace & plenty.

Also a letter from my darling Jane Perrin (93) who sold 2 water-colours but can't remember what I wanted for them! If you go to Connecticut you have got to call on her... She also still has 'a small showroom'... She was a great friend of the greats including Pierre Matisse & Chagall etc But mainly she's just a nice dame.

Am here all next week & hope to start on yr large frame picture.

No wine yet from the destitute.
lots of love
Adrian

---

19 | 11 | 91 HILL HOUSE

My dear Julian

I thought you'd like to know that the 'oil painting of Welsh Mountains' – (highly charged) is in fact a water-colour – probably with some body colour – of 'Mountains behind Toulon' – painted in the summer of 1950 when Bernard Hailstone & I stayed in Orovida PISSARRO's old farmhouse in Provence.

The Redfern exhibition – April 3–28 1951 was a great Flop – only three oils out of 38 sold (one to Eardley – 'Trout') & a few watercolours. Yours was the most expensive at 16 gns (of water-colours that is – E.K. paid 35 gns for his oil!) A grand Vodka party was attended by over a 100 guests (Evening Standard) among whom I read were Mrs Randolph Churchill, Sir Ed. Marsh & H.E. Bates – 'Twas still a flop!

I have just received a mammoth missive (or missile) from Sven, including an illustrated Poem – & a long letter with a coloured sketch of one of the 4 – 4 foot – oils of 'Lovers'... I can't describe them. They are v. Sven. He writes that Irving Grose is giving him an 80th year exhibition which will include them – 'There will be a few Cornish drawings' – but he is fed up with dealers insisting on giving 'the kiss of life to a dying prostitute.' I am finding it difficult to write an adequate reply.

Have a lovely time in America & be a good boy.
lots of love
Adrian

---

26 | 6 | 92 HILL HOUSE

My dear Julian

Many thanks for your thank you letter. Herewith mine. Your cash very welcome as Sue insisted I buy an etching by my friend Eric Brown! Numerous distinguished Goldsmithians added to my embarrassment but there was plenty of wine...

In the excitement of yr visit & sale of forgotten picture etc I omitted to ask how you were doing with the Historical Motor Racing number – or whether the paper still life had fitted the vast frame. I've done you another-sized-paper-pic of some kind of lily in a chinese pot. Masterly (just measured – 30 x 22 too BIG...A Nightmare!)

Rosie may have to wait while I hurl myself at Normandy. Am up fleetingly on Tuesday for the Execution bash at the Nattie Gal – & on Wednesday my annual vist to Jack Low in Kent. 89 years old has asked for a miniature bottle of cherry brandy. She and her dove don't drink much.

May I wish you luck with furniture sales as Sue has received a bill from the cupboard carpenter for £1,093 and says I can pay.

Beautiful weather & the garden's a jungle. Pretty twelve year old called to help but wouldn't bend over and use the shears – insisted on a thing called a stripper which sounded like an old Dentist drill – and not at all what you think.

lots of love
Adrian

3 | 7 | 92 HILL HOUSE

My dear Julian

Just a line to say I've had a letter from Sven enclosing a catalogue of the Bristol Ex. Artists in Cornwall etc which included his Albatross & was upset you & I weren't there etc. Didn't know it was <u>on</u>, & no one asked me to show in it!

However, reason for quick note is:– There's an Adv in the catalogue for Sotheby's 'this years sale of postwar & con Brit art in the autumn under heading St Ives Artists at Sothebys etc Do you think we should put one of mine in? & which one & of what kind? etc Apply Susannah Pollen etc?

Hope all well, love to Rosie. Love Adrian

Just received an invitation of some grandeur for Guy's Exhibition at Messums – I expect you got bowled over too. I don't think I'll be up for it – Am tres fatigue & workmen are in the studio in the kitchen in the shower but not I hope in the Lady's bedchamber. love A.

---

2 | 9 | 92 8 CAMDEN STUDIOS[3]

My dear Julian

Many thanks for yr two v. generous cheques & all yr help.

Dear Julian, you <u>must</u> stop me talking about my family & the past. The Memorabilia should be buried! & I have 25 Albums in Suffolk too! From now on I shall be like old Thomas Hardy & 'resolve to say no more... what I know I will not tell'... What shall we do about Lisa & her collages? Sleep on them?

With love Adrian
Nothing for naughty Rosie

3. Sent on a card with image of H. Bosch's, *Christ Mocked*

---

6 | 11 | 92 8 CAMDEN STUDIOS

My dear Julian

Welcome home! Many thanks for your postcard from S.F. So glad to hear you were enjoying life. You will have had the

American Election excitement – but have missed our own fun in the House of Commons, if I may say so – only the Liberals stuck to their principles – hence they never get elected.

Corsica was lovely but the weather dodgy – nevertheless Sue swam & I drew & drank. I am very busy now on too many water-colours & not enough oils (they get harder & harder!) but am pursuing my 'Post-Abstract' art with a fair amount of gusto.

My brother from Vancouver has hit town, after staying with Scarlett & then with Geraldine – luckily he books into his suite in Dolphin Square so cannot afford very often the bus fare to visit us. Best to meet half way at Trafalgar Square! Looking forward v. much to seeing you & hearing 'all abhout it.'

Love Adrian

P.S Enclosed!

Sue is having lunch with David Machin who wants to to know who was yr grandfather & great grandfather? Apparently one (or both) had 8 sons – some family! People keep sending him my Montauroux greetings card & asking Who is Julian? !!

---

25 | 1 | 94 8 CAMDEN STUDIOS

Dear Onlie Begetter

Thank you for your letter re fish. I have painted two lots of sardines but I don't think any pretty swam in. I am constantly reminded of the words of that old rogue P. Picasso 'the walls of our museums are hung with our mistakes' – not mine – yet – but with your help it shouldn't be long now.

Am painting her Lordship on Tuesday.

Sven's book is 'Launched' at the Book Gallery St Ives on June 18th & with an exhibition. The Artist will be there to sign copies. Pray for him.

love to Rosie
Adrian

29 | 4 | 94 8 CAMDEN STUDIOS

My dear Julian

A thank you letter for the vast cheque – and also for yr sensible criticism of my french boats – which has led to massive re-painting along with verbal abuse.

Sue was amazed (and grateful for) at yr vast consumption of bread + cheese.

May allah be with you
love Adrian

---

8 | 9 | 94 8 CAMDEN STUDIOS

My dear Julian

5.30 pm, am now on vodka (Wodka WYBOROWA). I don't know how to express my thanks (?) for what you have done, or for what you are, or will be, doing, for moi. But thank you very much I do. Also for the unexpected (as usual) cheque – also I didn't expect such an early departure from the easel as [for] the (V.J.D) 'Welcome home' – you may find the green fields will sink & a little varnish may be necessary later on. I don't know if the paintings you took were signed...

I shall have fun (I suppose) making out a list of names. * = come to the party. A figure (2) or (3) (maybe) = could the recipient have a couple of whatnots please–: Tim Tew for instance might like more than one to show his clients (?) – You can see I'm bracket mad – must add a line after Sue gets in – any moment now – what my yachting friend calls 'What Fun!' I'll tell all in the morning.

Friday AM. Didn't fool Sue for long that you hadn't told me. Now – after a restless night Grave doubts & neuroses setting in! How many pictures are you putting before so many people? And the fish painting Sue & I like best is here, (14 x 21 framed (ugh)) hanging over the canvases where you dived – Perhaps you don't like it? Sue suggests she leaves it in her office & you can pick it up anytime (if you'd like to) after yr holiday*

[Drawing of Whiting & shrimps appears on the sheet here]
'Whiting & shrimps' – Sue says you don't know what fish are

called – like Eric calling a daffodil a crocus. I told her she and Geraldine were cowards – she said you were worse. Can't trust anyone can you!

*I hope you get to Rhodes and have a relaxation. Seems after all this activity you need it. I gather this whole subterfuge has been going on for 4 or 5 months. Can't believe all those people Sue told haven't let on – especially the women involved! Forgive me if now I have the 'ze backlash' of Funk.

lots of love
Adrian

---

8 | 10 | 94 8 CAMDEN STUDIOS

My dear Julian

to you must go the first of my many thank you letters – even before the Hodges with their Chocolate 1kg Bar – Here goes:– a million thanks for the party & the Exhibition & the sweet speech & the tape – & the conducted tour & for so many other kindnesses beyond the call etc. I shall have a surprise for you one day if I can think of one!

I shall be returning to the scene of... etc next Wednesday with Polly, but unless you are very inquisitive I should keep away – she's a bit slaphappy with some of her remarks.

Everyone has said what a lovely party it was & some of them had seen the pictures.

With masses of love and gratitude
Adrian

P.S. Please thank Prunella Scales so much for her beautiful reading. 76 people on our list drank yr wine.

---

17 | 2 | 95 8 CAMDEN STUDIOS

My dear Julian

I am mortified that I didn't write to acknowledge your very generous cheque or reply to your witticisms. But now I can add a bar of beautiful chocolate to my thank yous.

I hope you enjoyed yr flying visit to Amsterdam & have a wonderful time in the US. Exhausted by last night's play & jabber-jabber.

lots of love
Adrian

---

26 | 6 | 95 ST MALO[4]

Sunshine & wind. Oysters & wine. Too many drawings and no swimmings – yet. Luxury appartment living up to its description. Spacious rooms full of pictures – Amateur good: professional bad. Chandeliers & knicknacks.

Sue sends love. How could she?
love A

4. Postcard

---

19 | 7 | 95 8 CAMDEN STUDIOS

My dear Julian

Thank you very much for the cheque but most of all for your generous supply of food & drink!

...Thank you more than I can say for yr offer of driving me down to Jack – if you don't want to drive to Sandwich I suggest you walk down the lane, through the churchyard of the 12c church... you will see signs of civilization on the horizon – and a hostelry with grub & grog. Then you walk back & should not lose your way. The date of all this Wed August 9th D.V.

Am gone crazy labeling Tim Tew's pictures – sent him a list of titles sizes dates – & after I had posted it discovered the paintings had different dates on the backs. I wonder if these divergences will tax his computer.

Am told my two grand children deserve rewards. Sell more pictures.

Lots of love & a million thanks as ever
Adrian

Later: PS. My stick on labels don't.

12 | 9 | 95 8 CAMDEN STUDIOS

My dear Julian

Yr letter arrived this morning, for which many thanks. Jack writes she hopes 'Julian will bring you down again in the Spring' – Nota Bene the last word & make plans accordingly per favore. As for the other matter I suggest we both 'wait & see (my dearest Godfather's father made his fortune by manufacturing 'wait & see' pills for that little matter that occupied our parents attentions so much) if K comes up with the cash (in which case you'll receive yr fabulous pressie). You can tell him how cheaply he got it & in spite of that Adrian gave you a whacking commission. If that doesn't make him feel awful, what will?

Meanwhile... Mendelssohn is rattling away on the third (post Beethoven's last quartets for yr informal instruction) & if he hammers away much more I shall be unwell.

Lots of love
Adrian

---

14 | 12 | 95 8 CAMDEN STUDIOS

My dear Julian

A Merry Christmas & a happy New Year to you. Just to make sure it will be, I would like to say I'm afraid you chose some old rejects for Eton & in my state of post-Guy depression I let you take them away. However today I shall go through my 8 or 10 books of better (?) domicilia (?) in the hopes that you will consider them before you start your mounting horse.

(Guy has just interrupted me on the phone with news that his ex wife Isabelle has just died (he arrived too late) & he has been asked to give an 'oration' next week...)

Meanwhile all is gloom here too, as the light is nix & the self portrait has a white gesso face – the hat remains, a ce moment...

However the postlady handed me a parcel – a book from Frances she had well received (Reviewed I suppose I should say) Susan Wicks 'Driving My Father'. And a handful of Christmas cards from people I haven't sent to.

Don't be cross with me!
Lots of love
Adrian

---

4 | 3 | 96 8 CAMDEN STUDIOS

My dear Julian

Very many thanks indeed for all your hard work & for framing all those pictures so beautifully & hanging them so well – & thanks too for all the wine & the drink purveyors! A jolly time was had by all and I'm very glad that some people actually bought a painting at such Astronomical prices!

There is a plan afoot to gather again on Sunday afternoon 17 March. Geraldine Alfie & Peg want to drive down & Sue wants to bring her mother – we intend to meet at 1.0 in the pub you disappeared into – can you let us know the name when we return – will you be likely to come? People won't stay long – all in a hurry to return before dark.

I could do with some more cards if you have them – they seem v 'desirable.' I gather you were selling them at 50p each! I'm keen to see the pictures cos I didn't take them in – some I saw mystified me.

Weather forecasts for Holland not good. We'll try to call on Mr Demandt Thursday PM if we can find him. I hope I shall survive the travel.

lots of love
Adrian

---

2 | 10 | 96 12 HIGH STREET CASTEL MERE

My dear Julian

Nous sommes ici – beautiful cottage (flint & brick) ditto village – ditto church, Castle… Priory seems different… yet to paint it…

Very many thanks for my E.K. present – look forward to its frame & finding a place to hang it not to mention deciphering (?) what it is all about.

...Can't remember if you knew Jack's bird Moth died before we came away – But the crisis is over – she is writing the 'Story of Moth' at my instigation – & without yr help – some people can...

We have been to Holkham Hall (good paintings unseeable) & Sandringham – bad paintings easily seen – we much preferred the latter house and grounds in spite of the unattractive facade. The roads round here are littered with squashed pheasants & the pubs think we are all yorkshire people with their barfood helpings. You'd love it. I have done a number of exquisite pastels. Double all prices.

Sue sends her love, she's reading Fifi's 'Perfectly Pure & Good' & thinks she's WEIRD!

Lots of love as ever
Adrian

---

3 | 7 | 97

GREECE[5]

Safe arrival nearly on time. Villa de luxe & garden glorious. Beach very busy and bosomy. Taverna & tourist souvenir shops abound. Nothing else. The waves knock me over before I'm waist deep. Sue chose the card for you – I can't think why. There's not a fishing boat in sight. Am learning to paint lemon trees and setting suns.

Lots of love S & A

5. Postcard

---

19 | 8 | 97

8 CAMDEN STUDIOS

My dear Julian

A thousand thousand thanks for yesterday – I hope you were not too exhausted. Thank you for returning all those crummy pictures. I can't see why you took them in the first place. I might be able to work on a few and tear up the others – except of course for the magnificent and historical grand prix.

With lots of love
Adrian

PS IMPORTANT – My foot clinic is 3.30pm 27th!

3 | 2 | 98[6]

Very many thanks as ever for the cheque… for a Paris Street Scene, which I can't remember. But all will be revealed when I study my immaculate filofaxfile.

Love A.

This is how it should be done. (the last sentence is written above where it's printed 'The Leaping Horse, John Constable R.A. …The Tate Gallery, London')

6. Picture postcard

---

14 | 3 | 98

8 CAMDEN STUDIOS

My dear Julian

Thank you very much for the cheque & for coming here – & collecting more pictures! The news you gave Sue on the phone re Abbott & Whatnot was amusing! (it was followed soon after by Peggy!)

Erotica is a bit pricey.

I forgot to tell you that after leaving Suffolk five years ago I have only just found, upstairs, tied up in bundles of dirty string 20 or more sketchbooks containing enough of my old watercolour paper to last me out – So I shall be able to do watercolours again if I can remember how to – just as I was warming to my easier pastels.

Inside one of the books I found… 'Holbrook 1974, Paint what you see and not what you know. Everybody knows what you know but nobody knows what you see.' You may quote me! I think I knows what I meant. Doesn't quite constitute a Delacroix Journal but its a start…

Lots of love
Adrian

---

27 | 5 | 98

8 CAMDEN STUDIOS

My dear Julian

a very quick note (off to the bloody isle) to thank you a million times for yesterday. Jack has been on the phone for hours in outcome, you can't buy the Dogs Head – she'll never sell her animals – the Mushrooms you can have if I send her £5 a week to lose. She was delighted with you & yr being interested in her work & I've told her that at last she has a dealer who will spread her work throughout the country if not the world.

The beach picture is Rye – I'd sent her down to Iden years & years ago to bother old Keith Baynes. All of which she reminded me of at breakfast.

Love & kisses
Adrian

PS simple mathematics made me realise I'd covered only one way petrol to little Stourmouth. Herewith the return, with more thanks.

---

18 | 6 | 98 8 CAMDEN STUDIOS

My dear Julian

Many thanks for the cheques & also for the Wine – and the lovely flowers. Whilst waiting for the irises to open I've been trying to paint the white flowers (what are they?) – bloody difficult. Wet and gloomy but a heatwave promised demain.

Monday I hear my doom.
Lots of love
Adrian

---

27 | 9 | 98 8 CAMDEN STUDIOS

My dear Julian

For the life of me I can't remember if I've written to thank you for all you did on Thursday – So v. many thanks!

Saturday we cleared a little path in the kitchen – 5 large sackfuls of ghastly rubbish & it doesn't look as if anything has been done! The gardener called & talked – so did Joyce. I did very little except drink & say 'my God' or 'ye Gods'. I have to do it all over again with Scarlett & Bruce on Wednesday. I shall never want to see the place after that!

Sue's in bed with a tummy bug & I've been entertaining

a meter-man under the kitchen sink. Our water will probably cost twice as much instead of half. Am not in an opeful mood. No painting.

Lots of love
Adrian.

---

4 | 9 | 98 8 CAMDEN STUDIOS

My dear Julian

...I'm very sorry to hear about yet another bereavement in your family – and yet another funeral to attend.

The way I feel it will be mine next – Sue is dragging me off to the doctors this evening – if I can get there – my legs don't want to go further than a few yards before painful aches in the shins. Very odd.

My indigestion continues uncomfortably & am unable to put brush to canvas. However I shall be well enough to welcome you anytime.

David Becker is back from a cloudless blueness... off Turkey & may come next week to take Jack's picture to clean.

Offers have been made for her cottage but you know how people back out at the last minute – having in this case probably fallen through the floorboards.

Scarlett's daughter Eleanor gave birth yesterday to a 'beautiful boy' so I can sign off with lots of love from a Great Grandfather

---

14 | 11 | 92 *Received September 2000, almost two years after Adrian's death*

HILL HOUSE

My dear Julian

...Don't suppose you'll ever receive this – but should you the news:–

Guy had a heart attack Christmas Eve & was rushed to Westminster hospital – Father Christmas called & gave him presents & lunch with a comic Les Dawson – + champagne & both coloured wines & port to boot. You'll hear his story so mustn't jump the gun – but that jollity was followed by a massive operation at the Brompton. However he is now out & staying with his daughters – one by one? – till well enough to look after himself.

I can't remember if before you left I had lost my £3300 cheque from Tim Tew in the post ? – which I had taken for granted was firmly in the hands of my bank – only for a rude or gracious letter to inform me of a massive overdraft – since generosity had ruled the Christmas waves. Tim has been over – unseen – but no replacement cheque yet received. Times are hard but Richard Cobbold is pumping me with good wines in exchange for bad pictures.

The light is rotten – fog & mist & cold – we have booked to go to Amsterdam early in March to see the Vuillard expo which we missed in Glasgow and Sheffield – luckily.

Sue is back at work in the Nat Gal & earning more in a year than I've earned in fifty. How to keep her when my last tooth drops out?

Happy New Year
lots of love
Adrian

Posthumous one-man shows

Paintings and Watercolours
Redfern Gallery, 12 September–12 October 2000

A Different Kettle of Fish
Penlee House Gallery & Museum, Penzance, 19 January–9 March 2002, curated by Julian Machin

Works on Paper
Redfern Gallery, 21 May–20 June 2002

Painting in France
Charleston Trust, 6 July–31 August 2003, curated by Julian Machin

Still Life Paintings
The National Trust, Sutton House, London, 3 February–6 March 2005, curated by Julian Machin

Oils, watercolours and etchings
Redfern Gallery, 31 January–3 March 2006

The Abstract Hinterland
Town Hall Galleries, Ipswich, 5 October–17 November 2007, curated by Julian Machin

The Ryan family tree

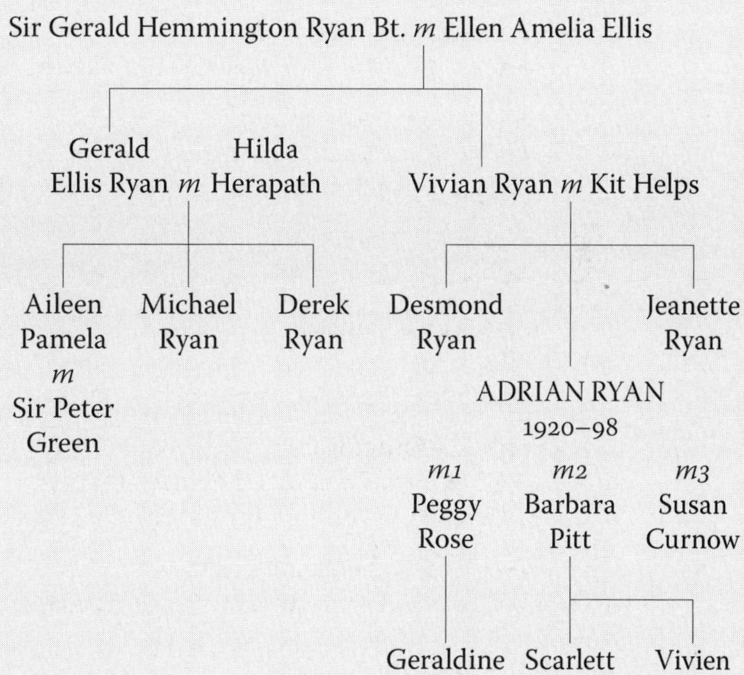

Tribute by Sven Berlin

From the service of memorial for Adrian Ryan, 30 March 1999, held at St James's Church, Piccadilly, a tribute by Sven Berlin (1911–99) edited and read out for him by Julian Machin:

When a painter dies it is a matter for the angels. To be a painter is to serve the first Creator, helping to complete his task. Whichever way, it is a sacred and difficult thing. This Adrian has done using his quiet genius to interpret the world about him. No need for me to praise this man whose passing we honour today. The tribute is in his life and work: a constant friend for over half a century; a beautiful painter for all time uncorrupted by modes of fashion. In my last letter to him, I wrote how disappointing it was that art has taken some of the direction it has during our life times. He replied:

'They have forgotten the ancient prayer of the Muses:
What is lovely is beloved by the angels,
What is unlovely, is unbeloved'

Hale and farewell, Adrian. See you soon – in Paradise.

Love,
Sven

Index